365 DAYS OF POSITIVE LIVING

Live a Joyful and Vibrant Life

NORMAN VINCENT PEALE

JAICO PUBLISHING HOUSE

Ahmedabad Bangalore Chennai
Delhi Hyderabad Kolkata Mumbai

Published by Jaico Publishing House
A-2 Jash Chambers, 7-A Sir Phirozshah Mehta Road
Fort, Mumbai - 400 001
jaicopub@jaicobooks.com
www.jaicobooks.com

Published in arrangement with
Guideposts
110 William Street, 9th floor
New York, NY 10038, USA

To be sold only in India, Bangladesh, Bhutan,
Pakistan, Nepal, Sri Lanka and the Maldives.

365 DAYS OF POSITIVE LIVING
ISBN 978-93-87944-06-0

First published as *Positive Living Day by Day* by Guideposts

First Jaico Impression: 2018
Second Jaico Impression (New Cover): 2024

Printed by
Trinity Academy For Corporate Training Limited, Mumbai

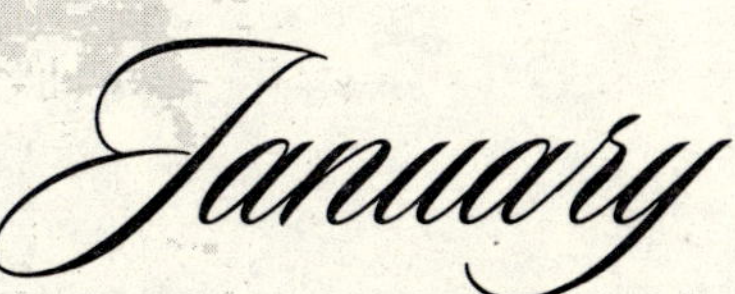

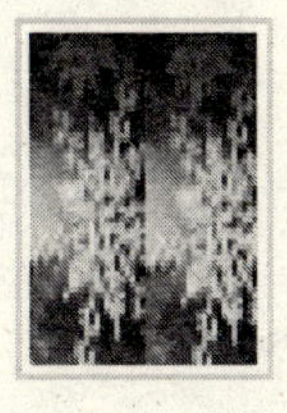

January

Jesus looked at them and said, "With man this is impossible, but with God all things are possible." Matthew 19:26

Not only so, but we also rejoice in our sufferings, because we know that suffering produces perseverance; perseverance, character; and character, hope. ROMANS 5:3–4

JANUARY 1

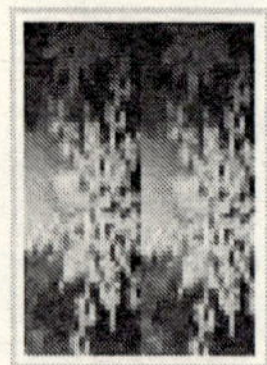

James Russell Lowell made a remark one time that has always fascinated me. He said, "Mishaps are like knives that either serve us or cut us, as we grasp them by the blade or the handle." If you grasp the blade of a difficulty, it will cut you; but if you grasp the handle of a difficulty, you can cut your way through all manner of obstructions.

The Russians have a proverb that I like: "The hammer shatters the glass, but forges steel." If you're glass, if you're superficial, if there's no faith in you, adversity will crack and shatter you. But if you have in you the victory that overcomes the world, then the hammer of circumstance hitting you forges you into a strong person. God knew what He was doing when He constructed this world so that there was difficulty in it. That is what makes it possible for us to grow in strength and understanding. There is conflict in the universe and that is what makes life go.

I know, O LORD, that a man's life is not his own; it is not for man to direct his steps. JEREMIAH 10:23

JANUARY 2

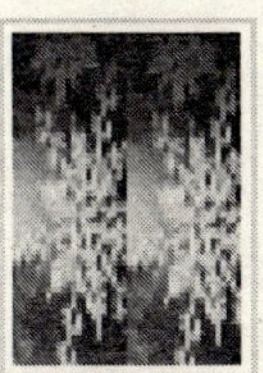

Once while in San Francisco, I climbed into one of the cable cars alongside the grip man—the man who runs it—and the car filled up with people. We were traveling down the Powell Street hill at high speed. It looked as though at each moment we were in imminent danger of destruction, but this made it a more exciting ride. I asked the grip man, "Don't you ever get nervous when this car starts plunging down this grade?"

"Nervous?" he replied. "Never. Because, you see, I know I'm in control of this car. So why should I be nervous?"

As we careen down the steep grades of our lives, we sometimes have dark apprehensions of what may happen. But if you know you are in emotional control, you then can handle any situation. It is when we finally relax in God that we find health and well-being and deep joy.

Jesus looked at them and said, "With man this is impossible, but with God all things are possible." MATTHEW 19:26

JANUARY 3

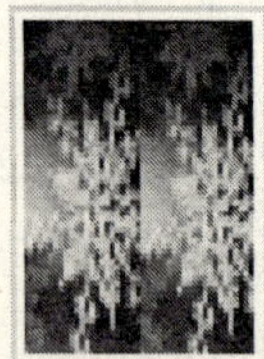

The Bible just bubbles over with spiritual food for the disheartened. Dig into the New Testament, and you come up with light and music and singing, health and hopefulness, and faith and love.

An important thing to realize is that it doesn't make any difference how much difficulty there is—there are always great possibilities in any situation. Generally, when people are disheartened, they can't see the possibilities. They see only the difficulties that are involved, not the solution. They magnify the difficulties, to blow them up, to make them bigger than they actually are. The thing to do when you are disheartened is the very opposite: go hunting around in your situation for the bright possibilities that are surely there.

Our Heavenly Father, help us to believe that even though great difficulties come against us, we can overcome them because You will help us. Through Jesus Christ, our Lord. Amen.

Surely God is my help; the Lord *is the one who sustains me.* Psalm 54:4

January 4

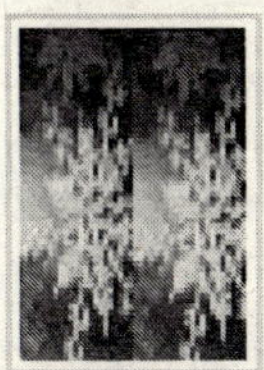

Several years ago, I was to speak at a dinner and was seated next to the United States Senator from New Jersey, Warren Barbour. He seemed fidgety and he surprised me by remarking, "I'm glad you're speaking first. Having to speak still scares the wits out of me."

"But why, if you were so afraid of speaking," I asked him, "did you run for public office?"

"Actually," he confided, "my fear of speaking was one reason I decided to run. I was determined that I wasn't going to go through life reeling because I was afraid to speak. I find that the more I do it, the less I fear it."

You and I, when experiencing fear, should remember to have a holy boldness. I call it that because it is of God. He put potential boldness into you. We cannot do it of our own unaided strength, but with God's ever-present help, we can.

The fear of the LORD *is the beginning of knowledge, but fools despise wisdom and discipline.* PROVERBS 1:7

JANUARY 5

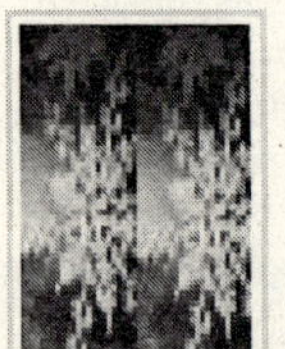

Truth is the wisdom of God in the mind and in the soul of man. So many people have so little grasp of truth that they are constantly plagued by mistakes.

A gentleman who was really concerned about himself asked me a question. As he put it, "Why am I so dumb? Why do I do so many dumb things?"

His IQ was very high. He was a graduate of a celebrated university. But this man had lost six jobs in ten years, and in every instance it was because he did something stupid. "Now," he said, "tell me what is wrong with me."

I remarked, "You aren't really stupid." And I pointed him to the answer that will help anyone in that situation: "Jim, if you will commit your life to Jesus Christ so that He takes over your thought processes, you will be guided and will not make all these mistakes."

Know also that wisdom is sweet to your soul; if you find it, there is a future hope for you, and your hope will not be cut off.
PROVERBS 24:14

JANUARY 6

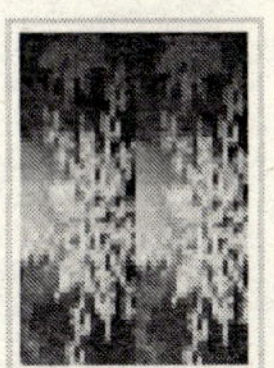

I used to sit down in the first pew, when I was still so small that my feet wouldn't touch the floor. I would watch my father up in the pulpit and hear him quote these familiar words: "Be firm in your faith. Stay brave and strong."

I haven't heard a sermon on 1 Corinthians 16:13 in years. But in the old days of rugged Protestant Christianity in this country, when ministers still had the idea that their function was to help develop great souls, you used to hear such texts, designed to call up the strength in human beings.

Accept Jesus Christ as your Savior, receive Him as your Divine Redeemer, let yourself be washed clean by Calvary's atonement, let your life be changed. Then you will be able to handle anything life brings. I don't mean to say it's going to be easy. It never will be easy. The Bible tells us we will face tribulation. You'll have trouble to the end. But you can be master of it in the name of Jesus.

I sought the Lord*, and he answered me; he delivered me from all my fears.* Psalm 34:4

January 7

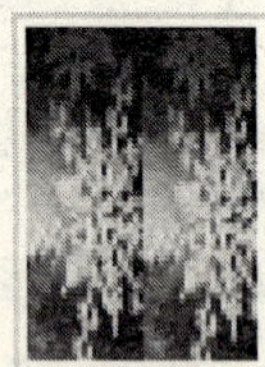

Some years ago I met a man named Oelroyd. He was the curator of the house in Washington, D.C., across from Ford's Theater, to which Abraham Lincoln was carried after the assassin shot him, and where he died. Mr. Oelroyd showed me a Bible which he said had been used by Lincoln during the critical days of the Civil War. Opening it to Psalm 34, he pointed to the fourth verse and to a slightly soiled indentation alongside it near the edge of the page, which looked as if it might have been made by a finger. Mr. Oelroyd liked to think that this was evidence that Lincoln frequently turned to that verse, which says: "I sought the Lord, and he answered me; he delivered me from all my fears."

Now the psalmist doesn't say that God delivered him from some of his fears, but from all his fears. I've always been impressed by the astonishing promises the Bible makes. There is nothing halfway about it. It offers you everything—including, here in Psalm 34, deliverance from all your fears.

For no matter how many promises God has made, they are "Yes" in Christ. And so through him the "Amen" is spoken by us to the glory of God. 2 CORINTHIANS 1:20

JANUARY 8

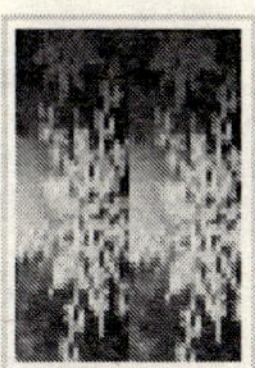

Do you think Christianity could have lasted for nearly two thousand years on its promises unless the Lord could deliver on them? Why, it would have been forgotten long since. Christianity still maintains its ancient power in today's world because there are always people who find out that these things are true. So whatever your problem may be—poor health, a confused mind, wrong relations with people, unhappiness in the home, business problems—whatever they may be, put them in the hands of Jesus Christ, who knows more about such problems than you or I ever could.

You may say this is claiming a lot. It certainly is. But it is not half of what we could claim. If we had the time, hundreds of people could be brought to pulpits everywhere who could bear witness to what happens in human lives when Jesus Christ takes over, when the God of the impossible is given control.

. . . and begged him to let the sick just touch the edge of his cloak, and all who touched him were healed. MATTHEW 14:36

JANUARY 9

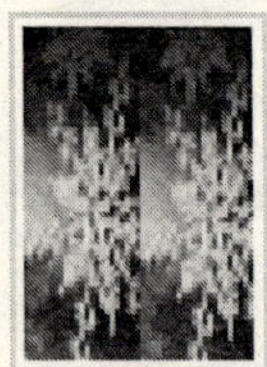

The key to becoming what we want to be is found in the fourteenth chapter of Matthew. In it we find a description of Jesus moving amid the multitude on the shores of Lake Galilee. Instinctively the people knew that He had the answer to their lives. They weren't going to go to school to learn the ways of faith. They were just going to touch His garment. And the passage goes on to say, "all who touched him were healed."

Don't feel you have to understand so much or do so many things. It isn't so complicated. I don't want to oversimplify, but what this passage says is: If you want to be a better person, just get hold of something of Him, even if it's only the hem of His garment. If your desire is real, you will be made perfectly whole. Think of that. You'll no longer be defeated by your fears, or torn asunder by inner conflict, or defeated by evil in your nature. You will be made perfectly whole.

But you, dear friends, build yourselves up in your most holy faith. . . . Keep yourselves in God's love as you wait for the mercy of our LORD Jesus Christ to bring you to eternal life. JUDE 1:20-21

JANUARY 10

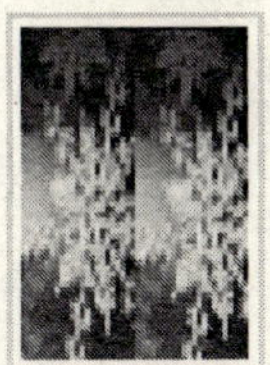

For many years I never experienced an operation firsthand. But my turn came. My doctor told me he had to remove my gallbladder. On the appointed morning, I told my wife that I loved her. And she told me the same. Then I asked the Lord to forgive me for any sins that I had committed. And I thanked Him for all His goodness. I looked out at the beautiful Dutchess County hillside and I said, "I love this world, Lord, and I'd like to go on and do a good job."

Now this is a simple thing I'm telling you. But what I did was let go. I committed my soul to God. Have you ever really done that? It's a tremendous experience. Friends, I want to tell you that in that one minute I had an experience of the Presence. I felt a sustaining power. I had a sense of reality. And it is going to live with me all the rest of my life. You don't have to wait for an operation or an illness to commit your life to Him. You can do it now.

He holds victory in store for the upright,
he is a shield to those whose walk is
blameless. . . . PROVERBS 2:7

JANUARY 11

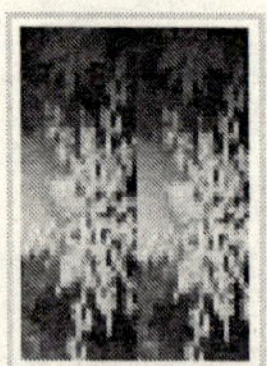

Phyllis Simolke was in New York City on a buying trip. After a happy reunion, she went with a friend to the subway and waited until a train came. Her friend got on, and they waved to each other as the train moved off. She started toward the exit. All at once, five thugs appeared and blocked her passage. The young woman froze. Mrs. Simolke had a committed faith. So she prayed to the Lord, saying, "For the sake of my two little boys and my husband, help me." And He did.

She walked straight up to the leader, a tall fellow with a scar on his face. Standing tall, she said gently but firmly, "Let me pass, please."

Like the parting of the Red Sea, they broke ranks. As she passed, one punk hissed, "You walk tall, woman. Walk tall!"—as though in his mind there glimmered a respect for the immense power available to renewed people. Phyllis Simolke is the kind of person who lives with unchanging truth in a changing world.

"Therefore I tell you, whatever you ask for in prayer, believe that you have received it, and it will be yours." MARK 11:24

JANUARY 12

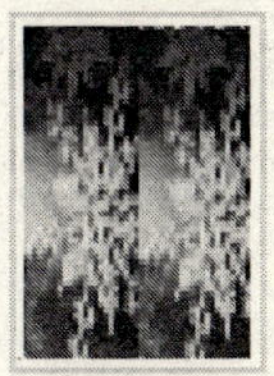

Prayer is the contact of the soul with God through the mental processes whereby the individual conquers his own weaknesses and enters into life abundant. If you have the idea that it is merely the mumbling of a few words, I almost think you're better off not to use it at all, for that is a degradation of this great process.

True prayer requires discipline, it requires pain, it requires the agony to think. But when you do think prayerfully, with Jesus as your guide, you break free from the defeats which have encompassed you. I do not believe there is any problem, any defeat, any difficulty that cannot be overcome through prayer. I do not believe there is any disease from which prayer cannot bring deliverance. One of the most devastating enemies of man is disease, but one reason it devastates is because we just accept it as inevitable. I believe in the power of Jesus Christ to resolve any difficulty, to remove any weakness, to heal any disease.

". . . you will be a blessing. Do not be afraid, but let your hands be strong."

ZECHARIAH 8:13

JANUARY 13

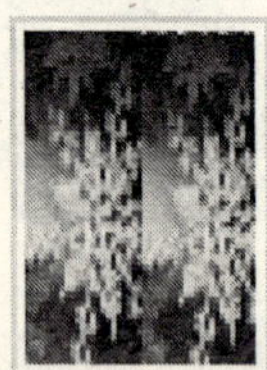

You may be full of fear. You have had fears all your life. You are so sick of these fears that you just don't know what to do, but you are in the habit of saying to yourself, "I've always been a fearful person. My grandfather was a fearful person, my mother was a fearful person—so I am a fearful person. That's just the way it is. That's just the way I'm made." What an evaluation of yourself!

Say instead: "Dear Jesus Christ, I believe that You came to give me power. I hereby repudiate these fears. I am from this minute on a person of courage." Then you will go out and live with courage. You'll do things you formerly were afraid to do. You'll live dangerously. And after a while you will find that your fears are gone.

The same is true of excitement and enthusiasm. Live on the basis of enthusiasm and excitement and you'll have them. And they will make a different person out of anyone who does it.

Be joyful always; pray continually; give thanks in all circumstances, for this is God's will for you in Christ Jesus. 1 THESSALONIANS 5:16–18

JANUARY 14

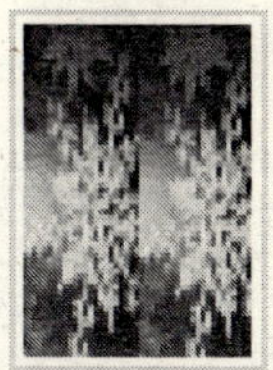

At a luncheon I was seated next to a distinguished woman who asked me what extra thing I was doing now. "Writing a book," I said. "The working title is *Enthusiasm Makes the Difference.*"

"I want to congratulate you on your audacity and your courage," she said, "that you would actually write a book on enthusiasm in a day and age like this."

Well, I was surprised to know that this required courage and audacity. But I shall persevere in encouraging people to sing in their spirit.

How does one have enthusiasm in his life? It is as simple as this: Cultivate the ability to love living. Love the people who live, love the sky under which you live, love the season in which we pass these days, love all of the facets of living. Jesus taught that the person who loves becomes happy. The person who loves everything becomes enthusiastic, filled with the zest and the joy of life. It is just that simple.

We were therefore buried with him through baptism into death in order that, just as Christ was raised from the dead through the glory of the Father, we too may live a new life. ROMANS 6:4

JANUARY 15

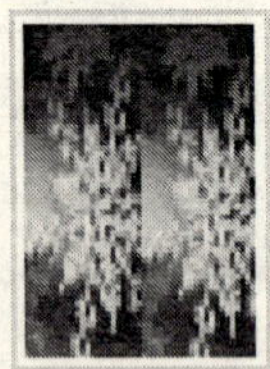

Paul says that we have been raised to life. What does that mean? It means we are supposed to get rid of all the old barnacles that have encrusted us for so long: our hates, our lusts, our dishonesties, our rationalizations, our fears, our weaknesses. These must all go, so that we may experience the power of Christ.

And how can you and I become new? The only way is to have contact with the power of God so that, like a lightning bolt, it may burst into our lives and change us. Maybe people have shaken their heads about me and said, "This man is becoming an old-time evangelist." Well, I'm not old-time, but I am an evangelist. An evangelist is a person who is trying to bring people the good news. And the good news is that we have been raised to new life in Christ.

But you will receive power when the Holy Spirit comes on you; and you will be my witnesses in Jerusalem, and in all Judea and Samaria, and to the ends of the earth." ACTS 1:8

JANUARY 16

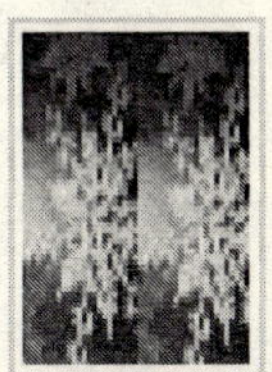

We use some words rather loosely because we repeat them so frequently. One such word is *power*. I decided to consult the dictionary on the subject. The Latin word from which *power* derives is the equivalent of the Greek word *dynamis*, a word used all through the New Testament. And from *dynamis* is derived the English word *dynamite*.

The Bible is filled with the most powerful ideas in this world. By substituting the word *dynamite* for the word *power*, you can begin to understand the greatness of it. Take Acts 1:8: The Holy Spirit will come upon you and give you *dynamite*. When the Holy Spirit comes upon you, you will experience an explosion that will change your whole life and, through you, help to change the world. It's really tremendous.

But the fruit of the Spirit is love, joy, peace, patience, kindness, goodness, faithfulness.

GALATIANS 5:22

JANUARY 17

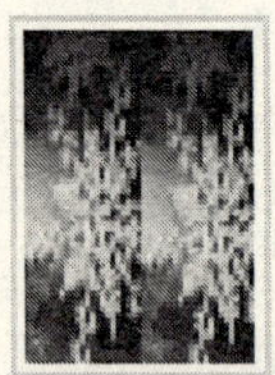

You were not made to live a dull life. You were not put into this exquisite world, filled with beauty and fascination, to be less than an interested, excited human being. It may seem strange to you that a minister of the gospel should talk about having an interesting and exciting life. A crime has been perpetrated against Christianity in the assumption, built up over many years, that the religion of Jesus Christ is dull, formalistic, something apart from vibrant life.

The most alive person who ever came into human existence was a man named Jesus Christ. He had an impact upon human beings as no other person who ever walked the earth. Could a nice, quiet, lifeless person have jolted humanity as He did? He was and is the personification of interest and excitement. The story of His life is told in only a small section of the total Bible. But in those pages there is more life than in any book or stack of books ever written.

"The LORD who delivered me from the paw of the lion and the paw of the bear will deliver me from the hand of this Philistine. . . ." 1 SAMUEL 17:37

JANUARY 18

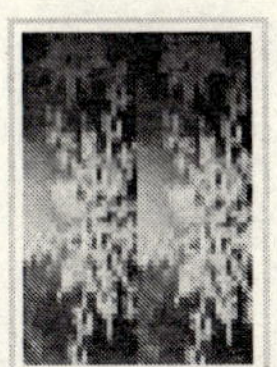

The story of David and Goliath might be told in this fashion: The Philistines had a giant named Goliath. He would yell at the Israelites, "Come out and fight. If your giant defeats me, we will be your slaves; but if I defeat him, you'll be our slaves."

David, a clear-minded boy, went to the king and said, "If you will let me, I will take care of this fellow." This went over well with the king. He said, "If you want to take on the giant, you may do it."

David collected five smooth stones and proceeded in the direction of the giant. He swung his slingshot, and the stone smacked the giant right on the forehead. And Goliath toppled over, dead.

What a story! And what does it teach? A simple truth. You are faced with a Goliath. Everybody is. But no difficulty is bigger than you are when you are united with God. Together you and God have the power to do mighty things of which you know not.

"Have faith in God," Jesus answered.

Mark 11:22

January 19

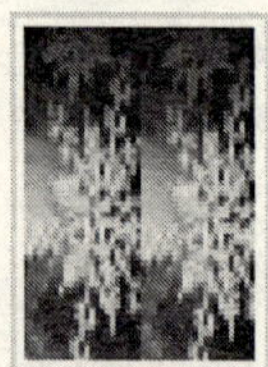

When you are up against a tough situation, the first essential is to stand up to it. Face it, think about it, study it, pray about it; then hit it and keep after it. You have within you enough force, put there by Almighty God, to overcome situations that seem overwhelming. If you practice faith constantly, if you keep in His spirit, if you stay in tune with Him, you can bring the necessary strength into play against all difficulties.

Don't ever think you're weak. Don't ever say you're weak. Don't ever believe you're weak. You're not weak. Draw upon your strength. And maybe it seems that you have very little strength, but you can bring it into play against difficulties and overcome them.

Each day declare, "I surrender myself into the hands of God, and I trust Him." Three times each day, thank God for all His goodness, and soon your life will be filled with God and emptied of apprehensions.

Let us then approach the throne of grace with confidence, so that we may receive mercy and find grace to help us in our time of need. HEBREWS 4:16

JANUARY 20

I believe a person should pray for courage as he prays for his daily bread. God will give it to you, because He will give you Himself. Let me illustrate.

At a prayer breakfast in Washington, General Harold K. Johnson, Chief of Staff of the United States Army, related an instance from his life. Fourteen years before, during the Korean War, General Johnson found himself in charge of a handful of men holding a dreary stretch of deserted road to cover a retreat.

"I was very troubled," he said, "so I just shut my eyes and talked to God, right there on that cold, frozen road. I asked His help. And out of the night, as if from a great distance, came God's voice saying, 'Be strong, have no fear, I am with you.'" From that moment he had no fear, only a deep sense of peace. And he and his men had the courage they needed to fight their way out of that situation.

But thanks be to God! He gives us the victory through our LORD Jesus Christ.

1 CORINTHIANS 15:57

JANUARY 21

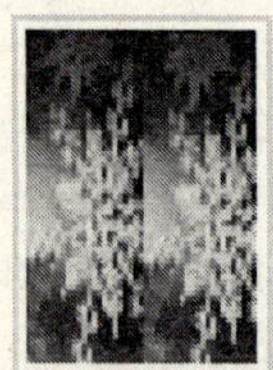

My wife and I were in England and went to Chartwell, Winston Churchill's home where he lived during the war. Outside the house we were shown where he stood every evening during the Battle of the Britain, watching the German bombers coming over in great waves. I asked our guide, "Did he ever lose hope?"

She laughed. "Churchill? No. Hope was built into him. He never expected anything but ultimate victory." That is why some men become immortal. They have hope and expectation built into them.

Well, you may think, I'm not Churchill; I'm just a plain human being. Certainly you are! But don't say you are going to let these things defeat you. Not when you have God, who will put such a glow of victory and health in you that it will be a thrill.

"Peace I leave with you; my peace I give you. I do not give to you as the world gives. Do not let your hearts be troubled and do not be afraid." JOHN 14:27

JANUARY 22

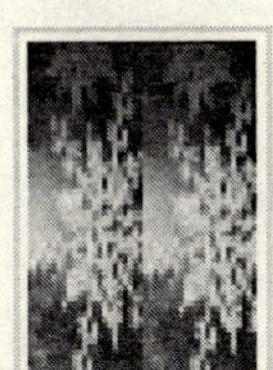

The two greatest forces in the world, ceaselessly contending with each other, are fear and faith. But faith is stronger than fear.

I am reminded of a talk I had with J. Edgar Hoover, who was head of the Federal Bureau of Investigation. In his early career, he was famous for his fearless pursuit of vicious criminals. I said to him, "When you were hunting those gangsters, were you ever afraid?"

"Of course I was afraid," he answered. "There were many times when I might have been shot to death at any moment. Of course I was afraid."

"How did you overcome your fear?" I asked.

Instantly he replied: "I lost my fear in the power of my Lord." He added, "Get the power of the Lord in your heart and you overcome your fear."

"Rejoice and be glad, because great is your reward in heaven. . . ." MATTHEW 5:12

JANUARY 23

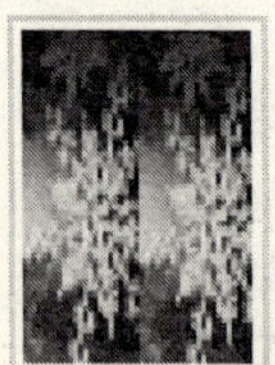

I consider it a travesty of the gospel of Jesus Christ to insist that there should be no expression of joy in this world. It was said of the first Christians that they had within them the song of the skylark and the babbling of brooks. But today that lilt seems, for the most part, to have gone out of Christian preaching. And this is a tragedy.

Now, of course, if you see only clouds, you naturally are not going to say, "It's good to be alive." But believe me, friends, there is much more in this world than clouds. And if that's all you see, then you should have a change of viewpoint. Take flight within yourself. It is a wonderful thing to have altitude in your thoughts. You can have it if you just take it. And altitude of the spirit makes all the difference in the world.

Whoever embarks upon the Christian life will have periods of testing. When such times come, fall further back on God; pray more earnestly and surrender more completely.

This is the day the LORD *has made;*
let us rejoice and be glad in it. PSALM 118:24

JANUARY 24

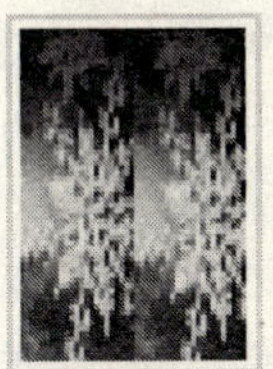

William Lyon Phelps, who in the early years of the twentieth century was one of the most famous of American professors at a great New England university, once wrote, "The happiest people are those who think the most interesting thoughts."

One morning in New York City, as I left my apartment for the day, the doorman, with a dour expression on his face, said to me, "This is one of the most miserable days I've ever seen."

For a moment it dashed my spirits, but I rose to the occasion and replied, "This is the day the LORD has made; let us rejoice and be glad in it." A new expression came over the man's face, so maybe I gave him a different idea. That's the way you've got to think. Your happiness in life depends upon how you think about everything.

How do you think about your future? Do you see it as gloomy? If you do, it will be so. Don't see it that way. See it as happy. See God in it. See God controlling your mind, and happiness will come.

I can do everything through him who gives me strength. PHILIPPIANS 4:13

JANUARY 25

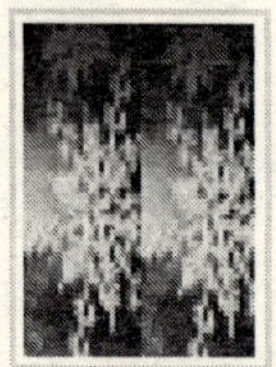

Your mind is a powerful instrument. If it controls you, you'll not be victorious. But if you control it, you will be. However, I don't believe that a human being by his own unaided strength can accomplish this. Something else needs to be added.

I once knew a distressed man who held steady and made his way back up with the help of a wonderful dynamic thought that changes everything. Given what little I know about human beings and about God, I will guarantee that this thought can help anybody under any circumstances to keep on keeping on. Everybody would do well to hold it in consciousness until it absorbs into the unconsciousness and live by it. It's found in Philippians, the fourth chapter, thirteenth verse. And this is it: I can do all things through—myself? No. "I can do everything through him who gives me strength." Christ will help you keep on keeping on.

The Lord is a refuge for the oppressed, a stronghold in times of trouble. PSALM 9:9

JANUARY 26

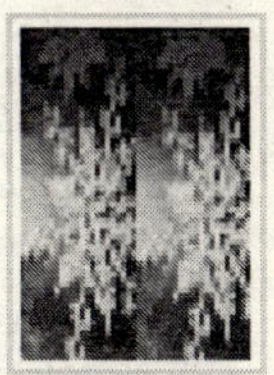

When you get turned on to the gospel—not just intellectually in agreement with it, but experiencing it really deep within you—then, no matter what you have to face or deal with, you have the power to do it. The Bible promises us this. Psalm 9:9 says God is "a stronghold in times of trouble." That means there is no time, ever, when He isn't there to help you, if you are there to turn Him on inside you.

Now how do you go about getting the help of God in this great way? You begin by having what we call spiritual experience. "Spiritual experience." What does that mean? It means a personal awareness of the presence and work of Jesus Christ in your life.

Our Heavenly Father, we give thanks for our faith. Help us to believe more deeply and with more dedication. Through Jesus Christ, our Lord. Amen.

For God did not give us a spirit of timidity, but a spirit of power, of love and of self-discipline. 2 TIMOTHY 1:7

JANUARY 27

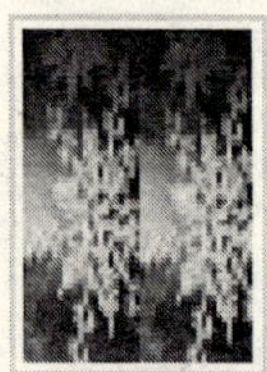

A university put out a questionnaire among six hundred psychology students and asked them, among other things, to reveal what they thought was their most pressing, painful, personal problem. Seventy percent of them said that it was lack of courage or self-confidence.

What, then, is the secret of self-confidence and courage? It hinges on the kinds of thoughts you think. Your subconscious is very accommodating. If you keep on sending it fearful thoughts and self-inadequacy thoughts, that is what it will feed back to you.

When you come right down to it, the secret of courage and self-confidence is to fill your life with God. Of course, you expect me to say that. And you are not going to be disappointed, because I've said it. And why do I say it? Because it's true. You were created by God and He made you right. If you haven't walked with God, you are making yourself wrong.

For the message of the cross is foolishness to those who are perishing, but to us who are being saved it is the power of God.

1 Corinthians 1:18

January 28

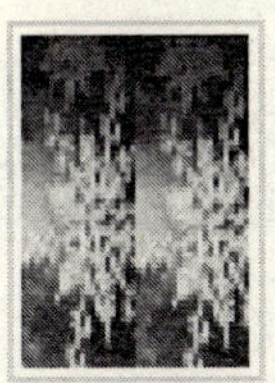

Your physical body is a marvelous instrument. Most everybody has a hand, and it seems to be an ordinary appliance. But consider the positions and motions you can make with your fingers and your hand. Think of the angles, the joints, the engineering that goes into the one small member of your body known as a hand! But your wonderful body isn't the greatest thing about you.

There is in you that indescribable thing called God's power. It is a power over yourself, a power over situations, a power over circumstance. If you exercise this power, amazing things can be done with it. Now you must be humble about it. It isn't your power. It is God living within you. This is why we constantly urge people to come into a closer relationship with Jesus Christ. Because what does He do? He releases power whereby anyone can transform himself or herself.

All Scripture is God-breathed and is useful for teaching, rebuking, correcting and training in righteousness. . . . 2 TIMOTHY 3:16–17

JANUARY 29

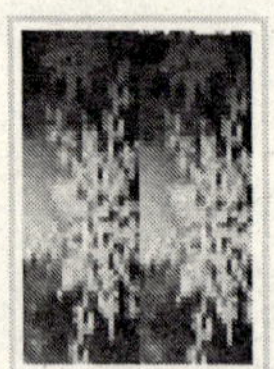

The Holy Bible contains some remarkable statements. It is probably a good thing that the canon of the Scriptures was written and settled generations ago. It was produced by men who were more naive than we are today, men whose faith was simpler; and they were not afraid of the great claims and promises which were written into the holy text.

What if leaders of religion today were to write the canon on the basis of traditions such as were given to the early biblical writers? I am sure that, with their more sophisticated scholarship and their smaller concepts, they would produce a Bible which, while it might be meticulously perfect from a literary point of view, wouldn't posses the rugged power and greatness of faith which this Book possesses.

Live by the sayings of Jesus Christ and become like that wise man who built his house upon the rock. You can have an inner serenity, strength and courage that defies all the storms of life.

"'If you can'?" said Jesus. "Everything is possible for him who believes." MARK 9:23

JANUARY 30

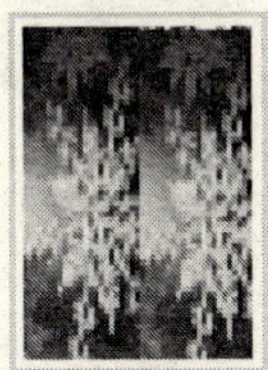

I call to your attention a text in the New Testament: Mark 9:23. And it is probably one of the greatest gems of truth you will find. It says: "Everything is possible for him who believes."

Notice that there is a condition. You are offered something tremendous, but only if you have faith. In-depth belief requires giving your whole self to it. It isn't the glib recital of a creed. But if you can overcome your doubts and your negative thinking and really, deeply believe, you will enter into a life transformed. This is the magic of believing. Belief is factual; it is truth. The magic of believing is a manifestation of one of the greatest powers in the universe: the power of thought. By our thoughts we either create or destroy. You can tear your life down by destructive thinking, but you can build your life up by thinking constructively.

". . . He has sent me to proclaim freedom for the prisoners and recovery of sight for the blind. . . ."

LUKE 4:18

JANUARY 31

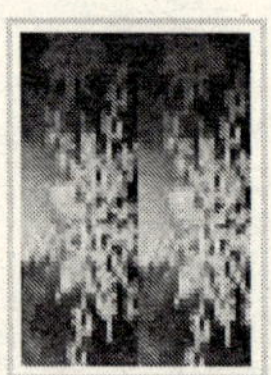

"[The LORD] has sent me to proclaim freedom for the prisoners . . ." (Luke 4:18). What prisoners? Those who were in jail? Jesus meant far more than that. People build their own prisons, forge their own chains. Held by self-imposed limitations, they are captives who wither and die.

But Jesus sets us free. He implies to each of us, *There is a giant within you.* Have you ever seen the giant within you? Have you ever felt him trying to burst out of the prison you have made for him? Let Jesus help you let him out. No child of God should ever be a slave to his passions or his ambitions or his hates or his weakness or his self-deprecation. Accept the truth that Jesus Christ has come to set the prisoners free. There is glorious joy in true freedom. Don't settle for your limitations.

February

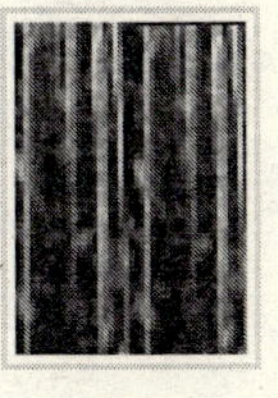

Now faith is being sure
of what we hope for
and certain of what we
do not see. Hebrews 11:1

Show me your ways, O LORD, teach me your paths; guide me in your truth and teach me, for you are God my Savior, and my hope is in you all day long. PSALM 25:4–5

FEBRUARY 1

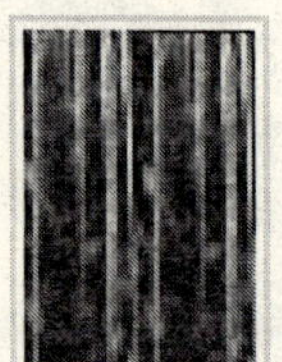

We live in the midst of the greatest scientific civilization in the history of the world. But the greatest wisdom walking our streets is not that of any laboratory scientist, but the wisdom of Jesus of Nazareth. When you have to solve perplexing problems and handle tough situations, He will give you the calm, quiet, orderly mind without which no solution can emerge. So the first thing is: don't panic. The second thing is: think. That's what Jesus Christ enables a person to do. He teaches you to think.

Write all the parts of the problem out. Talk it over with people whose intelligence and understanding you respect. Then do something about it. Do anything you can think of to find an answer. And never, never give up. Because there is an answer, and in God's leading, you will be guided to the answer if you keep on thinking, keep on working at it.

Praise the L*ORD, O my soul, and forget not all his benefits.* P*SALM* 103:2

FEBRUARY 2

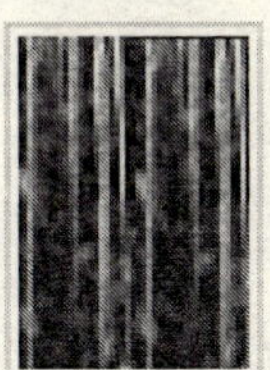

Psalm 103 is packed with wisdom. It is another way of telling us to thank God and to be sure that we do not forget all that He has done for us.

It is fitting and proper that we should have a special day of thanksgiving each year. But it would be most unfortunate if we were to limit our thanksgiving to one day. Thanksgiving is one of the most important, most creative capacities of the human mind. As we practice it assiduously and constantly, we develop a deep joy in living, despite the fact that life is filled with all manner of suffering and difficulty.

I truly believe that the individual who learns to practice thanksgiving activates within himself and around himself continuous victories and blessings from God. Become a practitioner of thanksgiving, and victory and joy and satisfaction will fill your life and will contribute to the happiness of those who touch your life.

In his name the nations will put their hope.

MATTHEW 12:21

FEBRUARY 3

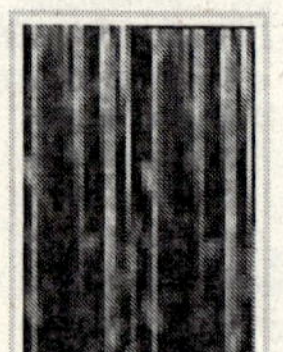

What is the hope of the world? Is it in the military? Is it in money? Is it in diplomacy? I would say that the diplomacy of the world hasn't succeeded too well, although without it we might be worse off by far than we are. Military force will never save the world. Education won't save it either. If all the people in the world are able to read, that is not going to guarantee anything, because what will they read?

I tell you, the hope of the world is in Jesus, because He alone can bridge the gap between people. He alone can establish a fellowship that is basic. He alone brings people together as brothers. Under Jesus, you no longer see people's race, nor their color, nor their background, nor their present condition; you see only a human soul, a child of God. If we could just get this world full of Jesus!

Then he said to them all: "If anyone would come after me, he must deny himself and take up his cross daily and follow me." LUKE 9:23

FEBRUARY 4

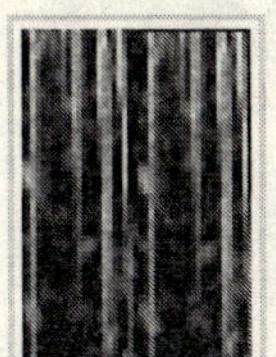

The most astonishing force that has been let loose in this world is Christianity. It is positively amazing what the Christian faith offers to its followers. They are offered peace of mind, victory over every defeat of the human spirit, a deep pulsating joy in their inmost souls, and, finally, the immortality of the soul.

These things are not offered cheaply. Christianity is not a superficial religion. You have to pay for everything it gives you. And what is the price? It is yourself. But if you give yourself to Jesus, He will give Himself to you, and life will be so wonderful that there is no describing it. You will be given the opportunity to be what Dostoyevsky, the great Russian writer, referred to as a citizen of eternity.

"The thief comes only to steal and kill and destroy; I have come that they may have life, and have it to the full." JOHN 10:10

FEBRUARY 5

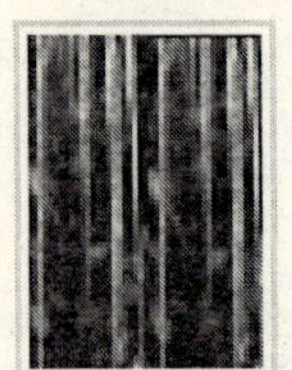

Part of having meaning in your life is to get lifted out of yourself, to get high, so to speak. Everybody needs a high experience once in awhile. You can't live adequately without great experiences. You must have great experiences at intervals. For instance, you can be caught up by some great music or be lifted by some beauty in nature or have some marvelous experience of love with other human beings. You need these elevated experiences. Christianity tells us this. Jesus said, "I have come that they may have life, and have it to the full" (John 10:10). In other words, that we might have it high—have meaning in your life.

Our Heavenly Father, help us to live grandly and greatly and joyously and victoriously, and to serve You better all our lives. Through Jesus Christ, our Lord. Amen.

When Jesus spoke again to the people, he said, "I am the light of the world. Whoever follows me will never walk in darkness, but will have the light of life." JOHN 8:12

FEBRUARY 6

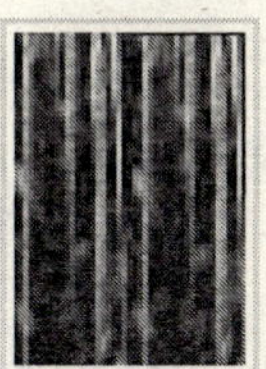

Everyone wants to make a new start. How can this be done? The formula is very simple. One sentence gives the answer to the whole matter. Put this thought at the center of your consciousness, stay with it, and you will keep it right every day: "I am the light of the world. Whoever follows me will never walk in darkness, but will have the light of life."

How many more years do you think you are going to have? Are you going to have fifty more? Thirty more? Ten more? One more? Very seldom does anybody have more than one hundred. Most people do not even have as many as eighty-five. It would seem that since we have so few years, we ought to figure out what is the best procedural wisdom to apply to them. I believe it is contained in the text, "I am the light of the world. Whoever follows me will never walk in darkness, but will have the light of life."

"Are not five sparrows sold for two pennies? Yet not one of them is forgotten by God. Indeed, the very hairs of your head are all numbered." LUKE 12:6–7

FEBRUARY 7

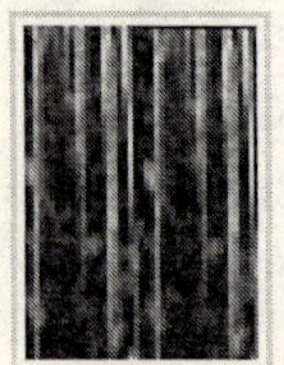

Howard M. LeSourd was a dean of one of the colleges of Boston University. He is not emotional about religion, yet he brings God into the little activities of life. He wrote me a note saying, "Thank you for the Sunday morning services, which have brought comfort and inspiration to us," and went on to tell of this incident: "Last night our car stalled on Forty-second Street. It would not start." His wife began to pray for help. "When she opened her eyes, a man was standing by the car saying, 'If you have a pair of pliers, I think I can help you.' I produced the pliers. He raised the hood, released the choke, and the engine started immediately." Isn't God wonderful?

This is a very simple illustration, but God always has His eyes on you. He notes the fall of a sparrow; even the very hairs of your head are numbered. So He is big enough to be interested in everyday human life.

But we have this treasure in jars of clay to show that this all-surpassing power is from God and not from us. 2 CORINTHIANS 4:7

FEBRUARY 8

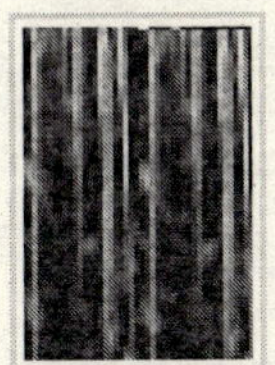

It may be that as a child you had experiences which made you doubt yourself, made you shy, withdrawn, and bashful. If you developed such a state of mind as a child, what you need to do is to take charge of your mind and begin to fill it with the healthiest, most powerful, most vital thoughts ever formulated. And where do you find them? In the Bible. The Bible is full of healing thoughts that, if put into your mind, will change your whole condition and fill you with courage and self-confidence.

You can always come back to God, and He will remake you. He remakes you in such a way that you no longer are a phony, but honest and real. If you try to become someone other than yourself, you do a bad job. When you are yourself, just the way God made you—real, honest and whole—then courage and confidence will flow into you, because you are right.

Though an army besiege me, my heart will not fear; though war break out against me, even then will I be confident. PSALM 27:3

FEBRUARY 9

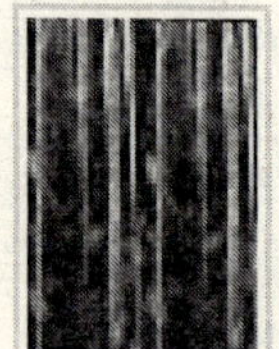

Years ago, a member of Marble Collegiate Church played guard on the Northwestern University football team. Apparently he wasn't exerting himself to the fullest, for the coach kept him back one day and told him, "You have it in you to be the greatest guard Northwestern ever had. But you've got to think bigger than you're thinking; you've got to believe bigger than you're believing." He added something the man says he never forgot—and which I have never forgotten since he told me. "Okay boy," said the coach, "go out there on the field running tall." What a phrase!

So I urge you as I urge myself: Get out there on the field running tall, thinking big, believing big, setting your goals high enough for the good that Almighty God has created for you. Think that good, believe that good, work for that good.

Jesus looked at them and said, "With man this is impossible, but with God all things are possible." MATTHEW 19:26

FEBRUARY 10

One of the most dynamic thoughts ever uttered in the history of mankind is found in Matthew 19:26, where it says: "with God all things are possible."

Ours is no little faith. If a person receives this thought, believes it and incorporates it into one's consciousness, there is a power, a vitality, and a force never felt before. Do you imagine that Christianity would have survived had it been based on little innocuous truths? The Christian faith was hewn out of truth itself. And it tells us: "with God all things are possible."

With man lots of things are impossible, but not with God. You should hold to this truth if you want to live a life that is filled with power.

She sets about her work vigorously; her arms are strong for her tasks. She sees that her trading is profitable, and her lamp does not go out at night. PROVERBS 31:17–18

FEBRUARY 11

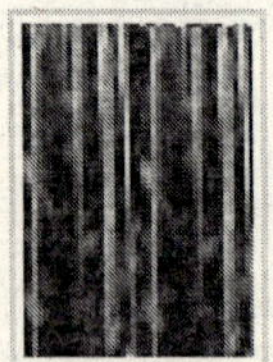

I once met a lady who lives in Mississippi who said, "I thought my husband would provide for me so that when he died I needn't worry. But his estate was eaten up, and I've got to go to work or go on relief."

I didn't know what to suggest. So I prayed, "Lord, give us an insight for Miss Lou." At the end of the prayer I hit on it. I asked, "Can you make candy?"

"Now that is something I can do," she answered.

"You go home," I said, "and make me a pound of it. Send it to me."

Actually she sent me a two-pound box and it was marvelous candy. So I wrote her saying, "Get busy merchandising that candy."

If you go to Edwards, Mississippi, you will find a shop there called "The Sweetest Spot." Miss Lou found that by thinking creatively, she could change her life. And by serving others, she became a great influence for good in the area where she lives.

Now faith is being sure of what we hope for and certain of what we do not see. HEBREWS 11:1

FEBRUARY 12

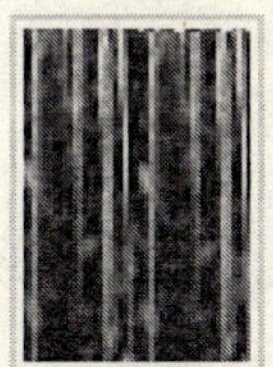

The Bible tells us that the great days of the Christian faith were when rugged believers preached to the people, giving them great Biblical examples of strong faith so that they would know that, if they would let God help them, they could overcome any difficulty they ever had to face.

We're dealing with something big. The Lord our God is with us to help us if we let Him. And how do you let Him? It is very simple: put everything in His hands, surrender to Him, take your problem—whatever it is—and say, "Lord, here it is. You tell me what to do with it. I'll do anything You say. I'm completely Yours." Then let go and let God. God then either relieves you of the problem or He gives you the ability to handle it. In either case you have a victory.

"I can do all things through Christ which strengtheneth me" is an antidote for every feeling of defeat. As you continue this affirmation, you will actually experience Christ's help. You will find yourself meeting problems with new mental force.

He went away a second time and prayed, "My Father, if it is not possible for this cup to be taken away unless I drink it, may your will be done." MATTHEW 26:42

FEBRUARY 13

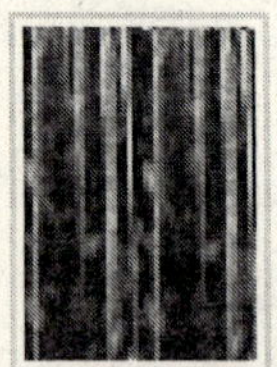

God in His wisdom isn't going to give you and me everything we want, because He knows what we need. I am reminded of Rabindranath Tagore, the great Indian mystic and poet, who said, "I have often been saved by God's hard refusals."

Not getting something you greatly desire isn't pleasant. It can be painful. It can be very bitter. But sometimes the greatest thing that ever happens to us is when God says, "No. I want it another way." Infantile people complain and say that God is cruel or that there is no God. Mature people, however, know that there is wisdom and sometimes an eternal kindness in God's refusals.

Our Heavenly Father, we thank You for the problems and difficulties of this life. We know it is a proper prayer, for at the heart of problems and difficulties lies the bright and glorious good You have prepared for those whom You love. For this we give You thanks in the name of Jesus Christ, our Lord. Amen.

Through him all things were made; without him nothing was made that has been made. In him was life, and that life was the light of men. JOHN 1:3–4

FEBRUARY 14

Jesus was so vital that they said of Him, "Everything that was created received its life from him, and his life gave light to everyone." Light, fire, power.

Have you ever gotten excited about Christianity? Have you ever gotten excited about life itself? Are you ever thrilled by the mere fact that you are alive? It is a great thing to be alive. It means that you can feel, you can sense, you can dream, you can think, you can love, you can have relationships with other people.

Yes, it's a great thing to be alive. But there are lots of people walking around who are only half-alive. Yet they can come alive. You can come alive right now, today. You can throw off all your darkness, your dullness, your dreariness, your negativism, and really live, if you open your mind and heart and receive Jesus.

Do not conform any longer to the pattern of this world, but be transformed by the renewing of your mind. ROMANS 12:2

FEBRUARY 15

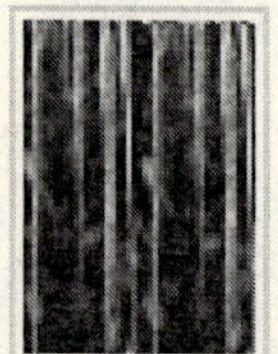

Not long ago, I saw a man whom I hadn't seen for a while. When I first knew him, he seemed to be only half alive and complained continually of not feeling well. At one time, he had a partial nervous breakdown. When I saw him later, I could hardly believe it was the same man. He had come alive.

His method consists of spending fifteen minutes every day filling his mind full of God. And how do you go about it? You think about God, you read or repeat to yourself scriptural statements about God, you talk to Him, you let Him bring you into a God-centered state of mind. Health and happiness are available to everyone. But they are gifts of God, for He is the source of health and happiness.

When tense or restless, sit quietly and allow these words to pass unhindered through your thoughts: "It is good to wait quietly for the salvation of the LORD." (Lamentations 3:26). Think of them spreading a healing balm throughout your mind.

My salvation and my honor depend on God; he is my mighty rock, my refuge.

Psalm 62:7

February 16

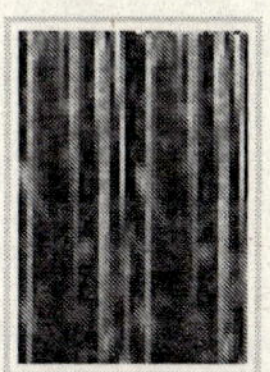

A woman tells this story of hope: "During the Depression, we had a terrible time. Only my married daughter's help—which she could ill afford—was keeping us alive. Things got to a point where I even thought of suicide as a way out. Then I thought, 'If I can depend on my daughter's love, why can't I depend on God's?' I got down on my knees, telling God I would leave everything in His hands. Then I prayed for those whose actions I had resented because they had injured us. And I arose from that prayer with joy in my heart.

"The next day my husband got temporary work. I went back to college to get my degree so I could teach. And it wasn't long before my husband had a permanent job and I became a regular teacher. We gradually paid off all our debts. When my husband was incapacitated, we were able to retire on pension.

"My own strength was not enough, but when I admitted it to God and put myself in His care, His strength was made perfect in my weakness."

"Therefore I tell you, do not worry about your life, what you will eat; or about your body, what you will wear. Life is more than food, and the body more than clothes." LUKE 12:22–23

FEBRUARY 17

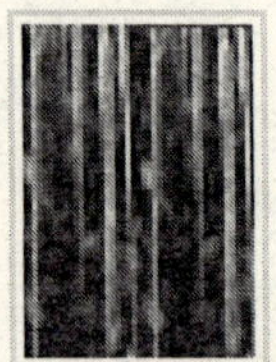

One of the worst things you can do is to permit a continuous trickle of worry across the mind, because like water it will ultimately dig a huge trench. Then every thought you think will be drained into this channel of fear and worry and come up tinctured with anxiety. You will be a person full of fear and worry.

The way to obliterate this is to start another stream. Let a stream of faith run across the mind and go deeper and deeper as you absorb faith thoughts into your consciousness—and after a while it will undercut the channel of fear and worry which will then fall into the channel of faith, and a great river of faith will surge through your mind so that every thought will come up bright and resplendent, optimistic and hopeful, and life will be good, very good. Cultivate a channel of faith to give you the deep security which you need.

Praise be to the God and Father of our LORD Jesus Christ, who has blessed us in the heavenly realms with every spiritual blessing in Christ. EPHESIANS 1:3

FEBRUARY 18

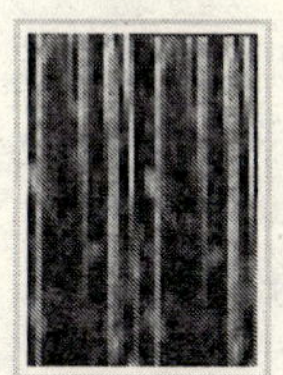

You may constantly think *scarcity*. I have observed that people who think scarcity tend in a strange way to manifest scarcity. The word scarcity is related to the word scarce. And there is only one letter difference between scarce and scare. It could be that if you think scarcity you scare money and prosperity away. This is, as I say, a little harder to demonstrate than the other correlations between attitudes and outcomes, but you might consider trying it out. Instead of saying, "How difficult everything is for me; how poor I am," affirm how God is helping you, how blessed you are. Avoid manifesting scarcity by avoiding scarcity thoughts.

By the same token, if in our minds we entertain thanksgiving, we manifest blessings. The more thankfulness a person cultivates, the more, I do believe, he will open to himself the power flow, the vast wealth of heaven, and blessings will pour out upon him.

Therefore confess your sins to each other and pray for each other so that you may be healed. The prayer of a righteous man is powerful and effective. JAMES 5:16

FEBRUARY 19

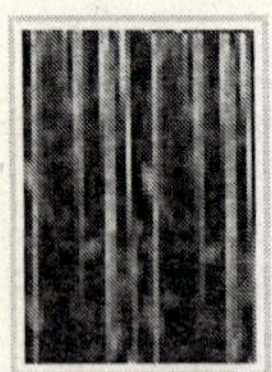

Some time ago I received a telephone call from a stranger who said, "I heard your talk tonight. I'm having a bad time. I know that my main problem is myself, but what I want to ask is, will you pray for me?"

"Of course," I said. "And I will do it right now." When I concluded the prayer, his reverent "Amen" echoed my own. After a moment he said, "Thanks a lot. I will get busy and follow through on that prayer."

When he had hung up, I asked myself: Do I follow through on my prayers? How often have I prayed "gimme" kind of prayers or desperation kind of prayers or bewildered prayers with no results? Having prayed, do I believe God has heard? Do I leave it with Him? Or do I shut out answers by continuing to expect the worst? Do I try to do something about the thing myself? I think everyone could ask these same questions. When you pray, do you follow through?

He who has the Son has life; he who does not have the Son of God does not have life. 1 JOHN 5:12

FEBRUARY 20

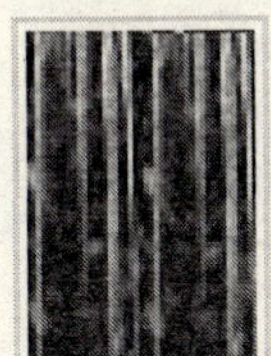

Jesus said "I have come that they may have life, and have it to the full" (John 10:10). Life. What is life? Life is vitality. It is excitement. It is enthusiasm. It is motion. And the Bible says, "His life gave life to everyone." Jesus was the most alive being who ever walked the earth. Even death couldn't crush Him. He said, "Because I live, you also will live" (John 14:19). And that statement in 1 John 5:12—that is really tremendous, a ringing message to anybody who wants to live.

Christianity is an either/or business. It lays it on the line. Either you have it, or you don't have it. Christianity tells us that if you want to have life—real life, life so exciting that you can hardly stand it, so thrilling that you never can erase it, so glorious that you can never get over it—then have the life that is in the Son. If you don't have this, you're not really alive.

But because of his great love for us, God, who is rich in mercy, made us alive with Christ even when we were dead in transgressions—it is by grace you have been saved. EPHESIANS 2:4–5

FEBRUARY 21

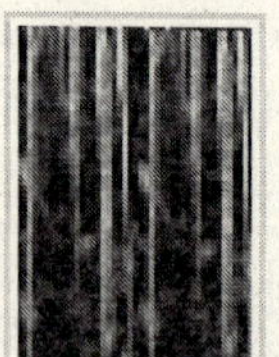

How wonderful life would be if we could just hold on to mystical experiences with perpetual enthusiasm! And some people do—like a man I met who told me, "I hate to go to bed at night, I'm so afraid I will miss something. I can hardly wait to get up in the morning, I am so happy. Since I met Jesus Christ and surrendered my life to Him, it just seems that He pours His power and glory into me every day. I am so wonderfully alive."

Are you alive? The Father wants to give you the Kingdom, so that you will delight in life. How is that done? By transferring life to you. This is the greatest thing about the Christian religion. Jesus wants to give us abundant, overflowing life. Because He lived it, you and I can live it, too, if we pay the price to get it.

Jesus Christ is the same yesterday and today and forever. HEBREWS 13:8

FEBRUARY 22

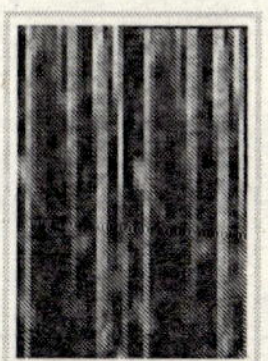

I was brought up on revival meetings, those of Billy Sunday and other evangelists. In churches each winter, they had what were called protracted meetings. These were strung out over many nights, and the whole impact and effort was to win people to Christ and away from their evil and indifferent living.

While I naturally changed my approach because I was living in a modern age, I feel that the gospel preached in 1840, 1890, and 1940 is the same gospel that the American people need today. I believe that Jesus Christ, Lord and Savior, divine Son of God, who died on the cross for our redemption, is the chief message of the church in any age. Christianity is timeless.

The only figure in history who endures is Jesus. Great statesmen arise, but they are a dim memory twenty years after they die. Their principles seem antique to the modern ear. Only Jesus is everlastingly modern. His gospel is as fresh as today's newspapers. That is why He lives while others fade into oblivion.

"In repentance and rest is your salvation, in quietness and trust is your strength, but you would have none of it." ISAIAH 30:15

FEBRUARY 23

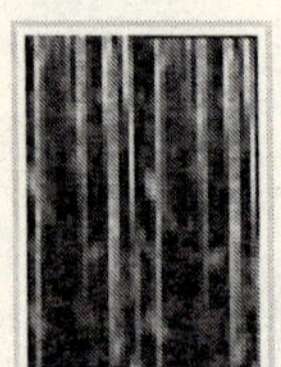

Dwell on this tremendous thought from Isaiah: "I will make you strong if you quietly trust me." One of the basic, fundamental ingredients of the Christian religion is strength. Those who built Christianity knew how the onslaughts of circumstance, difficulty, pain, sorrow, opposition, and resentment can break a human being down. But the prophets and apostles and, most of all, Jesus Himself built into the structure of our faith a power that can make us men and women who handle life majestically. Your job and mine is to handle life. If you don't handle life, it will handle you. So the issue is who handles what. You are created in the image of God. Go home and look in the mirror and tell yourself that through Him, this strength can be yours.

Our Heavenly Father, You have given us assurance that You are our refuge and our strength and our very present help in time of trouble. And for this we give thanks through Jesus Christ, our Lord. Amen.

Let us fix our eyes on Jesus . . . who for the joy set before him endured the cross, scorning its shame, and sat down at the right hand of the throne of God. HEBREWS 12:2

FEBRUARY 24

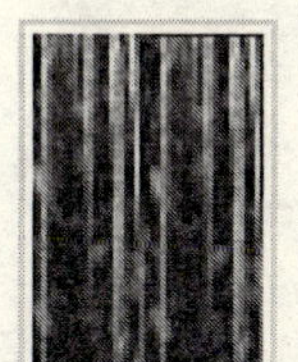

I have a letter from a woman who told me that if I wished to share her story I could. Here is what she says:

"They tell me I have heart disease and only one year to live. I don't believe they always know, especially about us Irish Christians, who are made of pretty tough stuff! I have buried two sons. I've had nine operations and rheumatic fever, in addition to this heart disease. You're probably thinking, 'That poor woman!' But don't you dare. Save your pity for some poor soul who isn't tough-minded and optimistic.

"I'm forty-five years young and I'm going to live to be ninety if the Lord wills it. I've never been in need since I found the Lord. I'm proud that God has chosen me to bear these crosses, and grateful that He gave me a strong back to bear them.

"I'm happy. My friends tell me I'm a character. I'm never quite sure just how they mean it. But if I'm a character because I can laugh and enjoy God's wonderful world we live in, then I'm a character."

". . . As I have loved you, so you must love one another. By this all men will know that you are my disciples, if you love one another." JOHN 13:34–35

FEBRUARY 25

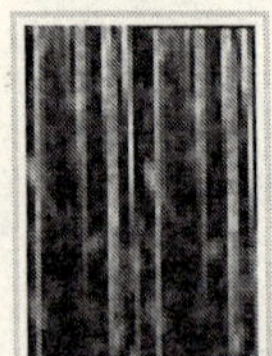

I believe that faithful following of these five rules will revolutionize the life of any person.

First: Be bold, and mighty forces will come to your aid. The person who is afraid cuts himself off from the flow of power, but when you venture boldly, there comes a flow of power in response.

Second: Deny adverse conditions. Don't go around saying or thinking: "Conditions are against me." Face facts, but realize that it often happens that a person is defeated not so much by the facts of a situation as by his negative interpretation of the facts. In every problem there is an inherent good. Believe that.

Third: Picture good outcomes. By envisioning good things, you actually bring good influences into play, both within yourself and in the world around you.

Fourth: Pray for every person you meet with by name, that he or she may benefit from the dealings you have with him or her.

Fifth: Practice Christian love toward everybody.

The Sovereign LORD is my strength; he makes my feet like the feet of a deer, he enables me to go on the heights. . . . HABAKKUK 3:19

FEBRUARY 26

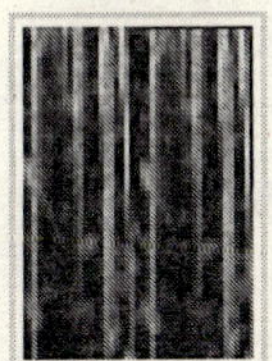

When you have experienced a defeat, you should promptly make a new endeavor. Otherwise you'll get the idea that life's too much for you and will keep defeating you. When you experience a defeat, take it to Jesus and say, "Lord, I messed this one up badly."

He'll say to you, "Just take more of Me into your heart and into your life."

That's the message which poor, defeated humanity needs to hear and heed. You cannot handle everything with just your own strength. But with Jesus Christ, we become "more than conquerors." God will not let us be tempted beyond our strength, which means we shall be equal to any circumstances or conditions we may encounter. And if we stay in contact with Jesus Christ, we continue to receive this power.

Keep your lives free from the love of money and be content with what you have, because God has said, "Never will I leave you; never will I forsake you." HEBREWS 13:5

FEBRUARY 27

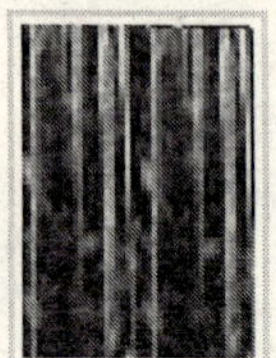

A couple consulted a minister in California and said, "We don't understand why we have money trouble all the time. You talk about the boundless generosity of God, but we never see anything of it." And they asked, "Will you pray for us?"

The minister gave them a strange task. "Tomorrow I want you to go to the beach. See if you can calculate how many grains of sand the Lord made. When you get tired of considering the sand, walk through the park and count all the leaves on the trees.

"I want you to realize," the minister told them, "that this God who has put all the sand on the beach and all the leaves on the trees is trying to put blessings into your life. But you're closed. Your belief is too little."

The couple went and talked it over with God. And they began to reappraise their lives. They started an enterprise that brought new value and prosperity to their lives. They learned to believe big, pray big, think big, and built themselves a full, rich, satisfying life.

My help comes from the LORD, *the Maker of heaven and earth.* PSALM 121:2

FEBRUARY 28

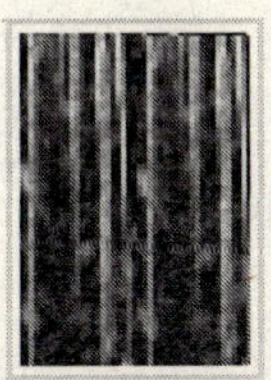

God will help you if you let Him. Even God, with all His power, cannot help you unless you will allow Him to do so, for He has made man a free agent, with power of choice. But one of the greatest of all facts is that God is ever-ready to help you with whatever difficulty you may have, however great it may be. With His help, you will either solve your problem, overcome your difficulty, or learn to live with it and get along with it.

Take any sizable group of people and you can find the whole range of human problems represented to one degree or another among them. There will be people who are very sad, laboring under a weight of grief; there will be people who are very discouraged, for whom things haven't gone well, who have encountered much resistance and to whom life seems very hard. But God will help them all if they will let Him.

"Turn to me and be saved, all you ends of the earth; for I am God, and there is no other." ISAIAH 45:22

FEBRUARY 29

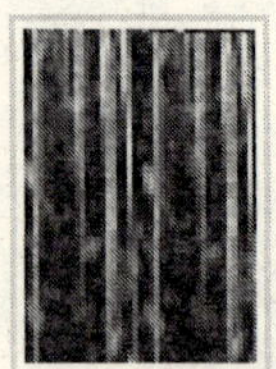

Once in Miami Beach, I spoke to a large audience of businessmen. Among those present was a man named Ford Philpot, who was one of the greatest demonstrations of power I have ever encountered. Ford was a young man with all kinds of personality, but he had become an alcoholic. In the grip of that complicated disease, he sank lower and lower. He was expelled from school and spent all his time in bars.

Everybody—family, friends, doctors, everybody—had tried to help him, but with no success. Then one night he unaccountably decided to reach for a power that could save him. Later the same night, he knelt in prayer with a group of dedicated men, and by midnight, was so completely delivered from his old weakness that it never again controlled him. He became a minister who helped and inspired many other human bcings.

March

And surely I am with you always, to the very end of the age. . . . Matthew 28:20

Wait for the LORD; *be strong and take heart and wait for the* LORD. PSALM 27:14

MARCH 1

You don't have to stand up to your problem alone, for God is with you. And this is really a great thing. If we had to stand up to tough problems alone, life would be very bitter. In the end, it would be a losing battle, for man isn't that big. The greatest among us is small in the presence of some problems of human life. So we should forever be mindful, and grateful, that we are not alone.

The secret, then, is to stand up to your problem by taking it and doing all you can about it. Then put it in God's hands, turning it over to Him. Turn away from the problem and turn to God. When you pick the problem up again, it will be the way He wants it. And that means it will be right. You'll get your answer. It may be "no," it may be "wait a while," it may be "yes," but it will be the right answer.

God is our refuge and strength, an ever-present help in trouble. Psalm 46:1

March 2

If you are troubled, spend half an hour doing nothing but reading the Bible. Open to Psalms, Proverbs, or to Matthew, Mark, Luke, or John. Let God give you quietness. Then, whatever anybody may be doing to trouble you, or whatever you have been doing to trouble yourself, it can trouble you no longer—you are above it.

A man who heard me preach a number of times said to me, "You know, you only have one sermon—just one message. You come at it a little differently each time, but it's the same message."

"What is it?" I asked.

"It is this: "Whatever the problem, surrender your life into the hands of Jesus Christ."

"I'll settle for that," I said. "It is the answer."

We have minds and we are supposed to use them. Heaven help us if we don't. God does help those who help themselves; but there are problems we cannot handle without a greater wisdom and power than our own.

My soul finds rest in God alone;
my salvation comes from him.
Psalm 62:1

March 3

I was on friendly terms with Jesse L. Lasky, a pioneer of the motion picture industry and a wonderful and spiritually minded man. One evening at his home, he said to me, "Before dinner I want you to spend fifteen minutes in my silence room." I was intrigued, of course.

He took me to a room used as a place to practice creative silence. On the table there was a Bible and a stack of cards on which he had written texts from the Bible which had to do with silence and peace.

"I will leave you here," he said, "to commune with God's silence." He was gone for fifteen minutes. It was a delightful, renewing experience.

Are you aware of inner silence even now? You can spend this very moment in the temple of silence, acquainting yourself with God and becoming peaceful. Practice creative silence.

"The Spirit of the L*ORD is on me, because he has anointed me to preach good news to the poor. . . ."* L*UKE 4:18*

MARCH 4

A physician told me that as a boy he was full of fear, anxiety, nervous tension, and apprehension. Perhaps because of his own emotional frailty, he decided that he wanted to help the sick find health again. But when he began his practice, he was stymied. There was no health in him; how could he give health to other people?

He went to one of his old professors and poured out his problem. The older doctor said, "Son, there is only one physician who can heal you and His name is Jesus Christ. You put your life in His hands, and He will heal you of your fears."

The young doctor found healing in the words of the Bible. They sank into his consciousness and into his subconscious mind, and drove out the disease of fear. He became a strong man of faith and a great healer.

The law of the LORD *is perfect, reviving the soul. The statutes of the* LORD *are trustworthy, making wise the simple.* PSALM 19:7

MARCH 5

Things go well when you get in tune with the Lord. Get on His side. Live His way. We can, I believe, take comfort in what may be called the law of opposites. This whole world is filled with opposites. There is up and its opposite, down. There is light and its opposite, dark. There is wet and its opposite, dry. There is heat and its opposite, cold. There is a problem and there is its opposite, a solution.

But the question is: How do you find this answer to every problem? Psalm 19:7 states: "The law of the LORD is perfect, reviving the soul. The statutes of the LORD are trustworthy, making wise the simple." There you have it in a capsule. You overcome your difficulties and you solve your problems by in-depth understanding, which you obtain from the precepts of God.

"Be strong and courageous. Do not be afraid or terrified because of them, for the LORD *your God goes with you; he will never leave you nor forsake you."* DEUTERONOMY 31:6

MARCH 6

There are plenty of people who experience fear continually without even having any notion what it is they are afraid of. Now, what can you do about the problem of fear? You can do either one of two things. One is to give in to your fears and permit yourself to be dominated by them all your life. Many people do just that. They carry their fears with them all the days of their lives, suffering misery and inner conflict until the very end of their days. That is a piteous thing.

The other course—the only alternative—is to rise up in the full stature of your manhood or womanhood and, with all the help of Almighty God and of the Lord Jesus Christ, dominate your fears. If you do that, you will have gained a victory that will make you worthy of eternal life. That kind of greatness is possible in every human being.

We proclaim to you what we have seen and heard, so that you also may have fellowship with us. And our fellowship is with the Father and with his Son, Jesus Christ. 1 JOHN 1:3

MARCH 7

A man once gave me an insight into overcoming problems. "My mother," he told me, "used to say, 'When you have a problem and you've worked as hard as you can at it and still haven't solved it, the thing to do is just walk away and think about God. But don't talk to God about the problem. Tell Him how much you love Him, thank Him for all He has done for you, tell Him you want to be His faithful follower. Have fellowship with God and with Jesus.'"

How wise that woman was! An irreligious person might advise you to put the problem aside and play a game of golf. But there is a vast difference between playing a game of golf and talking to Jesus—Jesus lifts you way up, so that when you go back to the problem you have grown, the problem has shrunk. Then, prayerfully, you can break it open and find the answer.

"I have come into the world as a light, so that no one who believes in me should stay in darkness." JOHN 12:46

MARCH 8

A friend of mine reads the Bible every morning. He always reads something written by Paul, he says, because he thinks Paul had the most acute and profound mind he knows. He says, "I like to sharpen my mind on the great, keen mind of Paul."

I did this myself once, and it did me good. I was in my study working on a sermon. It was raining and the rain was beating against the windowpane. I love the sound of the rain, and because I wasn't getting anywhere with the sermon, I turned around and watched the rain. Suddenly I asked myself: "Why are you preaching sermons?" I thought it over and I came to an answer. It is because I believe with all my heart in the immense power of Jesus Christ to change the life of the entire world. This is my greatest enthusiasm.

". . . See how the lilies of the field grow. They do not labor or spin. Yet I tell you that not even Solomon in all his splendor was dressed like one of these." MATTHEW 6:28–29

MARCH 9

I recall the wisdom of the man from whom I first heard of the law of supply. He went through fire and flood and depression and panic and made out all right. He used to say, "The law of supply never failed me once."

"What is this 'law of supply'?" I asked him. I had never heard of it in the schools I went to.

"It is an inclination of the universe to sustain you if you're in harmony with the flow of rightness. And you get in harmony with it by letting your thoughts open up big. Let the soul flower out," he said. "Speak big, pray big, ask big, give big, believe big, love big, and bigness will flow to you."

Now this doesn't mean that by being in harmony with the law of supply, you will necessarily get rich. God isn't going to line your pockets, but He will give you all you need if you are in harmony with His will, loving and serving others and forgetting yourself—in other words, if your soul gets big.

When he had finished speaking, he said to Simon, "Put out into deep water, and let down the nets for a catch." LUKE 5:4

MARCH 10

I was reading in the Gospel of Luke about the time when Jesus told his disciples to launch out into deep water if they wanted to get any fish. It's a message to anyone who wants to pack meaning into his life. Get away from yourself. Don't be tied up with yourself. Don't hang on to yourself. "Put out into deep water, and let down the nets for a catch"—and you'll pull up more values than you could imagine.

One of the ways you launch out into the deep is to embrace the profound principle that abiding, joyous life comes only through giving. The people who throw themselves into some great social issue—forgetting themselves, being willing to suffer hurt if necessary for their convictions and ideals—become the happiest people in the world because they are growing bigger. When you give, you get bigger, you grow, your personality expands. You become a far greater individual by giving yourself, your time, your money.

"But seek first his kingdom and his righteousness, and all these things will be given to you as well." MATTHEW 6:33

MARCH 11

Many years ago the president of a great corporation told me, "For years I have made decisions on problems and made them fast. Now I live in fear of making decisions. You're a spiritual doctor. Can you give me a prescription to cure me of this?"

So I gave him this prescription: "When you get up in the morning, say, 'Thank You, Lord, for giving me a good night's sleep. Now I'm going to go to work. And each time I have to make a decision, I'm going to talk with You about it. I can't go wrong with You helping me.' Before you go to sleep say, 'Thank You, Lord, for all the decisions we made today.'"

He assured me he would follow the prescription. And he did. He became a strong, effective man again, having discovered that if you seek the Lord, He will hear you and will deliver you from all your fears.

". . . I tell you the truth, if you have faith as small as a mustard seed, you can say to this mountain, 'Move from here to there' and it will move. Nothing will be impossible for you." MATTHEW 17:20

MARCH 12

Confidence is a vital ingredient of living. The Bible regards confidence—faith in God—as necessary to our well-being. One day you may notice a huge obstacle in your pathway. You can't get around it and you don't know what to do about it. That is your mountain. It has you licked. But you can knock it down if you have faith, if you believe.

You can overcome gigantic obstacles and have a life more wonderful than you ever imagined if you recondition your mind. Learn to reject small thinking. Never admit a negative thought. Never give utterance to defeatist fears. Talk it up, think it up, believe it up! As you think big, big results will come.

Our Heavenly Father, help us to be big enough to take the big things You offer and live the big life You intend for us. Through Jesus Christ, our Lord. Amen.

"Then you will know the truth, and the truth will set you free." JOHN 8:32

MARCH 13

After a speech one evening, a young man told me his story: "I was a salesman, but I couldn't sell," he said in a booming voice. "I knew the trouble was that I had clamps on me of shyness and self-doubt. These things held me tight and I couldn't get free. I went to my pastor and he said, 'Bill, turn to Jesus and ask Him to free you of these things. If you give your life to the Lord, He will give Himself to you.'

"So," Bill said, "I did and those clamps fell away, and I was able to sell. But I realized that the big thing that had happened was that I was free inside. It was as if I had moved out of a little cell into the big wide world."

The man's face glowed. People who stood listening had misty eyes, for they were seeing one of the greatest things in the world: a man set free by the power of Jesus Christ.

"'Call to me and I will answer you and tell you great and unsearchable things you do not know.'" JEREMIAH 33:3

MARCH 14

The Christian religion is far greater than anyone realizes. It tells weak people that they can become strong. It tells defeated people that they can become victorious. It tells unhappy, mixed-up people that they can become organized. It teaches that we can become great. There is nothing else like it in the whole wide world.

Listen to just this one statement from Jeremiah: "'Call to me and I will answer you and tell you great and unsearchable things you do not know.'" Call upon God, it says, and He will answer; He will show you tremendous things. And yet we make something small and indifferent out of our religion.

There is a very profound law of human nature which says that we become, to a very large degree, what we think. If you think little and believe little and act little, the results are likely to be little. If, on the other hand, you think big, believe big, and act big, the results are very likely to equate with bigness.

Yet to all who received him, to those who believed in his name, he gave the right to become children of God. JOHN 1:12

MARCH 15

Think what might be accomplished in the United States if only a few of the best young people among us would have the revolutionary spirit their forefathers had and would determine, "This great fair land shall not be destroyed. We'll make it clean, so that high leadership for the future may be certain and sure."

"Well," you may think, "I'm not a young person." Maybe not; but if all the men and women in this country who profess belief in God would live clean lives and would set those lives against the decay of our time, they would be contributing to a moral revolution. I believe the time has come for greatness. That is what built this country's splendor, power, and prestige. That is the only force that can hold its future secure. So get into the fight against evil. "Yet to all who received him, to those who believed in his name, he gave the right to become children of God" (John 1:12). That's the difference between a little life and a tremendous life.

When Jesus heard this, he was astonished and said to those following him, "I tell you the truth, I have not found anyone in Israel with such great faith." MATTHEW 8:10

MARCH 16

A man wandering outside on a moonless night decided to take a shortcut through the cemetery. He stepped in some loose dirt and fell to the bottom of a newly dug grave. He tried to climb out but couldn't, so he decided to just take it easy until morning.

He was half asleep when a second man slipped in the dirt and also fell into the grave. He struggled to get out and couldn't. In the darkness, the first man said, "You'll never get out of this grave." But the second man, startled, did get out. Fear sent him over the top.

Faith, however, is an even greater force. A ball will roll downhill, a flower will come out of a seed, and faith will cancel out fear. So the secret we must all master, if our lives are to be as effective as we want them to be, is how to get our faith built up, how to protect it, how to live by it.

Finally, brothers, whatever is true, whatever is noble, whatever is right, whatever is pure, whatever is lovely, whatever is admirable . . . think about such things. PHILIPPIANS 4:8

MARCH 17

You can't have a sound mind unless you have a clean mind. Any dirtiness in the mind will send out spiritual and intellectual disease and will create a pathological condition. There have probably been more worries and fears started and grown by guilt than by any other thing. An unclean mind grows fear, anxiety, and conflict. Here again is where the Gospel comes in. By the grace of Jesus Christ the mind can be cleansed. And when it is cleansed, it becomes sound once again.

So have a sound mind in which there is no guilt, in which there is statistical common sense, in which there is control of the spasm of emotions that grasp an obsessive idea. Do you see why Jesus Christ is called the Great Physician? He understands the intricacies of human nature as nobody else does. And in His touch, there is wondrous healing of fear, anxiety, and worry.

So we say with confidence, "The LORD is my helper; I will not be afraid. What can man do to me?" HEBREWS 13:6

MARCH 18

Fear is tenacious. It gets down into the intricacies of your consciousness. So how can you get it out? The first step is to know that fear, like every other deficiency of human personality, is removable. God didn't give it to you. You took it on yourself or it was put upon you by your environment. But it is removable.

Don't think that you've got to live with fear. Don't imagine that because your father or your mother had it, or your grandfather had it, you've got to have it. You only have to have what you're willing to have. If you want to live with fear, you can. But it is removable.

Once you know that it is removable, then comes the process of removing it. And this involves something which isn't very popular with this generation, but which this generation needs to relearn: self-discipline. You can do anything you want to with yourself if you have what it takes to discipline yourself.

Though you have not seen him, you love him; and even though you do not see him now, you believe in him and are filled with an inexpressible and glorious joy. 1 PETER 1:8

MARCH 19

Would you like to have a sense of well-being? Would you like to be filled with energy, vitality, eagerness, enthusiasm, even excitement? That is a healthy person. How enthusiastic are you? How thrilled are you? How excited are you?

One January night, I looked out the window at midnight to see a glorious snowstorm. I became so excited that I rushed back to the bedroom where my wife was sound asleep and said, "Ruth, get out of that bed. Let's get dressed and take a walk in the snow!"

Don't get to the point where you do not thrill to feel blood surging through your system. Don't get so you cannot breathe pure cold air down into your lungs and feel sheer exhilaration. Don't become withdrawn. Live with vitality and energy and excitement.

The Bible is full of life. Life is a big word in this Book. And one of the things life includes is to have the blessings of health, to be a whole, integrated, organized, enthusiastic human being.

". . . And surely I am with you always, to the very end of the age." MATTHEW 28:20

MARCH 20

The Democratic convention that nominated Grover Cleveland for president declared, "We love him for the enemies he has made." During the campaign, advisers kept reminding Cleveland that, in order to be elected, he would have to carry New York state. When his campaigning brought him to New York City, he attended a dinner at which two bosses of the notorious Tammany Hall political machine were present.

After dinner these men wanted to know, "What will you give us?" "I will not give you one single, solitary thing," Cleveland answered. The Tammany Hall bosses respected Cleveland's bluntness and integrity. They got behind him and helped him carry New York.

In a similar way, the presence of God helps us resist fear and intimidation. You are not alone in this great big universe. God is with you. You can stand in the presence of difficulties, pain, onslaughts, resistance, criticism, anything, and not be afraid. God is with you.

Worship the Lord *with gladness; come before him with joyful songs.* Psalm 100:2

March 21

I've noticed that the non-enthusiast, the pessimist, has a remarkably high score for faulty judgment. For example, in 1806, William Pitt, one of the greatest statesmen in history, declared, "There is scarcely anything around us but ruin and despair." In 1852, the Duke of Wellington, on his deathbed, stated, "I thank God I shall be spared from seeing the consummation of ruin that is gathering about us in this world."

Well, friends, do these comments strike you as familiar? Some people spend their lives insisting that the world is going to pieces. But the world blunders along, striving for something nobler. And the world will attain it if it keeps enthusiasm working for it. *Enthusiasm*! It is a word that is built deeply into the victorious spirit of humans. Enthusiasm literally means "full of God." God will help you overcome all difficulties, all tragedies, all sorrows, all heartaches, all defeats, and will give victory.

The earth is the LORD'S, and everything in it, the world, and all who live in it. PSALM 24:1

MARCH 22

There is no power in the world equal to spiritual power. Some people think atomic power is the greatest power in the world. Well, it is certainly an enormous, explosive power—there is no getting around that. It is a terrible power. But call to mind the sight of spring sunshine streaming through a window. There is more power there than there is in atomic energy—within a period of a few weeks, the earth awakens to that power and soon grass and flowers cover the earth, powered by something that makes no noise. That is more than atomic power can do. Just think about it. Don't judge power by the noise it makes. Judge it by the results it achieves.

Our Heavenly Father, help us to give our minds a new mental and spiritual guide—living on the great teachings of Jesus that have the power to change thinking, to change everything. Amen.

I am not ashamed of the gospel, because it is the power of God for the salvation of everyone who believes: first for the Jew, then for the Gentile. ROMANS 1:16

MARCH 23

I think one of the most heroic episodes in the human story is Paul standing at the gates of the eternal city with a smile on his lips. Probably he threw back his shoulders as he said to mighty Rome, "I, not you, have the lasting power."

Rome, the city of the caesars, was for its time the personification of earthly power. Nobody could take it; but Paul did. Three centuries after he passed through its gates, the Emperor Constantine declared the new faith of Christianity the religion of the Roman empire. Multitudes were baptized into the faith called by the name of the lowly Nazarene.

Paul declared in a statement that shall live as long as life lasts: "I am not ashamed of the gospel, because it is the power of God for the salvation of everyone who believes: first for the Jew, then for the Gentile" (Romans 1:16). So won't you believe, really believe? If you have never given your heart to Christ, never allowed Christianity in depth to take root in your heart, I beseech you to do so now.

Rejoice in the Lord and be glad, you righteous;
sing, all you who are upright in heart!
PSALM 32:11

MARCH 24

In 1907 Frank Bettger was playing baseball for Johnstown, Pennsylvania. One day, the manager fired Bettger because he was too lazy. The manager said, "Whatever you do next, for heaven's sake, put some enthusiasm into your work."

Bettger took the first job he could get, playing in a fourth-class league. He decided to begin acting enthusiastic, and this had an interesting result. An old ballplayer perceived that this boy had possibilities and persuaded New Haven, Connecticut, to give him a try. "From the minute I appeared on the field," Bettger would say, "I acted like a man electrified."

The next day the newspaper said, "This new player is a barrel of enthusiasm." They nicknamed him "Pep" Bettger. From there he went on to big league baseball, playing third base for the St. Louis Cardinals.

For God did not give us a spirit of timidity, but a spirit of power, of love and of self-discipline. 2 TIMOTHY 1:7

MARCH 25

We modern, civilized people live in a fear-ridden world. What things are we afraid of? We are afraid of money problems, of the boss, of the job; we are afraid of other people; we are afraid of ourselves—afraid that we will not have what it takes to do what we ought to do. Children are afraid of their parents and, heaven help us, parents today are oftentimes afraid of their children. There is a veritable plague of fears concerning health. We are afraid of cancer, of viruses, of being awakened in the middle of the night and having to be hurried off to the hospital.

As you go about your day, say to yourself, "I am strong in the Lord. I am not afraid. 'For God did not give us a spirit of timidity, but a spirit of power, of love and of self-discipline'" (2 Tmothy 1:7).

Finally, be strong in the LORD *and in his mighty power.* EPHESIANS 6:10

MARCH 26

Christians should never lack confidence. They, of all people, should be confident, for they are not like those who have no hope. Their lives are based upon something unshakable, something enduring, something completely secure—Almighty God, the Father of our Lord Jesus Christ, and our Savior Himself. Therefore, if you feel weak, defeated, and insecure, I call upon you to return to Jesus Christ and build Him into the center of your life. Then you will never be lacking in sound confidence.

Remember this great affirmation from Romans 8:38–39: "For I am convinced that neither death nor life, neither angels nor demons, neither the present nor the future, nor any powers, neither height nor depth, nor anything else in all creation, will be able to separate us from the love of God that is in Christ Jesus our Lord."

Consequently, faith comes from hearing the message, and the message is heard through the word of Christ. ROMANS 10:17

MARCH 27

Perhaps you've read the story about John Wesley, the famous religious leader, who came from England to Georgia in the eighteenth century, on a small ship. They encountered an enormous storm and Wesley, by his own admission later, was petrified.

There was a group of religious people on board, known as Moravians. They were calm and unaffected by the storm. When it was all over, Wesley asked the Moravian leader, "How did you manage to have such composure and such faith? How can I have faith?"

The man told him, "Act as though you have faith, and by and by, you will have faith."

So if you want to have enthusiasm, say to yourself, "The Lord God gave me enthusiasm. But this thing that God built into me has somehow escaped me. I know that potentially I have it. Therefore, I will act as though I were enthusiastic." By and by, that which God gave you at birth will reassert itself.

Therefore put on the full armor of God, so that when the day of evil comes, you may be able to stand your ground, and after you have done everything, to stand. EPHESIANS 6:13

MARCH 28

God helps you when you can't help yourself. Let's face it. You are strong and you can do lots of things, but there come times in life when you haven't got what it takes to do any more. You struggle with things and they won't come right. You face difficulties and you can't overcome them. Then you should turn and say, "Dear God, why am I doing it wrong? Why can't I handle it? I turn it over to You. I put it in Your hands."

God can do for us what we can't do for ourselves. So the principle, as Paul said, is that "when the day of evil comes, you may be able to stand your ground, and after you have done everything, to stand" (Ephesians 6:13). Having done everything you can do, then just put it in the hands of God and let it go. Of course, this is one of the most difficult things—to let something go. But let Him take it. Don't strain and strive and be under stress with it so much. Let it go! Let go and let God.

Because those who are led by the Spirit of God are sons of God. . . . And by him we cry, "Abba, Father." ROMANS 8:14–15

MARCH 29

Christianity provides the techniques for becoming strong in life. Christianity provides the formulas and principles by which a person can really live with certainty, conviction, and confidence in all the circumstances of this life. One must have a simple, humble, and active faith in God, not as an inscrutable idea, the far-removed Creator of the universe, but as a friend and helper who is with you all the time.

The greatest truth in this world, in many respects, is this: We are not alone. Whoever develops simply and humbly this confidence in the intimate presence of God will have one great shining word made real: *confidence*.

Our Heavenly Father, we give You thanks that we are not alone in this world, but that You are always and at any time here. In this will we be confident. In His name. Amen.

"Therefore do not worry about tomorrow,
for tomorrow will worry about itself.
Each day has enough trouble of its own."
MATTHEW 6:34

MARCH 30

Sometimes when I stand at the pulpit and look out at the congregation, I could almost swear that everybody present is inwardly confident and calm. But I know that if you could gather together all the fears lurking behind all those impassive faces, you would have a great load of fear.

I've often thought it would be wonderful if we could have two collections at each church service. The first would be the usual collection of money. Then I would ask everybody to come up and lay his fears on the altar and leave them there with God. Or maybe we could have the ushers go down the aisles and take up all the fears. Then I would say, "Let's stand and sing." Nobody would have to be told what to sing. Everybody would feel so free and released that the whole congregation would burst out singing "Praise God from whom all blessings flow . . ." so joyously it would knock off the church roof.

The Lord *is my light and my salvation—whom shall I fear? The* Lord *is the stronghold of my life—of whom shall I be afraid?* Psalm 27:1

March 31

Those many, many thousands, even millions, of people for whom life is very hard are asking themselves, "How can I have what it takes?" Christianity has an answer to this problem. When the going is hard, when difficulties mount up, when the stresses are great, when the resistances are overwhelming, Christianity tells us that through faith in God and commitment to Jesus Christ, we have within us all that is needed to handle anything that confronts us. Psalm 27:1, for instance, shows that Christianity is the most rugged, vital, powerful faith ever found among men. It says, "The Lord is my light and my salvation—whom shall I fear? The Lord is the stronghold of my life—of whom shall I be afraid?" Does anybody have more strength than the Lord does? No. This faith is so toughening that we can develop what it takes to stand up to anything life may hand us.

COMMIT TO THE LORD WHATEVER YOU DO, AND YOUR PLANS WILL SUCCEED. PROVERBS 16:3

"My grace is sufficient for you, for my power is made perfect in weakness."...

2 CORINTHIANS 12:9

APRIL 1

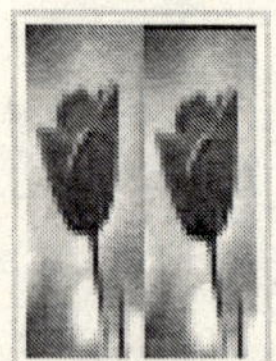

Do you think Christianity would be such a dynamic force in the world if it were not an extraordinary adventure for human beings? Just let it into your life. If you really let it in, not just as an idea, but as a power, you will experience the sure cure for depressive feelings and for every other ailment of the human spirit. You really will.

We find the secret stated many times in the Bible. I find it, for example, in 2 Corinthians 12:9, in the wonderful words: "My grace is sufficient for you." That is to say, nothing can ever happen to you that you cannot meet with faith in Him, because His kindness is sufficient. The text goes on to say, "my power is made perfect in weakness." That is to say, if in your weakness, you will turn to God, His strength will be manifested through that weakness. You have the kindness of God, which provides everything you need.

Seek the L*ORD* *while he may be found; call on him while he is near.* ISAIAH 55:6

APRIL 2

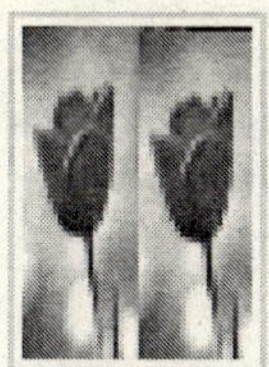

Do you ever consider your life? Does it need changing? Are you in control of yourself? Are you the master of yourself and of your life? Are you proud of the life you live or are you ashamed of yourself? Have you fallen for the notions of those who maintain that the morality of the Lord Jesus is outmoded? Do you listen to those who want to set Jesus aside? Why, time will set them aside. The ages don't set Him aside. "Heaven and earth will pass away, but my words will never pass away" (Mark 13:31).

What did He tell us? Be good, be honorable, be pure, be righteous, be loving. Well, have you lost the way? Many people do. But the wise person comes back to Christ and finds the way again.

He lifted me out of the slimy pit, out of the mud and mire; he set my feet on a rock and gave me a firm place to stand.

Psalm 40:2

April 3

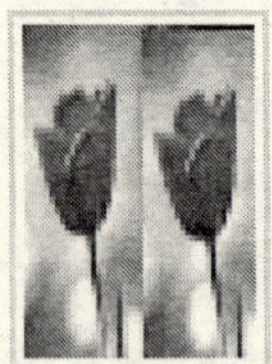

Why are you depressed? Why are you discouraged? Isn't it because your mind is full of shadows, full of gloom, full of ghosts? Most fears are ghosts, and they build up in the mind. I venture that if I could open your mind, I would cut through layer after layer of gloom and doubt and darkness. Maybe that is what we ought to do with our minds at very frequent intervals—open them up.

It's too bad, really, that we have such thick skulls. What the mind needs is ventilation to let out all the dark shadows. Naturally, you can't go around cutting holes in your head, but through the use of creative thought and prayer, you can ventilate your mind. How would you feel right now if every dark shadow and apprehension were lifted out of your mind? Why, let me tell you, people would meet you and they would say, "What in the world has come over you?" and you would be so excited and alive that you could scarcely contain yourself.

As a result, people brought the sick into the streets and laid them on beds and mats so that at least Peter's shadow might fall on some of them as he passed by. ACTS 5:15

APRIL 4

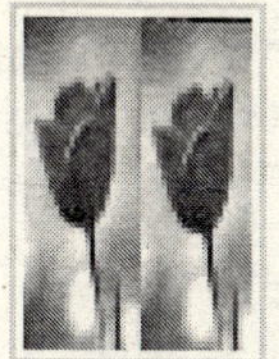

I follow the line of thought given to me by a gentleman I knew who was told by a competent doctor that he could not live more than a year. The doctor said, "There isn't anything specifically wrong with you, and yet everything seems to be wrong with you. Your whole organism seems to be deteriorating, and I believe it will give out within a year unless you get a tremendous infusion of faith into your mind. Affirm life. Say to yourself, 'I affirm that life is operating in me. Life is going through my nerves, my bloodstream; life is in me. I shall live by the life that is from God.'" The man took the doctor's advice and recovered from his illness.

Some cynics may say, "I don't believe in all that." Well, that is okay by me. The man I refer to is still alive and he does believe in it. Whatever works is legitimate, if it's in harmony with the will of God. In any case, many medical professionals today believe that the cultivation of harmony between the spirituality of man and his physical being is the future of healing.

"Blessed are the meek, for they will inherit the earth. Blessed are the peacemakers, for they will be called sons of God." MATTHEW 5:5, 9

APRIL 5

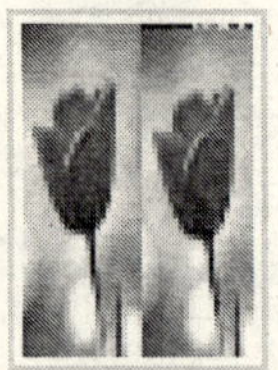

A woman telephoned me and said, "My problem is belligerence. Inside I'm a friendly person. But I have a quarrelsomeness in me and a lot of irritability." Then she told me about a time on the highway when her belligerence caused an accident. She said it was a miracle that nobody was hurt. "Talk about getting in your own way!" she said. "That sure is me!"

Christianity has an answer to this problem—many answers. If you accept the teachings and guidance and help that Jesus Christ offers you, you will be made free. You will be freed from your anger and hate, your depression, your discouragement, from whatever it is that gets you in your own way. You may be blocked by some defect, some failure in your personality. All can be healed by bringing the truth of God to bear upon it.

He who has clean hands and a pure heart, who does not lift up his soul to an idol or swear by what is false. He will receive blessing from the LORD and vindication from God his Savior. PSALM 24:4–5

APRIL 6

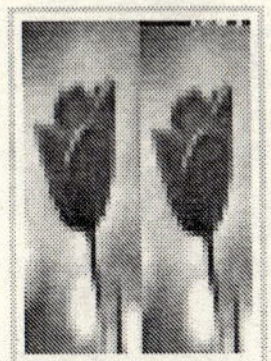

When you think of the world—how evil it seems to have become, how the old standards seem to have broken down, how mankind has reverted to the filth of Roman Empire days and wallows in it—remember also that there are beautiful mountains and rushing rivers and sounding seas and magnificent forests. Remember that the stars come nightly to the sky and that the sun still goes down in the west in radiant beauty.

Remember also that there are good people—people reaching for the good, people who will not let anything overwhelm them, people who see the surging fountains of the waters of life and wash themselves in them and become clean, fresh, and restored. Be glad that you have life. It is a precious thing. It is awfully good. Keep it good as long as you have it.

No, in all these things we are more than conquerors through him who loved us.

Romans 8:37

April 7

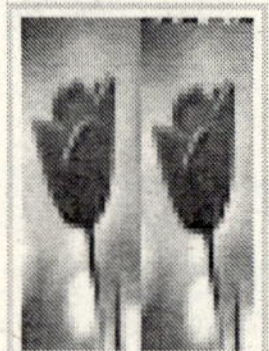

I went to Belfast to make three speeches. There is no central heating in Belfast. Every room has a fireplace or stove and its separate chimney. They are all smoking all the time and everything is grimy. It was raining and the smoke had no way to be lifted.

I stood at my window looking down at all the grimy houses. Then I saw something that changed the whole picture for me. As far as my eye could see, there were dozens of tall, soaring, graceful steeples. Why would any architect ever build a church without a steeple? A steeple is a symbol of the upthrust of faith in the midst of the smoke and the grime and the sin in human life, as if to say, "We believe in something higher, and this higher something must be visible to all the world." Jesus came to put the slender, soaring steeple into our souls and to move us to dedicate ourselves to the continuity of Christian idealism and faith.

Since we have these promises, dear friends, let us purify ourselves from everything that contaminates body and spirit, perfecting holiness out of reverence for God. 2 CORINTHIANS 7:1

APRIL 8

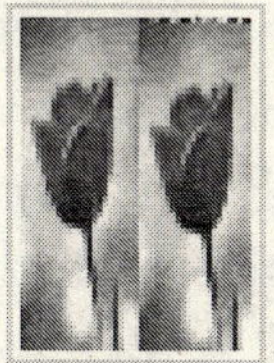

We must be careful, friends, not to be always basking in what Jesus does for us without ever asking what we can do for Him. He is at the forefront of a struggle going on continuously in this world. Some people call it the struggle between good and evil. Others call it the struggle between freedom and slavery, or the struggle between spiritual philosophy and crass materialism. It is a struggle between the greatness of humanity and the weakness of humanity.

And Jesus persistently holds before us ideals that we believe in but only half accept and hardly follow. H.G. Wells said once, "This Galilean is too much for our small hearts." There is a great deal of truth in that. But unless we have His greatness to pull us up, we sink down.

So David and his men went up to Baal Perazim, and there he defeated them. He said, "As waters break out, God has broken out against my enemies by my hand." . . . 1 CHRONICLES 14:11

APRIL 9

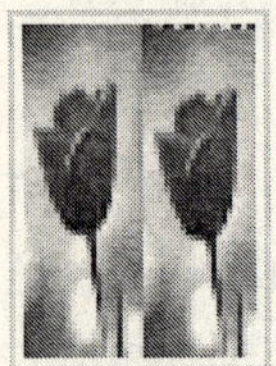

In the old days, Syracuse University had one of the greatest crew teams in the United States. Freshmen would watch them on the lake and they would go out for crew. The coach, Jim Ten Eyck, had them meet him at the football stadium. "You see all those aisles going up and down between the seats?" he would say. "I want you to walk up and down every one of those aisles." When they protested, he said, "You can't row until you've got good solid legs. You've got to have good lungs, lots of wind, deep diaphragms. You've got to be able to think too. I'll teach you how to think later on."

A man who had rowed on one of Jim's crews told me, "It paid off. I'll never forget the day when we pulled ahead of every other crew and won. We broke through into that power because we had practiced the work and the thinking and the discipline."

"'Then you will call upon me and come and pray to me, and I will listen to you. You will seek me and find me when you seek me with all your heart.'" JEREMIAH 29:12–13

APRIL 10

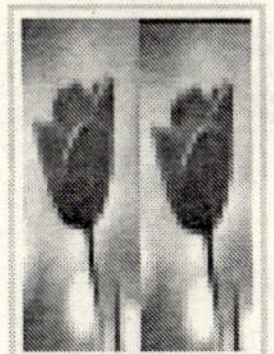

How deeply do we believe? Do we just believe superficially, without depth or commitment? In the book of Jeremiah we read, "Then you will call upon me and come and pray to me, and I will listen to you. You will seek me and find me when you seek me with all your heart." Nobody ever made anything great out of his life who didn't do it with his whole heart.

I remember talking to a celebrity years ago. I knew that she had had a great deal of trouble in her life. I asked, "How come you keep at it with such enthusiasm?"

"Why," she answered, "because I love it. I give my whole self to it." And she did; she threw everything she had into it. If you give yourself with all your heart to your business, to your children, to your marriage, to your future, to your hopes, you are going to come out with something that is lasting and strong.

Jesus replied, "Blessed are you, Simon son of Jonah, for this was not revealed to you by man, but by my Father in heaven." MATTHEW 16:17

APRIL 11

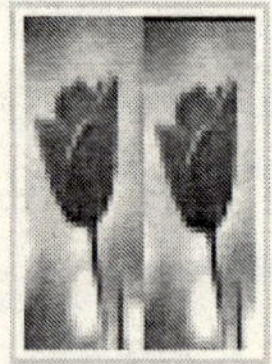

One time I crossed the Atlantic during hurricane season. I was lying in bed, seasick, and feeling helpless as the ship pitched mercilessly. Suddenly the door opened and a cheery fellow popped in. "What are you lying there for?" he said. "Let's go up on deck."

Well, that shamed me into it. We went up on deck and it was glorious. The waves were like horses with white manes thrown back. The wind drove streams of spray at us. My friend exclaimed, "Isn't this great?"

"It really is!" I agreed. I wasn't seasick at all after that. "You were lying there thinking error," observed my friend, "and up here you're thinking truth."

I realize there are serious diseases that may be difficult to handle in this way. Yet I have seen evidence that if you don't limit the power available to you, but allow it to move up and up, you can achieve tremendous results. Remember that you are called to be a disciple and to take power and authority over all devils and cure diseases—within you as well as in others.

Commit to the LORD *whatever you do, and your plans will succeed.* PROVERBS 16:3

APRIL 12

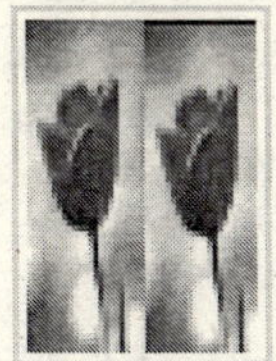

How can a better tomorrow be brought to pass? The real wisdom that answers this question is found in the greatest book of wisdom ever written. The book of Proverbs, chapter 16, verse 3, contains this gem of truth: "Commit to the LORD whatever you do, and your plans will succeed."

Now what does that mean? Dedicate to God everything you are doing. Place your activity, give all your works, into His hands. Your plans will work out; your hopes, your dreams, your ideals, your objectives, your goals will be realized. Your thoughts will be translated into actualities. This is an astonishing promise. This is worth its weight in gold. Commit into the hands of God what you are doing today and again what you are doing the next day, and again every day after that. Let God have everything and yourself along with it.

Our Heavenly Father, help us to let go of our straining and overpressing and gain peace and wisdom and power. Through Jesus Christ, our Lord. Amen.

On hearing this, Jesus said to them, "It is not the healthy who need a doctor, but the sick. I have not come to call the righteous, but sinners." MARK 2:17

APRIL 13

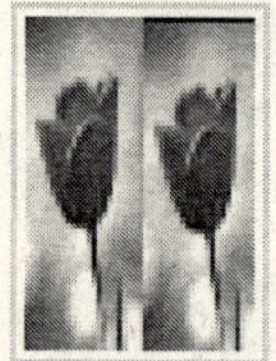

A physician once told me that he was convinced that countless thousands of people are ill from what he called "dammed-up anxiety." When anxiety can't find any outlet, it infects a person's whole psychology and his whole physical condition.

There is, however, healing in God's touch. This healing comes through Jesus Christ. If you want to get on top of your worries for good, you can do it best by surrendering your life to Jesus Christ, by identifying yourself with Him, and by giving your all to Him and having that most glorious of all experiences in this world, a spiritual experience.

People afflicted with discouragement, weakness, sickness, sinfulness, hate, prejudice, and fear have found a cure in the touch of Jesus. Say, "Dear Lord Jesus, You take me, I take You." And in this partnership comes healing.

Then Jesus went with his disciples to a place called Gethsemane, and he said to them, "Sit here while I go over there and pray." MATTHEW 26:36

APRIL 14

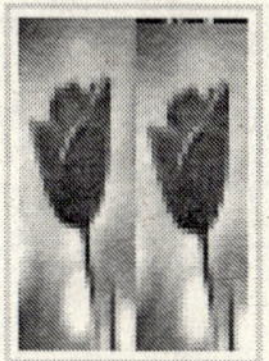

Years ago I was asked to speak to a gathering of advertising and sales people, a very sophisticated and dynamic audience. I remarked to the man who was sitting on my right that I felt power in the room. I thought it must be from the quality of those people.

"Oh," he said, "don't be so sure. I've been praying for this meeting." This remark startled me; I hadn't expected to encounter such ardor.

The man then said to me, "I found two things in life that have made everything different for me. The first—and it was the greatest single experience I ever had—was finding Jesus Christ and committing my life to Him. The second was that I learned to pray. These two things revolutionized my life."

This is what Jesus has been saying to us through the years. Really astute people make this discovery. Christ can change your life. Prayer can change your life.

"Today in the town of David a Savior has been born to you; he is Christ the LORD."

LUKE 2:11

APRIL 15

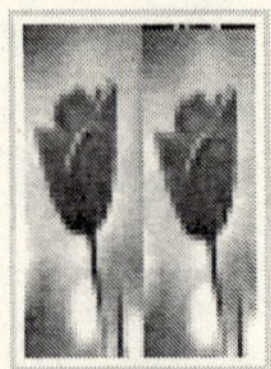

While we can sometimes do a great deal on our own to turn our defeats into victories, the supreme change in a defeated individual is not brought about by that individual himself or herself, but is effected by the grace of God through Jesus Christ. We refer to Jesus Christ as the Savior. That is a great term. It has not been used nearly enough or properly enough. The Savior.

If you are in a boat at sea and you're lost, you send out an SOS. Well, there are people lost on the sea of life. They have lost control of themselves and of their circumstances. They are defeated. Then they call upon Jesus and He saves them. He gives them power over their defeats, their sins, their weaknesses. This is the great message in the Bible. You have a Savior who will do for you what you can never do for yourself. The wonderful things that He can do would fill volumes. Indeed, they have filled volumes.

"I know that my Redeemer lives, and that in the end he will stand upon the earth."

Job 19:25

April 16

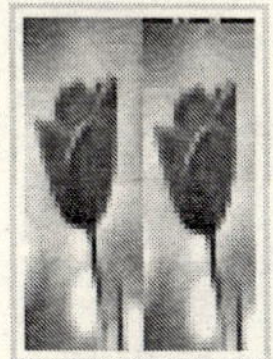

What do you want? See it clearly in your mind. Then check it with God; for if it isn't right, it's wrong, and no wrong thing ever turned out right. Then believe, and you will create. You want a happy life? You want a useful life? You want to be a part of the movements of our time for human good? Do you want to rise above all your sins, weaknesses, and fears? Faith will lead you on because faith leads to belief and belief creates. Have faith in the Lord and you will be established.

Keep dreaming dreams, having visions, having faith, and you'll create. Faith also helps in another way, by taking out of us that which holds us back. I tell you right now, on the authority of God's Word—and you can check it later on—that if you do a wrong thing, you will get a wrong result. But if you let God take wrong out of you, take fear out of you, and hate out of you, He will put life into you.

You were taught . . . to put off your old self . . . ; to be made new in the attitude of your minds; and to put on the new self, created to be like God in true righteousness and holiness. EPHESIANS 4:22–24

APRIL 17

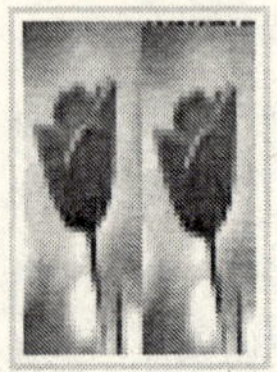

The Bible, in Ephesians 4:23, tells us to"be made new in the attitude of your minds." This is an extraordinarily interesting injunction. Paul tells us there should be an upbeat to the mind, an uplift. This verse embraces attitudes, perceptions, ideas. Keep the spirit of your mind high. Raise it high—high up to Jesus Christ himself. Then you will be renewed. Christianity works to help people who want to overcome their tendency to make mistakes. If you have the mind of Jesus in you, you will not be error prone.

There is an old truism that says we learn by our mistakes. And sometimes this is the case. But you also may reinforce a dangerous tendency: If you concentrate upon being educated by your mistakes, you may dwell on them too much. You may come to believe that making mistakes is the only teacher you have. Instead, whenever you make a mistake, you should extract from it all the know-how it may offer and then put it immediately out of your mind.

"Which is easier: to say, 'Your sins are forgiven,' or to say, 'Get up and walk'?" MATTHEW 9:5

APRIL 18

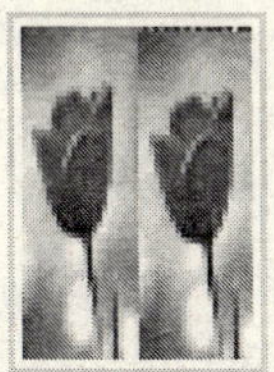

One evening, Mrs. Peale and I were sitting on the terrace of a hotel overlooking Lake Galilee. We were rereading parts of the Gospels and it was not difficult to sense the Holy Presence. I was startled upon this occasion by the emphasis that Jesus and the Gospel writers placed on healing. My sense of the importance of this emphasis grew on the following day as I walked along the shores of Lake Galilee where Jesus had walked, and I tried to mark the spots where He had healed people. His was a healing ministry.

How the church in the nineteenth century ever chose to neglect healing is beyond my comprehension. Healing came to be seen as a solely physical process and the effects of mental and moral conditions upon states of health were ignored completely. Nowadays, fortunately, there is a great new movement for healing in the church. We are bringing back the healing ministry of Jesus in a modern application.

. . . He said to them, "Let the little children come to me, and do not hinder them, for the kingdom of God belongs to such as these."

MARK 10:14

APRIL 19

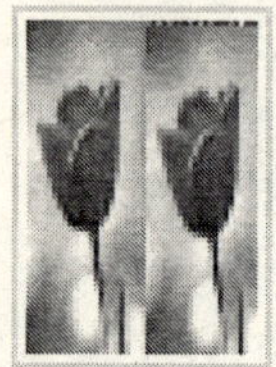

Each of us was born a baby—that is the only way we get into this world—and when God gives life to a baby, He does a wonderful thing: He wraps up this adorable little package and packs him or her full to overflowing with enthusiasm. It is the one thing that characterizes an infant.

Life is thrilling, exciting, and fabulous for a baby. The world is his oyster. He simply loves it. Everything is fresh and vital. Everything is fascinating and glorious. He has the time of his life. It's too bad, isn't it, that we cannot remain as babies? The writer Huxley said that the spirit of genius is to carry the attitude of the child into old age: to keep perpetual enthusiasm.

Every day, visualize yourself as plugged in to the spiritual line. Affirm that God's re-creative energy is restoring strength to every part of your body, mind, and soul. This brings vitality and energy and constant replenishment into your being.

"Come to me, all you who are weary and burdened, and I will give you rest."

MATTHEW 11:28

APRIL 20

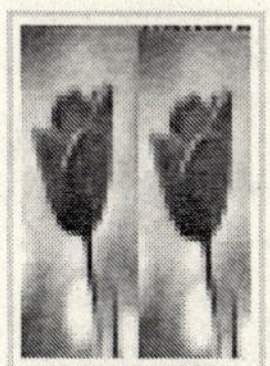

A woman from Minneapolis wrote: "I had migraine headaches for years. One evening I had to take the children to the library. I had a terrible headache. I thought I would read some books on the power of the mind. I saw your book and read it and liked it. You told me that with God's help, I could have health.

"I gave myself unreservedly into His care. Even though things in my life were upsetting, I began to get well. After about six months, I could tell others that I was rid of the headaches. I didn't say anything at first because I didn't want others to think He had failed me in case it was His decision that I continue to have the headaches. As for myself, I had made up my mind that if I still had the headaches, I would accept them because now that I had Him, nothing would be too hard to bear."

This woman couldn't solve her problems herself, so she went to the Lord and surrendered the problem to His care. If you have a difficult problem, you can get help by surrendering it to the Lord.

For his anger lasts only a moment, but his favor lasts a lifetime; weeping may remain for a night, but rejoicing comes in the morning. PSALM 30:5

APRIL 21

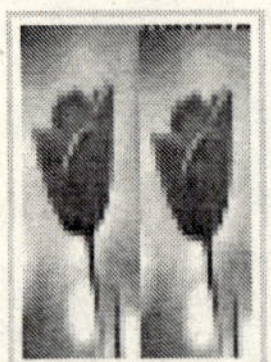

The attitude you take toward the day—when the day begins—determines the day. You may wake up and say to yourself, or to the people near you, "Oh, this is going to be a tough day. This is going to be one of the worst days I've ever been through. I can just feel it coming." And you may find that you are absolutely right, because you are bringing it on yourself.

But if you are a person of prayer, the first thing you will do in the morning is to thank God that He watched over you and your loved ones during the night and brought you to the light of another day with all its opportunity. God gave you this day and it is a day to rejoice in. In the course of my life, I have often observed that the more spiritually minded a person is, the more beautiful the day becomes and the more replete with opportunity it is. So if you want to have a good day every day, get your life changed by Jesus Christ. Then every day will be a great one.

So then, just as you received Christ Jesus as LORD, continue to live in him, rooted and built up in him, strengthened in the faith as you were taught. . . . COLOSSIANS 2:6–7

APRIL 22

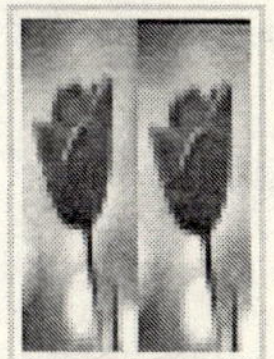

I was in a meeting not long ago where participants were talking about various difficulties and problems, both in our society and as individuals. They called upon a man to pray. I knew this man had experienced much difficulty and even then was experiencing much; and I was astonished by his prayer. He did not ask the Lord for a single thing except for His presence. And the man quickly affirmed His presence.

The prayer was full of giving of thanks and of affirmation of God's goodness. It was an entrancing prayer and I said to him, "Jim, I know something of the difficulties you face. How come you never ask God for anything?"

"Oh," he replied, "I've learned that the best way to pray is to thank God. He knows what I need. Why should I ask Him for anything? Let me just tell you all the wonderful things I have." And he began to enumerate his blessings.

No matter how much difficulty you have, and there may be much, you still have many, many things for which to be thankful.

Let us draw near to God with a sincere heart in full assurance of faith, having our hearts sprinkled to cleanse us from a guilty conscience and having our bodies washed with pure water. HEBREWS 10:22

APRIL 23

One of the main principles of the Japanese religion Tenrikyo is that disease begins in the mind and if you get your mind clean, you'll be at peace, happy, creative, an asset to society.

I especially like the way they have constructed their temples. Each altar is open to the elements. The rain falls on it, the snow falls on it, the wind blows on it, the sun shines on it. Everything—rain, snow, wind, and sun—is a cleansing agent, and the lesson is that if you let the rain and snow and wind and sun of the good God into your mind, He will cleanse you of that which destroys your peace of mind.

This same idea reaches its glorious fulfillment in Christianity. Not only does it cleanse, but it makes old creatures new. I've seen defeated people become victorious people, soiled people become clean people, dull people become excited. God doesn't merely create you, He repeatedly re-creates you.

Yet to all who received him, to those who believed in his name, he gave the right to become children of God. . . . JOHN 1:12

APRIL 24

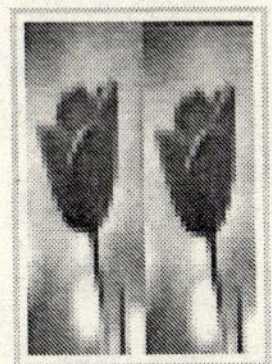

People have often asked me, "Why is it I do not have a sense of power that stays with me when the going gets hard?" Well, the Bible says that "To all who received him, to those who believed in his name, he gave the right to become children of God" (John 1:12). It is all there. Everything is offered to you. To as many as receive Him—that is, accept His guidance and help—He gives the power to become—that is, to grow and expand into—children of God.

Now what is a child of God? We believe that Jesus is the Son of God. But to some degree, we all become children of God. God, at creation, breathed into man the breath of life, and he became a living spirit. Humans are more than flesh and blood. We are of the divine. We come, as Wordsworth said, "trailing clouds of glory . . . from God, who is our home." And when we pass from this world, we pass to an eternal glory with God.

Paul looked directly at him, saw that he had faith to be healed and called out "Stand up on your feet!" At that, the man jumped up and began to walk. ACTS 14:9–10

APRIL 25

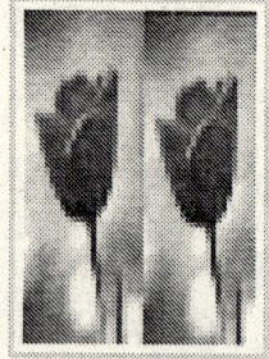

People are troubled by illness. They are either ill themselves or have loved ones who are ill. But God is the master of illness; He has the power to heal. And He has the power to give us understanding if it be His will that a loved one be taken from us. There is no problem I can conceive of, either individual or social, that God cannot help us with if we have the faith to let Him.

Now this is where the trouble is. How much faith do we have? Christian faith in earlier times was a very rugged thing. We are the descendants of a great breed of men and women who had strong, uncomplicated faith. They believed in God and that was that. They believed that God would help, that He would bring to their support an enormous power. And the Bible tells of people who are mature, not children; adults carrying out a challenging job. These people in the Bible had enormous faith. That is why they overcame enormous odds.

Although he [Jesus] was a son, he learned obedience from what he suffered and, once made perfect, he became the source of eternal salvation for all who obey him. HEBREWS 5:8–9

April 26

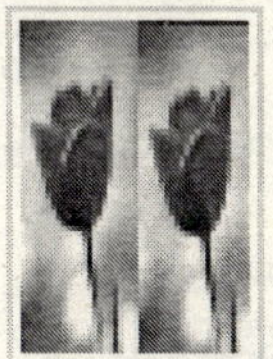

T. E. Lawrence once took some Arabs to London; what interested them more than anything else were the faucets in the bathrooms in their hotel. They would turn the water on and watch the enormous stream gushing out and exclaim "Look! All you have to do is turn that thing and you have all the water you want!"

When it was time to leave, Lawrence found these men trying to remove the faucets. Astounded, he asked them what they were doing. "We will take these back to the desert and then we will never lack for water." So Lawrence had to explain that the faucets had to be attached to a source of water.

Christians oftentimes do just the same thing. We try to get a flow from faucets that are not attached. Our faucets are all the little forms of faith and tradition: going to church regularly and all the rest.

May I never boast except in the cross of our LORD Jesus Christ, through which the world has been crucified to me, and I to the world. GALATIANS 6:14

APRIL 27

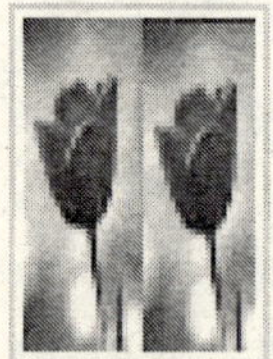

Christianity survives because it faces all of life, including the evil and the wickedness in humans. It paints the whole picture, but nevertheless affirms that in the midst of all this trouble, pain, and confusion, there is a good outcome, a way out of sorrow. The bright, pure lily comes up through the mud. There has never been a philosophy of life like Christianity. It deals realistically with all of the hardships of the human condition, but it concludes with victory.

At the heart of Christianity, there is a great, splintery, blood-spattered cross. You can't laugh that off: the sorrow and the suffering of life. But the lilting note of victory is never absent. That is why it was said of early Christians that there was something in them akin to the song of the skylark and the babbling of brooks. Optimism, hope, freshness, newness. One Bible text after another reminds us of these truths. Freshness, newness. That is Christianity in its essence.

He gives strength to the weary and increases the power of the weak. Isaiah 40:29

April 28

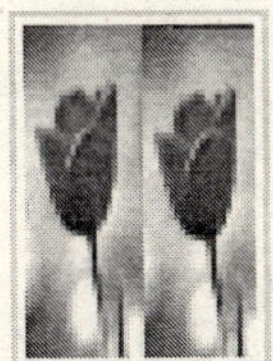

Nobody can live successfully in this world without being strong. You may be pampered and protected when you are a child, but you have to learn to be strong as you mature, because sooner or later, life will throw the book at you. Sometimes it will throw the whole book at you all at once. You have to get adjusted so you won't collapse under the trouble, or give way under difficulty, or fold under the blow of adversity. I sometimes think that the greatest virtue of all is to be strong.

Christianity is a way of life that makes people strong. You can have all the strength you will ever need if you build into yourself the love of God and stay close to Jesus until He becomes part of you.

Our Heavenly Father, we give You thanks for the great power that comes to us from You through Jesus Christ. Amen.

He has made everything beautiful in its time.
He has also set eternity in the hearts of men;
yet they cannot fathom what God has done
from beginning to end. ECCLESIASTES 3:11

APRIL 29

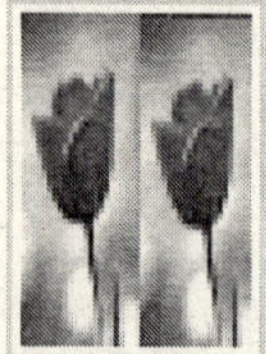

This world is a wonderful place. We were put into it by a God who loved us and wanted to surround us with that which would develop us, so that ultimately He could take us out of this world of the temporal into the world of the eternal.

Certain theological circles have put forth the notion that too much enjoyment of the physical world is pantheistic, even pagan, but I reject this attitude completely. I believe that the hills, the seas, the stars, the sky, the sun, the rain, and the snow reflect a greater spiritual world. The purpose of material forms is only to give substance and reality to the world of the spirit. The person who associates with the natural world, thinking of it spiritually, will find his spirit refreshed, his mind cleansed; he will be stimulated and inspired.

Why are you downcast, O my soul? Why so disturbed within me? Put your hope in God, for I will yet praise him, my Savior and my God. PSALM 42:11

APRIL 30

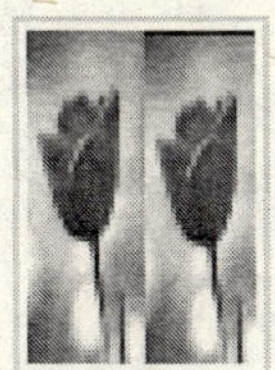

Hope and *expectation* are two dynamic words that can change your life. Write these words in gigantic letters across the sky of your life, as you sometimes see skywriting advertisements against the heavens. Deeply embed these until they become a motivational part of your whole being. Do this and your life will be good, very good, no matter how much pain or difficulty you experience.

The Bible—the wisest document ever known in human existence, which defies the ravages of time and change because it contains the truth that cannot be changed or invalidated,—says in Psalm 42:11: "Why are you downcast, O my soul? Why so disturbed within me? Put your hope in God, for I will yet praise him, my Savior and my God." What a text! There is power in it.

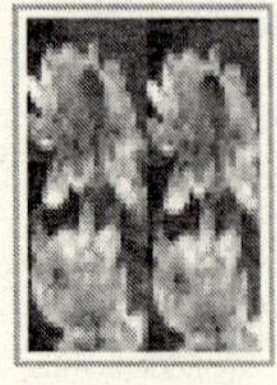

May

What, then, shall we say in response to this? If God is for us, who can be against us? Romans 8:31

For you have been my hope, O Sovereign
LORD, my confidence since my youth.
PSALM 71:5

MAY 1

I remember sitting on the porch with my mother and saying, "Mother, I want to amount to something. I'm going to make money and come back with enough to buy and sell some of these people around here."

But my mother said, "Ambition, Norman, is good if God controls it. But what I want you to be is a clean, decent, honorable, upright Christian man with love in your heart, serving God and His children; and I want you to live so that when you finish your course of life, I'll meet you somewhere in the eternities of our Lord."

That sounds sentimental. But this is the ideal that Christian mothers have put into us—or rather that they have fanned into flame, because it was God Himself who planted in us the instinct to be children of God. So touch the hem of His garment that you may be made perfectly whole.

He has caused his wonders to be remembered; the Lord is gracious and compassionate. PSALM 111:4

MAY 2

A man told me about a business associate who once enclosed a card in one of his letters. On one side, the card said, "Expect a miracle." And on the other, "God is on your side." The man was about to throw it out, but the card intrigued him. He put it in his wallet.

Every time he opened his wallet, this card would fall out: "Expect a miracle." "God is on your side." The message began to seep into his consciousness. He began to send up little prayers. Then he started adopting a positive attitude toward the problems that had baffled and frustrated and defeated him. And finally, he began expecting a miracle.

You get what you expect. Life is full of all kinds of disappointments and sorrows, but it is also full of wonders. And if you expect wonderful things, wonderful things will happen. When God is on your side, you can expect a miracle.

You made him a little lower than the heavenly beings and crowned him with glory and honor. PSALM 8:5

MAY 3

Listen to what the psalmist said: "You made him a little lower than the heavenly beings and crowned him with glory and honor. You made him ruler over the works of your hands; you put everything under his feet." Does this mean dominion over other people? Not at all. It means dominion over your weaknesses, your fears, your sins; dominion over your grief, your frustration, your disappointment, your sadness. Are you that way? Or are you a pushover for everything that comes along? Are you a weakling, a victim of everything and everybody?

"Lord, give me a high opinion of myself." You can pray this prayer, because you are, if you will allow yourself to be, a wonderful person. You are a wonderful person by realizing the best that is within you.

For with you is the fountain of life; in your light we see light. PSALM 36:9

MAY 4

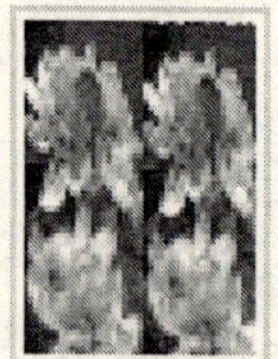

"For with you is the fountain of life." What a picture! An upsurging, sparkling fountain. And out of that fountain comes great goodness. Yet we are very painfully aware that not everyone comes to that source of goodness. "Morality in America is not crumbling; it has crumbled," claims one magazine.

Well, now, I don't know whether I am willing to accept that appraisal, but people who believe in God and in Jesus Christ and in the Ten Commandments and in the moral standards of our civilization should rise up and do something about it. Churches must attack current problems through spiritually oriented programs aimed at changing the lives of people.

For it is also true—thanks be to God—that there are thousands upon thousands of people who know that life is good and want what is good. The pity is that too often the churches fail to tell them that through the power and the grace of Jesus Christ, they can have life that is good and wonderful and ever new.

O Lord my God, I called to you for help and you healed me. Psalm 30:2

May 5

The Lord does speak to people. And there is such a thing as an inner ear with which you hear His voice. Where you really hear is deep in your soul. Stanley Jones heard. The Lord said to him, "I want you to do a job for Me in India. You can't do it the way you are, breaking down all the time. Will you give Me your worries, your anxieties? If you will, I'll give you such health as you never dreamed of."

"Lord" said Jones, "I'll close that bargain right away." I heard Dr. Jones say twenty years after this event, "Since that night I never had another breakdown. I had not only physical health, but I had mental and spiritual health as well. I seemed to have tapped new life for body, mind, and spirit. And I had done nothing but take it!"

I tell you, friends, what can be done for a human being seems so incredible that the person who hasn't the eye or the ear of faith can hardly understand it. So let God help you. He will help you and He will do it soon.

"'You have made known to me the paths of life; you will fill me with joy in your presence.'" Acts 2:28

May 6

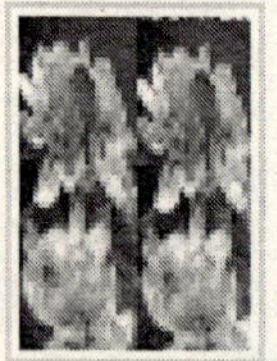

I have always maintained that it is an objective of Jesus that people shall live happy lives. Of course, the word *happiness* is sometimes used in a very superficial sense. Maybe the word *joy* is better, for it suggests something deeper. The Gospel never promises that a Christian shall be free from the difficulties of this world. But Jesus says that those who do what He asks will find happiness. He wants people to live joyously.

I realize that the minute I make that statement, I am bound to be criticized by the small, supercilious, sophisticated group of articulate preachers who seem to think that nobody should be happy. I don't know what they want for humanity unless they want everybody to be miserable. In some circles there seems to be a notion that a person cannot be a true Christian unless he goes around with a sour look on his face. This is a distortion of what Jesus taught. It is a carry-over of a mistaken notion that it is a sin to enjoy life.

Be strong and take heart, all you who hope in the LORD. PSALM 31:24

MAY 7

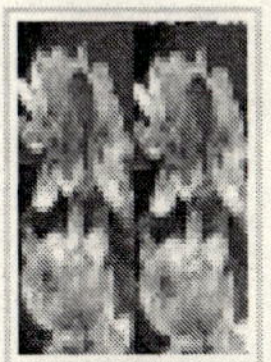

One day I was on a Boeing 707, and the pilot came back and sat down beside me for a few minutes. I happened to look out the window and saw something I didn't understand. I said, "Captain, out there along the wing, there are blades set at intervals. What are those things?"

"Those are vortex generators," he replied. "When we have a smooth flow of air, these big planes don't steer as perfectly as they do when there is slight turbulence. The flow of air swirling around those blades gives us enough turbulence for perfect performance."

If you had nothing but absolutely smooth flight conditions on the voyage of life, you wouldn't attain the objective for which you are designed. So the Lord has put vortex generators into human existence in order that we may grow strong and learn to steer our course and arrive at the destination He has set for us. These vortex generators seem very big sometimes, and we feel defeated by them. But a person is lifted above defeat by getting hold of the hope we have in Christ.

What, then, shall we say in response to this?
If God is for us, who can be against us?
ROMANS 8:31

MAY 8

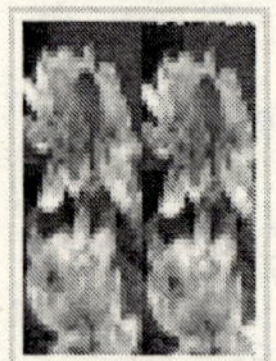

This morning while having breakfast, I listened by radio to a Baptist minister who was preaching a sermon about the end of the world. It was the kind of preaching I used to hear when I was a boy—very powerful. It is a sad thing that Christianity is seldom preached that way today, and many people look upon it as a kind of country club adjunct to a respectable life.

We all have problems and difficulties, and sometimes these seem overwhelming. But the Bible says, "If God is for us, who can be against us?" No matter what problems or difficulties you may have, you can conquer them and, not only that, you can be more than a conqueror through Jesus Christ who loved you so much that He died on the cross for your salvation.

This is what Christianity teaches. Some people take it and run with it and have a tremendous time in their lives. Others stay bogged down and defeated. It is startling what vast differences there are between people. And the force that makes the biggest difference is a powerful faith.

Honest scales and balances are from the LORD; all the weights in the bag are of his making. PROVERBS 16:11

MAY 9

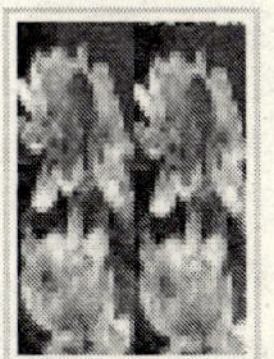

The Bible is a straightforward, honest book. It does not guarantee freedom from pain, sorrow, trouble, difficulty, or heartache, but it does promise inner happiness and good days. So to have better ways to better days, keep all this in the background of your mind.

One way to realize better days is to live honestly. How many people live with absolute honesty? Have you ever been completely honest with yourself? Have you ever told yourself the whole truth about yourself? Have you ever faced yourself, not as you think you are, but as you really are? How long has it been since you made an appraisal of your strengths and your weaknesses? Do you know whether you are deteriorating or growing? Are you a better, more confident, more knowledgeable person now than you were ten years ago—or are you a worse person now than you were ten years ago? Honesty is the first principle for having better ways to better days.

Now if we are children, then we are heirs — heirs of God and co-heirs with Christ, if indeed we share in his sufferings in order that we may also share in his glory. ROMANS 8:17

MAY 10

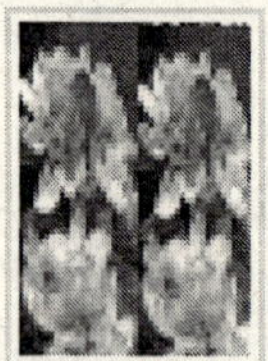

Faith is an acceptance of spiritual truth, a belief in yourself as a child of God. I think everybody, once every day, ought to draw himself up and say, "I am a child of God." And when you believe that, you begin to release powers within your mind, your soul, that can lift you above your defeats. If you just stay at your earthly level, then when you look up at these great big defeating problems, they will overwhelm you.

But as a child of God, you are much taller than you are on your own. You have an extension in you and with this extension, by the power of faith, you can overcome any difficulty in this world. The problems of life are infinitesimal in comparison with the extension powers that are in you as a child of God. You may have problems; they may seem very big to you. But you yourself are much bigger than you think. I've seen it happen again and again: God comes into a man's mind, into his thought; and the inspiration produces an explosion, and the man rises above his difficulty.

. . . to the only God our Savior be glory, majesty, power and authority, through Jesus Christ our LORD, before all ages, now and forevermore! JUDE 1:25

MAY 11

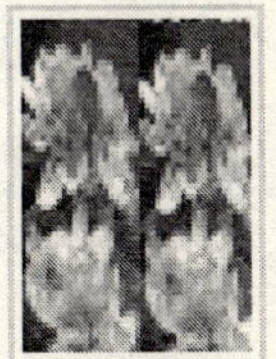

People practice different kinds of religion. They observe a formal kind, which means carrying out precepts and following the proper forms. They practice a doctrinal religion, which is acknowledging certain truths and creeds. Unfortunately, that is as far as most people ever get.

But there are those who find a lifesaving, life-changing religion. They come upon a power, and it helps them to overcome pain, weakness, sorrow, frustrations, and defeats. It gives them a sparkle in their eyes, a glow on their face, and an elasticity in their step. It changes them so that they love everybody. Their whole life flows out to bless humankind. This is vital Christianity, religion in depth.

He who humbly depends upon God will receive a vast strength. Get close to God and God will be very near to you.

. . . how much more will those who receive God's abundant provision of grace and of the gift of righteousness reign in life through the one man, Jesus Christ. ROMANS 5:17

MAY 12

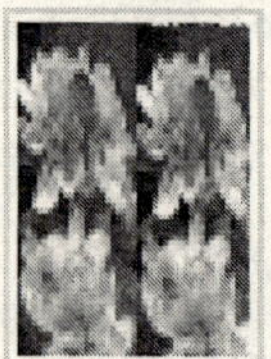

Do you know the meaning of the word *abundance*? I didn't, until I looked it up one time. And I was thrilled. The derivation of the word goes back to the Latin verb *undare*, which means "to rise up in waves." Isn't that great? Life rises up in waves. Have you got any waves of life? Or are you living on little dribbles? Almighty God is a generous God. He never meant that we should dribble through life. He intended us to live in abundance.

Of all handicaps that hold people back from being successful in their living, from overcoming weakness and having strength, the worst is a lack of love. There is no wisdom like that of the Bible, which tells us not to be angry with people and not to hate them, but to love them; not to be irritable with people, but to love and serve them. If you so live, life will flow back to you in great waves.

"In the same way, let your light shine before men, that they may see your good deeds and praise your Father in heaven." MATTHEW 5:16

MAY 13

One day I was reading the fifth chapter of Matthew. I've read that chapter hundreds of times, but this time I had a revelation about it: It is a blueprint for happiness. The descriptions of what you must do to be happy go on through the whole chapter. And it says not only to love your friends, but also to love your enemies and pray for those who mistreat you. Then the great sermon rises to a climax when it says, "Be perfect, therefore, as your heavenly Father is perfect."

You may say, "That is unattainable. That is too hard."

That is why Jesus is Jesus. He put it high because He believed that there was something great in human beings. He tried to get us to see that if you have what it takes to rise to this challenge, you will find happiness in a way you cannot find it anywhere else. If you are courageous enough to take it, your life will be great.

"If you then . . . know how to give good gifts to your children, how much more will your Father in heaven give the Holy Spirit to those who ask him!" Luke 11:13

May 14

You can judge the depth of a person's Christianity by how big a person it makes of him. The person who has it in depth becomes a strong character, becomes a victorious person. One thing such a person characteristically has is a recognition of the fact that in difficulty, there is potential good. That is basic in the Christian philosophy of life. The philosophy known as optimism is related to it.

True optimism is the belief that the good of life outweighs the evil, and there is always an inherent good behind a difficulty. When faced with difficulties, the optimist does not say, "Isn't this awful?" but says to the Lord, "Lord, You've given me a difficulty, but I know there must be good in it, and I will seek to find that good."

Let God's words sink deeply into your consciousness, and the experience of God's protection will be yours.

When a mocker is punished, the simple gain wisdom; when a wise man is instructed, he gets knowledge. PROVERBS 21:11

MAY 15

A mixed-up, defeated man started coming to Marble Collegiate Church; one day he found Someone here, that Someone who can change any individual. This is a letter that he wrote me.

Dear Dr. Peale:

As you well know, alcohol was not the only problem I had six years ago. I was one of the most negative people anybody ever met. I was one of the most super-critical, impatient, cocky individuals that you could imagine. Now, please don't think that I have overcome all these things. I haven't. At times I become discouraged with my progress. Gradually, by trying to follow the teachings of Jesus, I am learning to control myself and be less critical. It is like being released from a prison. I never dreamed life could be so wonderful.

Do as this man did and you will say to yourself with gladness in your heart, "How good God is."

How great is the love the Father has lavished on us, that we should be called children of God! And that is what we are!

1 John 3:1

May 16

Faith is an acceptance of spiritual truth. Faith is belief in something. Faith is belief in yourself as a child of God. I think everybody, once every day, ought to draw himself up and say, "I am a child of God." You have to stand tall to say that. And when you believe that, then you begin to release powers within your mind and your soul that can lift you above your defeats.

If you stay at your earthly level, when you look up at these great, big defeating problems, they will overwhelm you. But as a child of God, you are much taller than you are of yourself. You have an extension within you, and with this extension of faith, you can overcome any difficulty in this world. The problems of life are infinitesimal in comparison with the extension powers that are in you as a child of God.

Remember me, O LORD, *that I may enjoy the prosperity of your chosen ones, that I may share in the joy of your nation and join your inheritance in giving praise.* PSALM 106:4–5

MAY 17

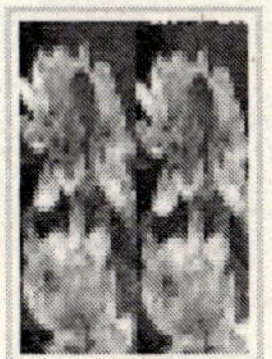

God's Kingdom radiates with love and health and happiness and goodness. Our God is so completely outgoing, so overwhelmingly generous, that He wants to give you every good thing. If this is God's good pleasure, why don't we experience everything that is good and beneficial? Perhaps one reason is that we block the flow of good by the miserable, negative attitudes we develop toward life, toward other people, and even toward God.

How can one overcome failure that comes from negative attitudes? One way, and a very important one, is to practice seeing everything as developing rather than as deteriorating. See only good coming to you. Practice visualizing it. Practice being conscious of it. Really see it coming to you and practice thanking God for it. There is a law whereby in so doing, you actually attract it to yourself.

I will give you a new heart and put a new spirit in you; I will remove from you your heart of stone and give you a heart of flesh. EZEKIEL 36:26

MAY 18

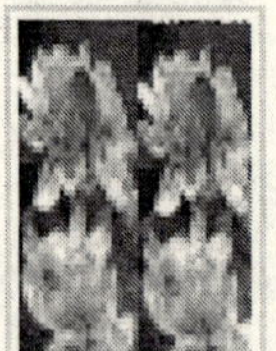

A friend of mine has always impressed me with his vivacity, his sense of delight in life, his eagerness. I asked him once how he managed this, and he said, "I pass expectancy thoughts through my mind every morning." What a technique!

Another vibrant friend explains his secret for living joyously and without boredom this way: "Every morning I read the Bible, spend ten minutes in quiet meditation, and close by saying, 'O Lord, thank You so much for the eventful day You are going to give me.' And I do have one eventful day after another, days filled with joy and excitement."

How is your heart? Everyone needs a new heart at times, for the old one gets tired. How is your spirit? Everyone needs a new spirit at times, for the old spirit often becomes weary. If you haven't got a joyous heart and spirit, let God give it to you.

Our Heavenly Father, let that light, which You commanded to shine out of darkness, come into our minds to change us with new faith and new heart. Through Jesus Christ, our Lord. Amen.

"He is not the God of the dead, but of the living, for to him all are alive." LUKE 20:38

MAY 19

How much of Christianity do you want? Are you content to have merely a set of ethics? Or would you like to be deeply stirred and released? James Russell Lowell in his poem, "The Cathedral," wrote:

I, that still pray at morning and at eve . . .
Thrice in my life perhaps have truly prayed,
Thrice, stirred below my conscious self, have felt
That perfect disenthrallment which is God.

There is a power that can lift us above ourselves; give us victory over all our weaknesses; fill our minds with courage and make us count in the day and age in which we live; make us flaming tongues of fire to live with power. And only a few people reach for it. The others are content with something halfway alive. But a human being is meant to be a tremendous person.

One way to start becoming such a person is to say, "By the grace and power of the Lord Jesus Christ, I'm going to find interest in life. I'm going to put interest into my living. I'm going to live with delight. I'm going to live with enthusiasm."

Sing to the LORD a new song, for he has done marvelous things; his right hand and his holy arm have worked salvation for him.

PSALM 98:1

MAY 20

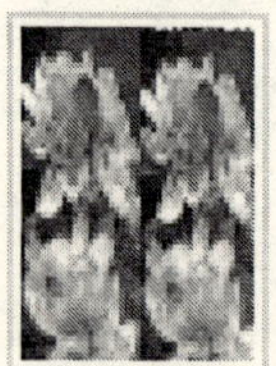

Arriving by train to speak at a rally in Pennsylvania, I headed for a cab. A somber man was sitting in the front seat with the driver, and a woman was in one corner of the back seat. I got in and took the other corner. Then along came another woman with a suitcase and a couple of paper bags. I moved over and she got in. Then she took us all into her love. She asked, "How are you all today?" I said I felt fine.

The man in front turned around and asked, "What makes you so happy?"

"Jesus makes me happy," the woman replied. "I used to be the most miserable woman in Pennsylvania. But I found Jesus and He resurrected me." And by the time she got out, she had made us all happy.

If you are feeling weak, tired, sick, defeated, or unhappy, you can be made new. And once this resurrection by Jesus Christ takes hold, you will becomes strong. Resurrection makes strong people.

He who was seated on the throne said,
"I am making everything new!" Then
he said, "Write this down, for these words
are trustworthy and true." REVELATION 21:5

MAY 21

The New Testament begins with a star and a song, and it marches up to a cross and another song, the song of the redeemed. It is a tremendous story. Toward the end of the Bible, in Revelation 21:5, we find these glorious words: "I am making everything new!" It doesn't matter how much you may have failed, how you may have messed up things, how many defeats you may have experienced.

But how are you going to keep this newness, this freshness, this wonder in life? There is one big fact which I think you ought to have in mind as you approach the future, and it is that life will give back to you just exactly what you give to life. That is the deal. That is the way life is. So if you want to know what the future is going to mean to you, you have to decide what you are going to mean to it.

Life is very fair. It pays in the same coin. It is scrupulously honest. It gives to you what you give to it.

Therefore, if anyone is in Christ, he is a new creation; the old has gone, the new has come! 2 CORINTHIANS 5:17

MAY 22

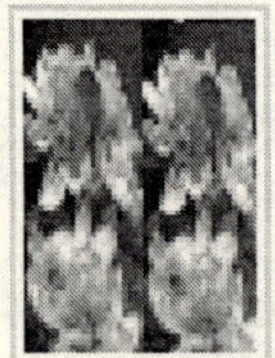

A few years ago, a Rotarian came to the New York club laboring under terrible sorrow. His son Steve had fallen into trouble; he had driven a stolen car over several state lines and was in jail in New York. The father had come to the Rotary Club for comfort and assistance.

The club turned the problem over to two laymen. They got in touch with me and explained that they'd been appointed as a committee to handle this case and asked if I would help. They said, "We want Jesus Christ on this committee, too, because only He can help this father and this boy." Later they came to my study and we prayed together, putting Steve and his father in the hands of Jesus. And Jesus, the alive Christ, took charge.

We went to the judge in the case and the boy was paroled to us. A few years later, Steve became a pastor. Moreover, his seminary sent him to other seminaries to testify to the students what can happen to an individual who meets the living Christ.

You intended to harm me, but God intended it for good to accomplish what is now being done, the saving of many lives. GENESIS 50:20

MAY 23

My friend Richard Prentice Ettinger, who founded the Prentice-Hall publishing company, was present at a breakfast I attended. He'd had throat cancer and had a little tube in his throat, but he spoke distinctly and well.

That morning we had a wonderful conversation. In the course of it he said, "You know my theory that whatever happens, happens for the best? When I got cancer I thought, 'Oh, oh! How is this going to be for the best?' The cancer took twenty pounds off me. The doctors said afterward that the weight had been affecting my heart. Because the excess weight is gone, I will live ten years longer. Whatever happens, happens for the best."

One of the greatest things that ever happened for the best in my life was to know an undefeatable man like Richard Prentice Ettinger, who demonstrated in the most difficult circumstances that if you do your best and you put it in the hands of God, you can make things happen for the best.

Your beauty . . . should be that of your inner self, the unfading beauty of a gentle and quiet spirit, which is of great worth in God's sight. 1 PETER 3:3–4

MAY 24

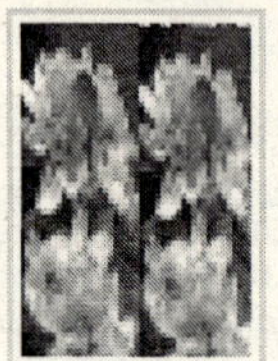

Quietness is a profoundly creative element. Who was the tallest character who ever rose up from among the American people? Well, in my book, it was Abraham Lincoln. Now Lincoln in his early years was fortunate enough to live in the virgin forests of the Middle West. As a distinguished writer on Lincoln once observed, "In the making of him, the element of silence was immense." Great trees that seemed to scrape the sky were his companions, the silence of the forest whispered its wisdom to him, and later, in the days of crisis, he was sustained because he had within him quietness, from which he drew confidence.

We're too noisy; we're too hectic. We're too disturbed; we're too confused. We have noise all the time. Consequently, we have noise inside. So we lose our confidence. Then we lose our strength. Remember: "I will make you strong if you quietly trust me."

Light is shed upon the righteous and joy on the upright in heart. PSALM 97:11

MAY 25

Sir Arnold Lunn was an authority on the geography of Switzerland. He traveled over practically every valley, every mountain and wrote about them with the fervor of a poet. In the summer of 1940, when the German army was marching into France, Lunn was summoned to England. At Berne he looked at the mountains and wondered whether he would be back.

The war ceased. Lunn arrived at Berne in the late afternoon. The sky was overcast, the mountains invisible. Suddenly the clouds parted, and there they stood. The light of the sun upon them seemed to say that there are certain things in life which no cloud, no war, no hate, no force can destroy. This was for Arnold Lunn a spiritual experience, reassuring him that no matter how much suffering exists, God remains.

So I would say that there are two pillars upon which happiness rests. One is moral decency, mastery over self. The other is the knowledge of the love of God and of His presence at all times, come what may.

I pray that out of his glorious riches he may strengthen you with power through his Spirit in your inner being. . . . EPHESIANS 3:16

MAY 26

It is not necessary to be victimized by depression. There is a sure cure for depressive feelings. I think the Bible defines it pretty clearly in Ephesians 3:16. The answer is to ask God's help and allow the Spirit to make you a strong follower.

We find great subtlety and significance in these words. What your life is on the outside depends on what you are on the inside. The outer world is but a reflection of the inner world. And what Jesus Christ does for people who are smart enough to get near to Him is this: He strengthens them by His Spirit so that they drive the shadows off. They rise above depression, they experience the sure cure for depressive feelings. I have personally seen this miracle so many times that, I confess, I am filled with a boundless enthusiasm for what a person's life can become if he or she experiences this wonderful gift.

Our Heavenly Father, help us to know that if we expect great things of You, great things will come. Through Jesus Christ, our Lord. Amen.

You have made known to me the path of life; you will fill me with joy in your presence, with eternal pleasures at your right hand. PSALM 16:11

MAY 27

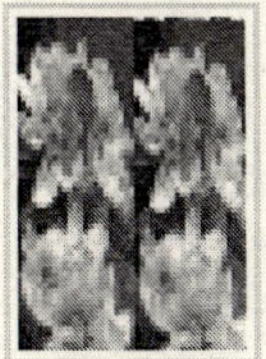

If we believe in the Holy Bible, we ought to realize that no matter how many difficulties we face, through Jesus Christ we find release from, and victory over, all depressing things and wondrous joy.

"Oh," you say, "but you're overly enthusiastic. You are unrealistic." What am I supposed to be? Am I supposed to tell you that you might as well go around in dark gloom, shedding tears all the time, hopeless and negative? I'll never do that, because I don't believe it. Jesus came so that we might have a joyful and abundant life.

"Oh," you say, "life is hard. You don't know the gloom that fills my mind." But I do. And don't think I haven't had plenty of it myself. We should remember that we are children of God, and that God has built what you might call "altitude" into us. That means that we are not meant to be denizens of the dark overcast, the cloud blanket, because above it—always above it and touching it and exercising the power to pierce it—is the powerful joy of Almighty God.

Everyone must submit himself to the governing authorities, for there is no authority except that which God has established. The authorities that exist have been established by God. ROMANS 13:1

MAY 28

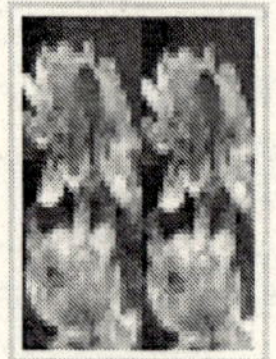

The Bible says the only power in this world is of God. And the earthly powers that be are ordained by God. We are created by this wondrous power. Are you living on the great flow of it? Or on a mere trickle?

"Well," you say, "how can God's power be released?" One way you can release it is by getting a higher opinion of yourself. It is my conviction that most human beings have a much lower opinion of themselves than the facts justify. If you see a person who seems to have an extraordinary opinion of himself, it may be that he is just overcompensating. Actually he may be throwing his weight around to give the impression that he amounts to quite a lot, while inside he feels he amounts to nothing.

Most people underestimate themselves. And if you underestimate yourself, you will be underestimated by others. Your achievements in life agree with your own appraisal of your capacities.

Create in me a pure heart, O God, and renew a steadfast spirit within me. PSALM 51:10

MAY 29

There is a verse in Psalm 51 that says, "Create in me a pure heart, O God, and renew a steadfast spirit within me." But can you get a new heart when you are old and tired and worn and weak and sick and discouraged? Of course you can. I'm not referring to the physical organ known as the heart. When we ask God for a new heart, what we are asking is for a new inner motivation, a new depth of feeling, a new basic attitude. Such heart transplants never fail.

When you come to the point where you commit your life to Jesus Christ and stop trying to run it yourself, you will experience the most amazing, dramatic, fascinating, and exciting changes. There are people who knew that they needed a new heart but couldn't get it themselves. They turned to the Lord Jesus Christ as their Savior, and He saved them from themselves.

Keep me as the apple of your eye; hide me in the shadow of your wings. PSALM 17:8

MAY 30

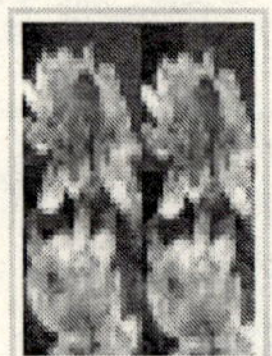

Leo Tolstoy went through his whole calendar of sins trying to make life good. But it was dust and ashes. He knew he had to find the secret of life. He went out into the country where he met peasants and said to them, "My friends, you must teach me your secret."

They said, "When you stay in contact with God, joy is continuous. But if you get away from God, you get away from the life force. Return to God. Return to His Son, and you will find good days."

Tolstoy wrestled with himself, because there were some things he didn't want to let go. Then one day he gave it all up; he accepted Christ and gave himself to God. He wrote later that he had no sooner done this than joyous waves of life seemed to surge through him.

You can make your days good. But in the deeper sense of the word, they are made good by God. I like that picture of Tolstoy—joyous waves of life surging in and out of him.

But as for me, I will always have hope; I will praise you more and more.

Psalm 71:14

May 31

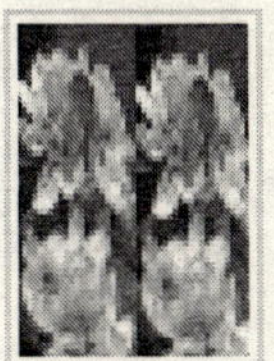

An analysis was made of the experiences of two thousand American soldiers in World War II who were taken prisoner by the Nazis. All had been in concentration camps where they were brainwashed, beaten, starved, and treated with indignity. Many died; others became physical wrecks; others were emotionally maimed.

But a small group of men emerged unhurt mentally, spiritually, or physically. These men had decided that they wouldn't let the terrible circumstances destroy them. They kept their spirits up by telling one another about how wonderful life was going to be when they got back to the United States. They described the girls they were going to marry and their plans for the futures of their children. In other words, they practiced hope. And they were saved by hope. Hope is one of the great blessings offered to us by Jesus Christ. Put on the helmet of hope and change your thought processes.

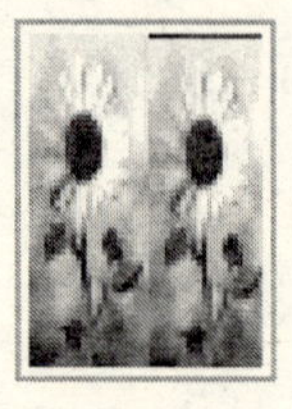

June

From the fullness of
his grace we have all
received one blessing
after another. John 1:16

"Blessed are those who hunger and thirst for righteousness, for they will be filled." MATTHEW 5:6

JUNE 1

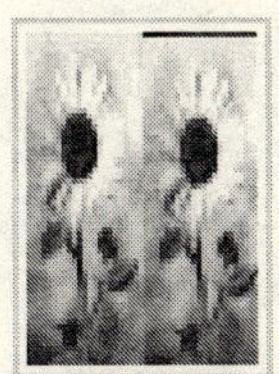

So how do you find good days? It is very simple. If you want to be happy, if you want to have good days, just skip the evil and go for the good. It is just that open and shut. Sit down with yourself and ask, what is my worst weakness? Don't ask your spouse what your chief weakness is. He or she will probably name a half dozen. Just ask yourself, What is my chief fault?

When you find it, study it. Maybe it is the thing that has been holding you back from better days. Once having isolated it, once having faced it honestly, you can decide what you are going to do about it, with the help of the Lord Jesus Christ. A person who is honest with himself, who has isolated his faults and taken them to God, can do something about them. And when a real fault is out of your way, what glorious, better days you can have!

"You became imitators of us and of the LORD; in spite of severe suffering, you welcomed the message with the joy given by the Holy Spirit." 1 THESSALONIANS 1:6

JUNE 2

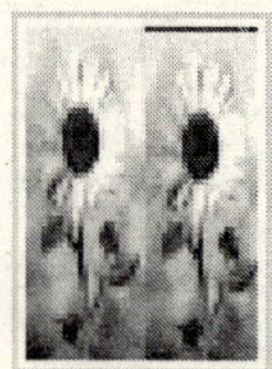

Getting acquainted with Jesus Christ means that you get to know His mind, that you develop the ability to think, that you are at peace. Out of inner peace comes intelligent understanding, and, as a result, good will come to you. I'm impressed with the power of the Bible to say something great in a highly understandable manner. The Bible knows how to communicate.

Knowing this, you can find an answer to your problems. The answer may be what you desire and want, what you have hoped for. And if this should be the case, I rejoice with you; that is wonderful. On the other hand, the answer may not be what you want. But if it has been hammered out with God, it is the right answer. There is nobody who has a problem for which there is not an answer through the wisdom and the guidance of God.

"I have told you this so that my joy may be in you and that your joy may be complete." JOHN 15:11

JUNE 3

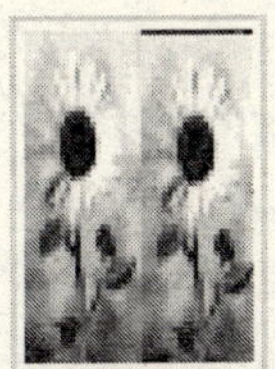

Christianity is one of the most joyful religions in all the history of the world. In fact, it may not be claiming too much to say that it is the most joyful religious faith that has ever been developed. This, I know, runs counter to a rather general conception of Christianity. It has been portrayed—for altogether too long, I believe—as a dour, ultra-serious, sad way of thought.

Now it is true that Jesus Christ was a man of sorrows and that He was afflicted with grief. The true Christian is sensitive to the pain and the sorrow and the injustice in our world and tries always to do something about it. But there is built into Christianity, in its very essence, an upbeat, victorious presence that can lift a person above every valley in human life. It is never flippant; it is always concerned. And always there is in it inherent joy.

All this is evidence that God's judgment is right, and as a result you will be counted worthy of the kingdom of God, for which you are suffering.

2 THESSALONIANS 1:5

JUNE 4

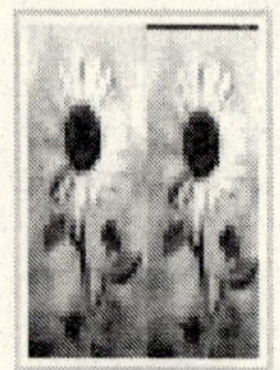

Christianity was established on this earth two thousand years ago by the wisest man who ever entered into human affairs. He knew the relationship between human beings and the divine. He knew the workings of the human mind. He understood well the handling of a problem. And one of the great things that He taught us was to let God help us. This may seem to you an overly simple theme. But how often we try to do the whole thing ourselves! We tug and we pull and we strain over our problems, trying to handle them with a strength we haven't got. We were not meant to proceed in this manner. We were meant to understand that the illimitable power of God is at our disposal and that if we will yield ourselves to Him wholeheartedly, God will let His power flow to our aid.

Our Heavenly Father, help us to put our lives and whatever is bothering us into the hands of the One who can give us the power to overcome, to grow, and to be. Through Jesus Christ our Lord. Amen.

When Jesus saw their faith, he said,
"Friend, your sins are forgiven." LUKE 5:20

JUNE 5

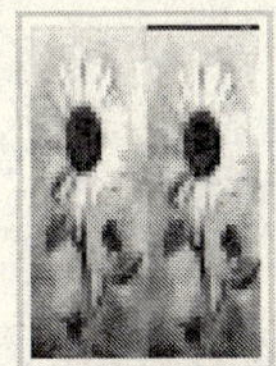

While I was vacationing in Switzerland, a troubled young man visited me. We went to a little cafe in Interlaken. There is a meadow in the heart of the town, and towering over this meadow is the great mountain, the Jungfrau (Young Wife). Like a coy young wife, she often throws a veil of clouds over her face. That morning, however, the veil had been cast aside and there she was, in all of her white, sparkling, radiant glory. We sat at the cafe. The boy gazed at the mountain and said, "That's the way I want to be: clean, like that!"

"You can be," I said, "if you will bring Jesus Christ into your life."

"Oh," he exclaimed, "thank God! That's what I wanted to hear you say!" Apparently nobody else had said that to him. He leaned over the table where we were having coffee and at my urging gave his heart to Jesus Christ.

"Go up there among the mountains where it is clean and talk with God," I said. That boy now knows that not only is there real good in life, but he knows where to find it.

They said to the woman, "We no longer believe just because of what you said; now we have heard for ourselves, and we know that this man really is the Savior of the world." JOHN 4:42

JUNE 6

If you have no confidence; if you're defeated; if you're being beat down; if you're troubled by fear, diffidence, apprehension, or weakness; then come to where the power is, where the confidence is to be found: in your faith, in the Savior. It is good that we should call Him Savior, because that is what He does. He saves you from your defeats and gives you confidence with which you can handle life with mastery, satisfaction, and happiness. You can have confidence. You must have confidence if you are going to live well. Never let anything get you down—no matter how difficult, how black, how hard it is; no matter how hopeless it may seem or how utterly depressed you may become. Whatever the quality and the character of the circumstances involved, never let anything get you down. Always, there is help and hope for you.

So Peter was kept in prison, but the church was earnestly praying to God for him. ACTS 12:5

JUNE 7

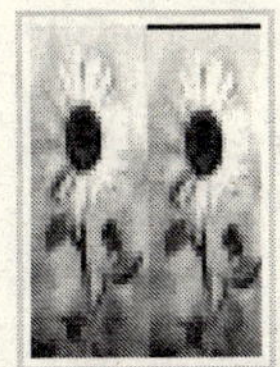

When faced with a difficult problem—whether it be a health problem, a money problem, or a domestic problem—walk around it prayerfully. Now that phrase is not my own—I only wish it were. It was given to me by one of the greatest Christians I ever knew. He used to say, "Let's lay the problem out there on the table, boys, and walk around it prayerfully." And he would tell us there is no problem in this world that doesn't have a soft spot somewhere. "Walk around it prayerfully," he would say. "Poke at it until you find the soft spot."

"Well," you say, "that may be all right, but you don't know my problem. My problem is a hard one." I know. Sure, your problem is a hard one. Just walk around it a little more—prayerfully—and you'll get your answer.

Our Heavenly Father, grant that into our weakness may come Your strength, that into our ineffective lives may come Your incredible power. Through Jesus Christ our Lord. Amen.

The one who sows to please his sinful nature, from that nature will reap destruction; the one who sows to please the Spirit, from the Spirit will reap eternal life. GALATIANS 6:8

JUNE 8

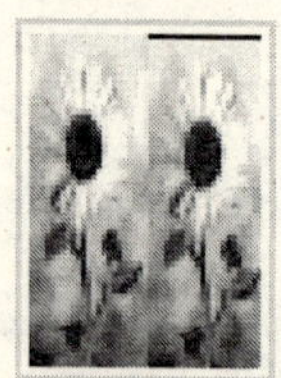

God gives us life, and this life continually re-creates itself if we stay in harmony with Him. For He not only creates, He re-creates. But if you abandon Him, if you cut Him off, if you stop the practice of devotion, if you cease the cultivation of your spiritual understanding, then disabilities creep in and you begin to deteriorate.

The next question is: How can we recover our identification with God so that we become vital and well? Important in this are the thought patterns we constantly employ, the attitudes by which we live, the pictures of ourselves that we form in our consciousness. There is a great life force that should work for health in us through God, and we must release it. To release it we must believe in it, and we must cooperate with it. That may be done by affirmation: I hereby affirm that I have within me the life given to me by God and that it is in charge of me, it is encompassing me. It is directing my life.

. . . the LORD *Jesus Christ, who, by the power that enables him to bring everything under his control, will transform our lowly bodies so that they will be like his glorious body.* PHILIPPIANS 3:20–21

JUNE 9

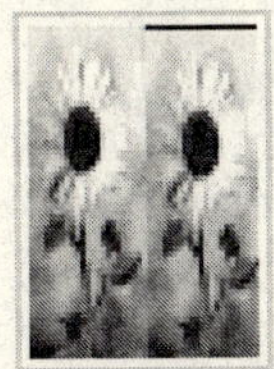

Knowing yourself and getting yourself healed can be a long, hard process if you try to do it by yourself. But the mysterious power of Jesus Christ is such that He comes into the life of anyone who will permit Him to do so and transforms it utterly, releasing the person.

As we go along through life, our minds get clouded so that they do not function in a clear, clean-cut manner anymore. Nervous apprehension or ill will, sinfulness or vindictiveness creeps in; you take yourself too seriously or you live with yourself too much so that your mind gets confused.

There are behaviors and ways of thought which just are not compatible with real happiness. Most of the frustration in our lives is self-imposed frustration. And Jesus Christ offers us release from it, calling us to know the truth, so that the truth may sweep the dust from our minds and we may be free.

Jesus turned and saw her. "Take heart, daughter," he said, "your faith has healed you." And the woman was healed from that moment. MATTHEW 9:22

JUNE 10

You want to live a successful, meaningful existence. How much do you want that? Well, the Bible tells us that things will happen to us according to our faith.

You may say, "That's okay; I go for that and I believe it; but it is awfully hard to have that kind of faith." That's right. It is. Because faith has to be practiced. Some people have a greater capacity to believe than others, and it is part of the job of a therapist or counselor to help an ill or disturbed person to develop his capacity to believe. When such a person gets to the point where he can truly believe, where he can trust faith, he can get well. Faith will heal.

Faith may seem to be an unsubstantial thing to put your feet down on, and you may be inclined to think that the wise ways of the world are better. But if you learn to have faith in faith and believe in it, it will see you through.

On arriving there, they gathered the church together and reported all that God had done through them and how he had opened the door of faith. ACTS 14:27

JUNE 11

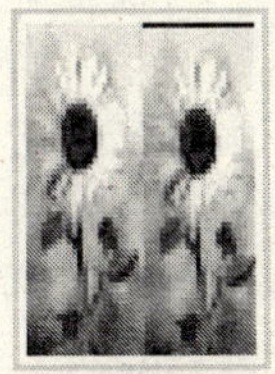

I never steer away from the pathos of human life. Everybody in our congregation needs help of one kind or another. I can certainly tell you that I need help very badly. Take, for example, a man who has been hounded by fear all his life—does he need help? Is it pointless to help him? Or consider a couple whose marriage is about to break up. They need a lot of help. Is it irrelevant to help them? One might say they are just two individuals out of the billions on this planet. But are we now concerned only with masses? Don't we see the pain on a human face? Have we no longer compassion for heavily burdened human hearts? What has come over us, that helping the individual should seem trite and insignificant?

A church alive in Jesus Christ helps both the masses and the hurting individual. Both missions deserve your dedication. We must help the world and we must also help individuals, the poor souls who live in it.

"What is the kingdom of God like? . . . It is like a mustard seed, which a man took and planted in his garden. It grew and became a tree, and the birds of the air perched in its branches." LUKE 13:18–19

JUNE 12

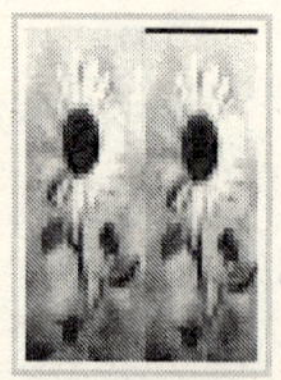

A young man I knew wanted to be a social worker, but he did not have enough education to qualify. He worked nights driving a rickety truck. One Sunday he had the radio on. A voice was saying, "Believe in the potential you possess, and yield to the One who has the infinite skills to bring your potential into action."

He wasn't too impressed, but he took to listening to that program every week. Finally one night he said, "Okay, Lord, if this is true, please help me." He described his goal and said, "I can't do it without You."

Soon he began to work days and went to school at night. Not long ago, he wrote a letter telling me: "I am now a social worker, and I am having the time of my life helping people. I will never quit. I will believe."

Now what do you call that? A miracle of real faith! Jesus doesn't say you have to have a lot of faith, just a little real faith. Quite an offer, isn't it?

"My command is this: Love each other as I have loved you." JOHN 15:12

JUNE 13

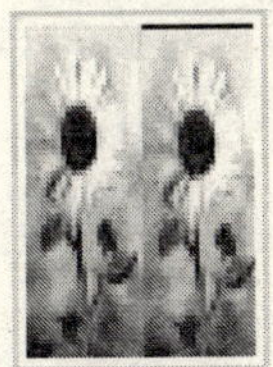

All of us are concerned today that there be found a constructive American and Christian solution to the problem of race relationships. This problem has burst violently upon the people of this land who, surprisingly, seem rather ill-prepared to meet it. When you break down this problem into its basic components, it is a human problem. It will take more than new laws to bring about brotherhood, respect, and understanding between people of different races in this country.

Here is an area where we should turn once again to the practical, problem-solving power of Christianity that teaches that all human relationships can be brought to a higher level where people live in mutual respect, understanding, and esteem. This is the great message of the New Testament. It is the only ground upon which the great social question of race relations will ever be resolved, now and in the future.

From the fullness of his grace we have all received one blessing after another. JOHN 1:16

JUNE 14

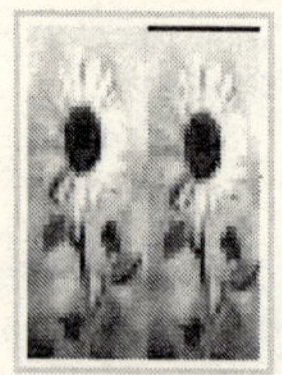

Health and prosperity can be yours. I realize that you may regard this as a very extravagant assertion—a big order, so to speak; but please remember that I do not make this assertion on my own authority. I have this on the authority of the wisest Book ever written. The Bible isn't as fearful of promising big things as some of the more timid, halfhearted preachers of the gospel. The Bible makes superlative promises, because its promises are inspired by a loving and omnipotent God.

But the Bible is also very subtle. And it points out that the blessings of health and prosperity are not easily given or easily received. Parenthetically, I want to say that by prosperity, the Bible does not mean merely material affluence; it means to enter abundantly into the blessings of God's grace. And it tells us that health and prosperity come to us when our soul is in harmony with God.

"The world cannot accept him, because it neither sees him nor knows him. But you know him, for he lives with you and will be in you." JOHN 14:16–17

JUNE 15

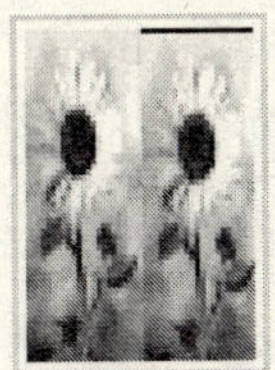

My wife taught me one of the greatest truths in the world: God is always with you. And I can guarantee to you what she guaranteed to me: if you put your problems in His hands and trust Him, He will guide you and bless you and take care of you till the day you die. And He won't stop there. He will take care of you the rest of the way.

"Well," you may say, "that is sensible; that is logical, but I never felt any closeness to God." I'm sorry to hear anyone say that. Are you going to live all your life and never feel the presence of God? Haven't you had some high moments spiritually, when you felt lifted out of yourself, lifted to a higher level? At some time in your life, you should feel deeply the presence of God. Then, even though there be times when you feel that He is far away from you; you know He is with you, and then nothing can overcome you.

"You have heard that it was said, 'Love your neighbor and hate your enemy.' But I tell you: Love your enemies and pray for those who persecute you. . . ." MATTHEW 5:43–44

JUNE 16

One part of learning to live successfully under pressure is to analyze our lives and honestly face any of our attitudes that would be a cause of pressure. What most often breaks people down is an impairment of the mental processes by negative thoughts and feelings, or the weight of sin upon their souls. Fear, hate, and resentment give rise to tensions that become continuous, preventing adequate relaxation between peaks of activity. Eventually they so impair a person's resiliency that the daily pressures get him down.

If you are so fortunate as never to have had a crisis, you can count on one thing—you will have a crisis sooner or later. And it will take all your faith, all your strength, all your thought, everything you've got, to meet it. But remember that in any crisis, you have a big God you can turn to in order to find the answer that answers.

He replied, "If you have faith as small as a mustard seed, you can say to this mulberry tree, 'Be uprooted and planted in the sea,' and it will obey you." LUKE 17:6

JUNE 17

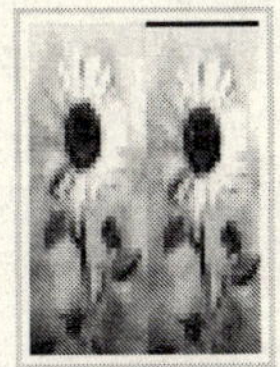

Mary B. Crowe rose from humble circumstances to become one of the most successful insurance agents in the United States. At the age of twelve, Mary was left in charge at home. She got the meals for a family of ten, cleaned the house, did the laundry, and went to school.

Later, after she became the first college graduate in the history of her family, she decided she wanted to be a life insurance agent. At that time, the idea of women selling life insurance was practically unheard of. She asked to see a manager about selling insurance, and he did his best to discourage her. Long after he had retired, that agency manager was present at a luncheon in honor of Mary B. Crowe's twenty-fifth anniversary.

If you remember God's everlasting presence and look to Him for help, nothing will be so hard that you cannot think it through and see it through. So you need never let anything ever get you down, you wonderful person, you immortal child of God.

". . . You have made them to be a kingdom and priests to serve our God, and they will reign on the earth." REVELATION 5:9–10

JUNE 18

Christianity not only outlines procedures and a methodology for solving problems, but provides the "go-power" that gets solutions into working order. You name the problem, and practical Christianity has an answer for it. A problem can be very pesky, difficult, and complicated, but there is an answer. This applies to individual and social problems alike.

Marble Collegiate Church began years ago the practice of recognizing no difference whatsoever between the races. Neither have we ever had any regard for differences in economic or social status. To think that the church of Almighty God should receive some persons differently than others because of differences in economic condition, social position, or color is a blasphemy. And if this church has spiritual power, it is because we have tried to follow the teachings of Jesus, who said: "A new command I give you: Love one another. As I have loved you, so you must love one another" (John 13:34). This sounds very idealistic, but is utterly practical.

But thanks be to God, who always leads us in triumphal procession in Christ and through us spreads everywhere the fragrance of the knowledge of him. 2 CORINTHIANS 2:14

JUNE 19

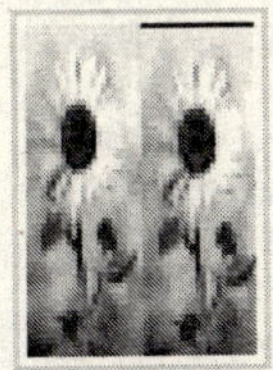

If you want enthusiasm, a good place to look for it is in the Bible; the Bible is packed full of enthusiasm. What does it talk about? In 2 Corinthians 2:14, we read these marvelous words: "But thanks be to God, who always leads us in triumphal procession in Christ." If you really surrender your life to Jesus Christ and follow Him—alive, vital Jesus Christ who has the answers that really answer—you will have enthusiasm. He will keep enthusiasm going for you, so that you can overcome your defeats, so that you can make a real contribution to humanity.

If you are constantly in the company of negative people, you will take on a negative mind—your mental reactions will be negative. So you have to practice enthusiasm. You do that by thinking it, by believing it, by praying it, by talking it, until enthusiasm becomes part of your better nature.

Each one should use whatever gift he has received to serve others, faithfully administering God's grace in its various forms. 1 PETER 4:10

JUNE 20

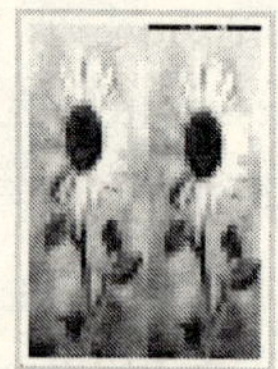

I spent several days with Leslie Carver, a reticent man, visiting camps for Palestinian refugees. We talked about everything. But if I touched on religion, he'd only say, "I lost myself and found myself in Jerusalem." One day we met an old man in the cellar of a bombed-out building. Carver sat down, took the man's hand and chatted with him in Arabic. When Carver stood up, I saw wondrous love written on the old man's face.

When we came out of the cellar, I saw the Garden of Gethsemane straight ahead of us. I said, "You found a Man in that Garden, and He put love in your heart. You love the people because you love Jesus Christ."

He just answered, almost gruffly, "Didn't I tell you I lost myself and found myself in Jerusalem?" I returned home and about six weeks later I received a letter that said Leslie Carver had died in an accident while "on one of his usual errands of love."

That is the way to get excited about life. Lose yourself, for in so doing, you find yourself.

We were therefore buried with him through baptism into death in order that, just as Christ was raised from the dead through the glory of the Father, we too may live a new life. ROMANS 6:4

JUNE 21

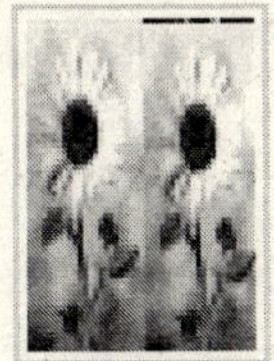

Paul told the Romans that we are raised to new life. Life should never grow dull or flat to us. It should never lose its luster. So if you want enthusiasm that never runs down, then run (don't walk) to a nearby church. Because wherever the Gospel is believed in and preached, people learn to walk in newness of life.

What a wonderful concept this is—newness of life! It means a renewal of the soul. God built enthusiasm into us when we were created. You should never let it run down. But if your enthusiasm for life has run down, it can be rejuvenated, it can be reactivated, it can be built up again. It can be enhanced with a powerful new upthrust. And when this happens, this thing that we call rebirth, then a person becomes perpetually enthusiastic and excited. In rebirth a person comes alive; it is where he comes up out of death and decadence into life and vitality.

He guides the humble in what is right and teaches them his way. PSALM 25:9

JUNE 22

After a speaking engagement in Florida, my hosts assigned a Navy captain to fly me home. En route, the captain told me that there was a very heavy overcast in New York. "As a matter of fact," he said, "we'll have to go in on instruments." We went down, down, down. And finally, I saw the lights of the runway and we came right up to the ramp. It was a beautiful landing.

The captain said, "The primary ingredient for a good landing is faith. I have to have faith in these instruments. If I didn't, I might think, 'Well, maybe this instrument isn't exactly right, so I'll make this adjustment.' And that could have tragic consequences."

Your religious education is your instrument panel for safe navigation through the long flight of the years. When clouds gather, storms develop, and trouble looms, if you lose faith in your instruments, you can be lost. But if you have faith in the teachings of the Bible, in prayer, in the church, in goodness, love, and hope, your instruments will bring you through.

Then Jesus said, "Did I not tell you that if you believed, you would see the glory of God?" John 11:40

June 23

My friend built a house in Topanga Canyon—a beautiful place in an attractive, wild setting. I was in Los Angeles when a fire swept through the canyon and destroyed 565 houses. My friend's house was among the ruined buildings. I telephoned and said, "I'm sorry that your house burned down."

"Why, what are you worrying about me for?" he said. "Sure it burned. But my wife and kids are safe."

"Did you save anything from the house?" I asked.

"Nothing but my philosophy and my faith," he said, "But that's all I need. I'm going to build again. Don't worry about me until I get into some real trouble."

That is the kind of talk I like to hear: Nothing left but "my philosophy and my faith!" If you'll start digging into the Christian faith and applying its principles, you will be able to meet and handle victoriously the tough situations of life.

The heavens declare the glory of God; the skies proclaim the work of his hands. PSALM 19:1

JUNE 24

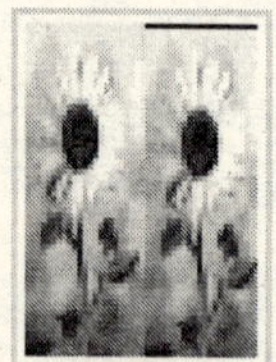

A young man was sitting next to me on a plane. It was so dark that the lights had to be turned on. But we took off with clockwork precision, and in seconds we were above the overcast and into the clear afternoon sky.

I was in the window seat. Suddenly I felt a boy leaning over to see this marvelous sight. He exclaimed, "Did you ever see anything like it? To come out of darkness into this glorious light—isn't it something? Don't tell me God isn't in His heaven!"

I looked at the young man's face. It was the great, full face of someone who loved life and loved the world. And he poured out to me his hopes, his dreams, his ideals and objectives. All of them had to do with human justice and making the world a better place. He had meaning packed into his life.

There are people everywhere who pack meaning into their lives because they pack something else into their lives: faith and goodness and love and hope and fellowship, and every other good thing.

And how can they hear without someone preaching to them? And how can they preach unless they are sent? As it is written, "How beautiful are the feet of those who bring good news!" Romans 10:14–15

June 25

I once met a man known as Brother Andrew. Hearing that people in Communist lands wanted the Word of God, he went to the missionary society in Amsterdam and asked them to send him to Eastern Europe. They said, "No, it's too dangerous."

"Will you pray for me if I go on my own?" he asked. He fixed up a car so it could conceal a supply of Bibles, and he crossed the border with them. Finally he was caught. But the border agents knew how valuable the Bibles were; they confiscated them and sold them for high prices. This didn't bother Brother Andrew, because at least his Bibles were getting into circulation. He returned to that border seven more times to get the agents to sell more Bibles.

Sitting and talking with this dedicated man, I asked him, "Why do you do this?"

He looked at me and answered, "I do it because the Lord set me free, and the only thing that can set these people free is the Word of God."

I will pray with my spirit, but I will also pray with my mind; I will sing with my spirit, but I will also sing with my mind. . . .

1 Corinthians 14:15

June 26

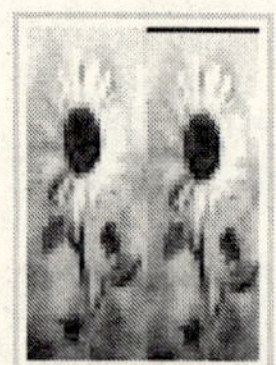

We are either destroyed or made whole by the kind of thoughts we think. You can cancel out a fearful thought or an apprehensive thought with a faith thought. Don't be afraid—just believe. If you have been victimized by the fear of some sinister thing that might happen down the road, just believe and healing will start. If you believe strongly enough, you can drive any apprehensive fear out of your mind. So the number one antidote for fear is to fill your mind full of God.

This may seem to you to be a strange expression. How can you get your mind full of God? Well, you read about God, you think about God, you talk to God, you try to serve God, you try to live God's way. After a while your mind gets full of God. And when your mind is full of God, it cannot have anything negative in it. It can't have prejudice; it can't have hate; it can't have resentment; it can't have impurities of any kind. It is holy, wholesome and good.

But you, O Lord, are a compassionate and gracious God, slow to anger, abounding in love and faithfulness. Psalm 86:15

June 27

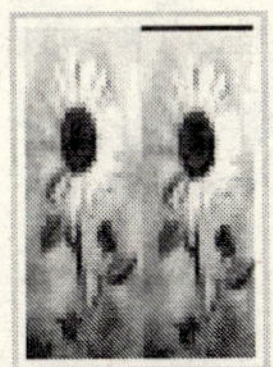

I was invited to a gathering to honor the mothers who had lost sons in the war. I went with the understanding that I was to give an invocation. But when I picked up the program I saw that I was on the program to make a speech! I was aghast. I had no confidence.

General Theodore Roosevelt, Jr. was sitting next to me. He said, "Each of those mothers has lost the idol of her heart. Can't you get up and tell them that God loves them and their country loves them and at some time, somewhere, in the mercy of God, they will meet their sons again? Forget about yourself, son. Put yourself in the hands of God and do the best you can."

To this day I love that man, for he taught me a tremendous principle: love other people, do the best you can, and put your faith in God. These are the secrets of confidence and security in an insecure world.

"The virgin will be with child and will give birth to a son, and they will call him Immanuel"—which means, "God with us." MATTHEW 1:23

JUNE 28

Almighty God put you and me in a hard, tough universe. Oh, He filled it with sunshine and babbling brooks and beautiful forests and misty valleys filled with eternal peace. He sprinkled the heavens with unlimited stars. He gave us dawn and sunset, lovely eyes to look into, dear friends to cling to. He gave us all that.

But He wanted to grow His human creatures, so He also made it hard. He knew it would get so hard that His creatures would want to quit the hard highway and abandon the upper climb, so He gave them support. He said, "I'll send Jesus to them and call His name Emmanuel, which means they will never be alone, that God is with them always."

Jesus Himself said, "And surely I am with you always, to the very end of the age." (Matthew 28:20) So, you children of God, thank God for that truth, because He is with us and nothing in this world can overwhelm us. You can be strong enough.

And we know that in all things God works for the good of those who love him, who have been called according to his purpose. ROMANS 8:28

JUNE 29

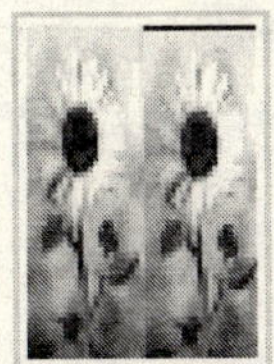

Romans 8:28 is a tremendous text. It means that everything that happens in your life—harsh, painful, hard though it may be—combines with all the rest of your experience for your good, if your life is dedicated to God. This is one of the deepest philosophies ever declared. We are to take all things—what we think is good and what we think is bad—and draw them all together into a symphony of creativity and make it work for good. And that's the way it is, if we are in harmony with God's will and mindful of His love. So I submit that this is the secret of having a bright future in this chaotic world. If enough people were to take hold of this idea and live attuned to it, moving out from the churches into the world outside, we could make all things work together for good in the world too.

To ask in Jesus' name means complete unselfishness and a sacrificial spirit. The great secret is to ask for that which He wants us to ask for. And it shall be granted overwhelmingly.

Now all has been heard; here is the conclusion of the matter: Fear God and keep his commandments, for this is the whole [duty] of man. ECCLESIASTES 12:13

JUNE 30

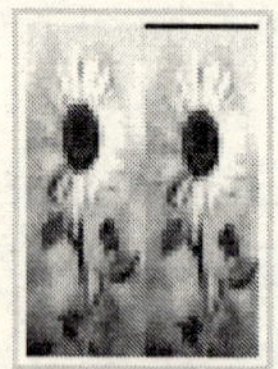

What kind of people are happy people? In reply to this question, some would say that the mood of unhappiness today is very high. A distinguished writer declared in a magazine article that unhappiness is the commonest thing there is. And T.S. Eliot, the famous British poet and literary critic, once asked plaintively, "Where is the life we have lost in living?"

A great many writers, perhaps because they themselves have lost the secret of happiness, dwell on the prevalence of unhappiness. But I believe there are untold numbers of people who have discovered a precious secret, the secret of how to have happiness in depth. And, as a matter of fact, unless there is depth in happiness, it isn't genuine. It is spurious and of little value. Apparently many people are discovering this. They are finding out how to live in this confused and bewildering world, while at the same time having peace within their hearts and a deep happiness within their natures.

July

The Lord gives strength to his people; the Lord blesses his people with peace. Psalm 29:11

Let us not become weary in doing good, for at the proper time we will reap a harvest if we do not give up. GALATIANS 6:9

JULY 1

It is really unworthy of a Christian to say, "Well, I guess I've had it. It's too much for me. I can't handle it anymore. I will just accept defeat."

You say, "Look at all the difficulties." I am looking at them. Our forefathers made a new world. Were our forefathers any greater than we are? We too can make a new world if we think we can and if we have the same quality of faith as they had. No, we don't need to be defeated by anything. Never accept defeat.

If you feel defeated and you think, "I'm tired and weary and I've had it," that is exactly how it will be. You can count on it for sure. You will be what you accept in your mind. But if, on the contrary, when the going gets difficult, you think, "I won't accept this—I will continue to think victory and not defeat," then what happens is that all the resources of your nature flow toward effecting a victory situation and circumventing a defeat condition.

Be at rest once more, O my soul, for the LORD *has been good to you.* PSALM 116:7

JULY 2

Carl Erskine, the great pitcher for the Brooklyn Dodgers, once told me, "The simplest and greatest truth that I have ever learned in my whole life is this: Whatever the problem, whatever the challenge, difficulty, hardship, pain, or suffering—you need never have confidence knocked out of your heart if you believe and remember that God is with you, and if you submit your life into His hands."

I know this sounds simple. The greatest things in this world are simple. Christianity is not a religion of complexity. It has taken the complex and inscrutable and made it so simple that a child can understand. Just put your life in God's hands; do the best you can, trust it to Him, and you will have the blessing of confidence. It does not come easily. It requires practice. But when you get it, then you have the secret of peace and confidence.

But you, O LORD, be not far off; O my Strength, come quickly to help me.
PSALM 22:19

JULY 3

A company was building a bridge and discovered a sunken ship in the channel where they had to put down some footings. They had to get it out of the way. A young crewman suggested a solution. He said to the foreman, "Sir, if I were you, I would send down a diver to work chains underneath the hulk and attach the chains to flat boats on either side. Let the tide float it out."

The foreman saw the reasonableness in the suggestion and adopted it, and presently the ocean tide came surging into the harbor. The shoulders of the sea got under those flat boats and lifted the hulk free.

Now haven't you seen people wearing themselves out, trying to lift a great weight, when through surrender to God, they could get the mighty shoulders of God under it? Let God help you. The power of God will flow to your aid if you give yourself to Him, commit yourself to Him, and have faith in Him.

"All men are like grass, and all their glory is like the flowers of the field. . . . The grass withers and the flowers fall, but the word of our God stands forever." ISAIAH 40:6, 8

JULY 4

The problem of preserving our country is acute. We do not realize how easily a civilization can decay. I have been to Byblos, at the eastern end of the Mediterranean Sea, where you can see at a glance the excavated traces of seven successive civilizations (thanks to the skill with which the excavations there have been performed): Egyptian, Persian, Greek, Roman, and others—all mighty civilizations.

If at the height of any of those civilizations, a preacher had stood in a pulpit and said, "This civilization can die," he would have been laughed at. But they all did die, and their cities were covered over by dirt and sand and a few crumbling monuments. That is all that is left of them. This mighty civilization of ours likewise has within it the seeds of death. All human beings have within them the seeds of death. You have them; I have them. It is necessary to counteract these seeds of death with those of life. Our civilization can die, or our civilization can live.

You will keep in perfect peace him whose mind is steadfast, because he trusts in you. ISAIAH 26:3

JULY 5

If people will love the dear Lord and love others and love this beautiful world, they will overcome fear. A great factor in overcoming fear is in getting a sound mind. Think of all the tangled ideas to which we have been subjected and from which we may never have escaped—quirks, notions, ghosts, shadows in the mind—affecting our attitudes toward ourselves and toward the world. A sound, clean, wholesome mind is a mental machine in which there is no sand—finely lubricated and working with precision.

When you have a mind like that, you have a mental engine that delivers power. Difficulties start with obsessive things that you pick up over the years: prejudices, hates, notions, fears, tensions, opinions of yourself that are incorrect. When you begin to know God, when you learn to love Jesus, then you begin to see yourself as you really are, not as you had thought you were. You cast out defeatist elements.

Humility and the fear of the L*ORD* *bring wealth and honor and life.* PROVERBS 22:4

JULY 6

A popular local television host invited me to his studio for an interview. When I met him, I was rather startled. He was abnormally short, and his hands were disproportionately large with stubby fingers. He had an unimaginative face, but when he began to talk, his countenance became animated; his eyes flashed with depths of understanding. There was a tremendous charm about the man.

Before we went on the air he told me, "I was a defeated person. I was self-conscious and resentful. I think you can understand why: you have only to look at me. However, some instinct kept telling me that being bitter would only make things worse. In my unhappiness I began to read the Bible. Gradually a big idea dawned upon me: changed thinking changes everything. So I resolved that I would learn to think spiritually about my handicap. And as I did so, everything changed for me."

I knew why his show was so popular. Even when he talked about ordinary things, he gave people something special.

Do not be anxious about anything, but in everything, by prayer and petition, with thanksgiving, present your requests to God.

PHILIPPIANS 4:6

JULY 7

Just what does the process of praying do for you to relieve you of worry? One thing it does is release and activate your built-in strength. Every one of us has more strength by far than he ever dreamed of. Have you ever used all your strength? *All* of it? No, you have never used one-half of your strength, nor have I. I'll go further and say that I doubt that any of us has ever used one-tenth of his strength.

We have tremendous reservoirs of power that we could call into action if we wanted to. The greatest achievement in life is to know how to continually break out from yourself the strength that is there. You pray the strength out, you believe it out, you practice it out. And then the worry fades away. It is amazing the strength that people have—that you have, that I have.

If power isn't coming through, find the block and remove it. Always poke around a problem, looking for its soft spot, for nearly every problem has one. Then break the problem open and find the solution.

Let the morning bring me word of your unfailing love, for I have put my trust in you. Show me the way I should go, for to you I lift up my soul. PSALM 143:8

JULY 8

I had a friend who managed a hotel in Florida who was one of the happiest men I ever saw. He had a very interesting way of starting the day. The first thing he did in the morning was go down to the ocean and take a dip. No matter what the weather was, he did this every morning. And just before plunging in he would offer this prayer: "O God, as I breathe into me this fresh morning air, so I breathe in Your Holy Spirit. Come fill me with Your holiness, fill me with Your peace, fill me with Your kindness, Your purity and wisdom. Fill me with Your joy. And O, God, fill me with Yourself." Then he would plunge into the sea and come out feeling alive to his fingertips, a song on his lips, vital and vibrant for the day. That was how he began his daily practice of happiness. And his joyous personality was impressive evidence that by practice we can be happy people, notwithstanding difficulties and adversities. So don't continue practicing old unhappiness. Practice happiness.

So God created man in his own image, in the image of God he created him; male and female he created them. GENESIS 1:27

JULY 9

What is the highest form of God's creation? Human nature—with its weaknesses, but with its strength; with its defeat, but with its victory; with its sins, but with its goodness; with its illimitable possibility under God? What, then, would you like to be? You name it, and by God's grace, you can be it.

You may say, "That is going too far. That is promising too much." But I have not said you can attain this through your own strength, because you cannot. You are weak. You are of the world, earthly. But you are also of heaven, heavenly. And through God's grace, you can realize your highest dreams.

As a child, you had long, long thoughts of what you might become. Have you now become so old and tired and cynical that you have forgotten these dreams of your youth, these high expectations of yourself? Never lose them, no matter what else you lose. Lose your stock certificates, lose your property; but don't lose your dreams. For this urge to be someone, to be something, was put into you by Almighty God.

"I will remain in the world no longer, but they are still in the world, and I am coming to you. Holy Father, protect them by the power of your name . . . so that they may be one as we are one." JOHN 17:11

JULY 10

If you are discouraged, I have news for you—good news. There is a way to end discouragement. And the word itself gives the clue. *Discouragement* is formed by putting the prefix *dis-* before the word *courage*. In effect, you have a discounting of courage. Therefore, the way to end discouragement is to remove the prefix and to lay under your life a solid foundation of courage. Winston Churchill expresses it well. He says, "Success is never final. Failure is never fatal. It's courage that counts."

It is a pity that the Christian religion is often presented as a genial philosophy, but with no power in it. Few speak of the tremendous power that Jesus Christ can let loose in a human being, power that can change even the cyclical rise and fall of your mental and emotional life so that you become a controlled human being—not the victim of your moods, but the master of them.

But I will sing of your strength, in the morning I will sing of your love; for you are my fortress, my refuge in times of trouble. PSALM 59:16

JULY 11

Some people must be revised in order that they may have a new life every morning. If you become a revised, new person, your tomorrows will be altogether different. I'd like to relate to you a letter that illustrates this point. It is from a woman who lives in Columbia, Missouri. She says: "I never before knew the effective use of faith. Now I find myself practicing my beliefs and, as a result, I have a cheerful outlook. I have been able to make new friends out of old enemies. I finally learned and accepted the fact that no one was against me but myself. I have come out of my shell at long last. I cannot adequately describe the happiness I now feel, instead of the self-pity and self-hate that once was me."

This woman walked away from her yesterdays. She applied the principle that by personal revision with God's help, you can become a new person. It is a simple formula. It takes discipline, it takes effort; but you can work it if you really want it, and thus be able to start life new every morning.

"Give, and it will be given to you. A good measure . . . will be poured into your lap. For with the measure you use, it will be measured to you." LUKE 6:38

JULY 12

Belief is the key to a transformed life. Hear the words of the Gospel of Luke, chapter 6, verse 38: "Give, and it will be given to you." Now the question is: Do we believe that? Do you believe that if you do so it will work?

The first thing is to believe in faith and trust it. The second thing is to go out and practice faith. Actually, there isn't much of a distinction between believing in faith and practicing it, because if you truly do believe, you practice it. For the person who learns the techniques of faith and practices them, nothing is too good to be true. If you are sick, you believe that God with the doctor will heal you; if you are weak, you believe you will become strong; if you have a great opportunity, you believe that you can handle it. You trust and you do the best you can. Whatever the situation is, you believe in and practice faith.

"The fear of the LORD is the beginning of wisdom, and knowledge of the Holy One is understanding." PROVERBS 9:10

JULY 13

You can find amazing truth all caught up in one verse from the Bible: "The fear of the LORD is the beginning of wisdom, and knowledge of the Holy One is understanding" (Proverbs 9:10). Any person who needs a change within himself or within his life can have this take place by changing his mind. But this cannot be a superficial mental change; it must be one in depth. Such a change can be extremely effective.

Are you perhaps facing a hard situation? Are you involved in some unsatisfactory personal relationship? Is there some other kind of trouble in your life? We could hardly enumerate all the problems a human being has to deal with. But there is a great answer to them all—and it is this: they can all be changed, and you can be changed—everything for the better—through the magic of a positive mental attitude.

May the words of my mouth and the meditation of my heart be pleasing in your sight, O LORD, my Rock and my Redeemer. PSALM 19:14

JULY 14

We are given instruments of faith and silence and meditation and prayer and unselfishness and love. And if we believe in these instruments and always trust them, we can come through any overcast sky to a safe landing. I don't mean to make this sound too easy. It isn't easy. But neither do I mean to make it sound impossible, for it is possible. Simply apply to each problem in life the love and the faith and the unselfishness and the spiritual perceptiveness that Jesus Christ gives to those who identify their lives with Him.

Our Heavenly Father, we thank You for this wondrous, sparkling, vital gift called Christianity. We know that Jesus Christ came to set us free from ourselves, and that we, in losing ourselves, may find life exciting, thrilling, wonderful, good. For this we give thanks. Amen.

Then Jesus answered, "Woman, you have great faith! Your request is granted." And her daughter was healed from that very hour. MATTHEW 15:28

JULY 15

One day after a speech I gave in Chicago, a young woman in a waitress's uniform rushed up to me and told me her amazing story.

"I have a little boy. When he was five years old, he got sick. The doctor prepared me for the worst. I felt my whole world would go to pieces if I lost my boy. Then a neighbor gave me one of your sermons to read. And in that sermon you said, 'If you have a loved one who is ill or about whom you are worried, give the loved one to God.' So I prayed and I put my boy in God's hands. And He let me keep my boy. And now God and I are raising him together."

And so when we separated, I went my way refreshed by yet another wonderful drama of human life rising to high places even out of humble circumstances.

John answered them all, ". . . But one more powerful than I will come, the thongs of whose sandals I am not worthy to untie. He will baptize you with the Holy Spirit and with fire." LUKE 3:16

JULY 16

A church in the South periodically holds what they call a "thought-burning" service. They bring urns before the altar and light fires in them. Each person in the congregation is given paper on which he is to write the thoughts he wants to be rid of—then, one by one, the congregants file down the aisle, drop their thoughts into the urn, and watch them curl up into ashes. I can well imagine the service ending with the hymn, "Praise God, From Whom All Blessings Flow."

Well, you don't need an urn to burn your regrets and hates and failures. You can set fire to them in your mind through the cleansing power of the Holy Spirit. Forget past failures. When you have failed, ask God to show you how to do the thing better the next time, and then go back at it and give it all you've got.

The LORD gives strength to his people; the LORD blesses his people with peace.

PSALM 29:11

JULY 17

Some time ago, after giving a speech, I returned to my hotel where the desk clerk informed me, "A woman has been waiting for you, and she has two of the noisiest children I've ever seen."

The minute she saw me, she rushed over. "I just prayed and asked the Lord to help me," she said. "I want to tell you my problem."

Now I've heard a lot of problems in my life, but this was really something. "Well," I said, "let's pray and let us turn all these problems over to Jesus." I prayed as best I could, and at the end, she and her children said in unison, "Hear our prayer, blessed Jesus."

Later the woman wrote to me: "Driving home that night, my heart was full of peace and my mind was full of cleanness. I knew that Jesus had answered my prayer and given me victory over everything. It hasn't been easy, but the victory of that moment has held."

When I applied my mind to know wisdom and to observe man's labor on earth—his eyes not seeing sleep day or night—then I saw all that God has done. . . . ECCLESIASTES 8:16–17

JULY 18

Look at a tough situation this way: "Well, it does present difficulties. I'm not going to be flippant about it. I know I have a problem here. But God is with me. I have a few friends. And Jesus Christ is helping me. Other people have solved problems like this. So I'm going to pour what confidence I've got right on this difficulty."

I hope those who read this meditation will start thinking about God, who gives abundantly above all we ask or even think. This is a big promise, isn't it? He gives us abundance, according to what we ask, more than we ask, above what we can ask, and more than we can even think. That is what He wants to give us all. But whether we receive or take it depends on the power that is working within us. The essence of the matter is the way we think. What goes on in the mind determines everything.

I eagerly expect and hope that I will in no way be ashamed, but will have sufficient courage so that now as always Christ will be exalted in my body. . . . PHILIPPIANS 1:20

JULY 19

Once when I was sitting in a hotel coffee shop having an early breakfast alone, a man came in. With a cheerful good morning to the cashier at the door and to the waiters, he came walking through the place, saw me, and apparently knew me, for he pulled up a chair, asking, "May I sit with you?" Before I could say yes or no, there he was. He shook out his napkin and exclaimed, "Boy, this is going to be another great day!"

I was astonished to hear this kind of conversation so early in the morning. "I gather you've had many good days," I said.

"Oh, yes," he assured me. "I learned that if I pass a series of expectancy thoughts through my mind every morning, God will bring my great expectations to pass. He can bring the good out. Therefore I just go along with Him, passing expectancy thoughts through my mind."

May I ask you, my reader, a question? What kind of expectatancy thoughts have you in your mind right now?

Do not conform any longer to the pattern of this world, but be transformed by the renewing of your mind. Then you will be able to test and approve what God's will is. . . . ROMANS 12:2

JULY 20

Some time ago, I met with a group of doctors and one of them asked me, "How many times a year do you discuss the problem of stress and tension from the pulpit?"

"About once a year," I replied.

He pulled a prescription pad from his pocket, wrote something on it, and pushed it across the table to me. "This is a prescription I give to patients after I have done everything I can do for them medically."

On the pad he had written: "Romans 12:2: Let God change the way you think." And lest you think this particular physician is odd, I assure you that his professional standing is extremely high.

I believe that the Bible has the answer to every personal and social problem. And I believe that by using such a great treatment as Romans 12:2, you can cure yourself of being victimized by pressure.

Cast your bread upon the waters, for after many days you will find it again.

ECCLESIASTES 11:1

JULY 21

The more you give, the more you shall receive. I saw an example of this at a luncheon for businessmen. The speakers were mostly in their forties, I would say, except for one man who was obviously older than all the rest. I sat down beside him and asked, "Are you head of one of these businesses here?"

"Sure am," he answered. "Why? Don't I look like I could handle it?"

I said, "I just heard you are eighty years old."

"Well," he demanded, "what's wrong with being eighty years old? It isn't how long you've been around; it's what you've done while you've been around. Don't think that just because I have a game leg, I can't handle the business. You don't run a business with your leg; you run it with your head."

Naturally, the man had found this zest where it really comes from: through the teachings of the Lord Jesus Christ, who says He has come that we might have life and have it more abundantly. That is what He offers us. Take it!

"Be still, and know that I am God; I will be exalted among the nations, I will be exalted in the earth." PSALM 46:10

JULY 22

I had a chat with an old friend who had been his state's attorney general. Some years ago, this man said to me, "If I don't find a way to reduce the tension in my life, I'm going to die." I discussed the problem with him and advised him to have a quiet time every day for communing with God and the Lord Jesus Christ. Later I saw him and he was quiet, calm, composed, and stronger physically than when he was ten years younger. He told me this was due to the beneficial effect of practicing creative silence.

You are a child of God. God never meant you to be victimized by pressure. He meant you to live in an effective, powerful manner. But that is only possible when you keep Him at the center of your life and in your own thinking. He will keep you in perfect peace if you keep your mind on Him.

To drop tension from your life, practice getting tranquility by passing peaceful words and thoughts through your mind daily and nightly.

For he does not willingly bring affliction or grief to the children of men. LAMENTATIONS 3:33

JULY 23

When he was thirty-one, Ludwig van Beethoven wrote of the "disastrous affliction," the growing deafness, that had befallen him. "I was soon compelled to keep apart, to live a life of loneliness," he wrote. "How could I possibly admit an inferiority in the one sense that should have been more acute in me than in others? I almost reached the point of putting an end to my life. Only art, it was, that held me back. It seemed impossible to depart this world until I had brought forth all the things I felt inspired to create. And so I went on living this miserable life. O God, You who lookest into the depths of my soul, You understandest me, You knowest that the love of mankind and the desire to do good live with me!"

Beethoven overcame that discouragement. He lived for another twenty-five years, the years of his greatest creativity. Such is the struggle that people have with black moods, and such are the victories of great faith. With the help of God, out of our discouragement and struggle, we may bring messages to bless mankind.

How great is your goodness, which you have stored up for those who fear you, which you bestow in the sight of men on those who take refuge in you. PSALM 31:19

JULY 24

Dr. Robert Schuller grew up in Iowa, and he tells an awe-inspiring story about a tornado. One afternoon Bob and his father heard a rumbling like many freight trains. The sky grew dark. Then out from the dark clouds bulged an enormous funnel.

Seconds later, the whole family was in the car racing down the road. They stopped and watched the tornado hit with elemental force. In ten minutes, it was gone. They saw the whole terrible sight; not one building was still standing—their house had vanished. Mr. Schuller told his wife and young Bob to wait where they were and got out of the car. He went poking in the ruins and brought back a battered motto that had hung in the kitchen. It said, "Keep looking to Jesus."

Some people would have lost their faith. But Mr. Schuller rebuilt. He replaced the lost livestock and buildings and equipment. A few years later, farm prices rose sharply. Before long, the mortgage was paid off! He died the prosperous owner of a thriving farm.

And we have the word of the prophets made more certain, and you will do well to pay attention to it . . . until the day dawns and the morning star rises in your hearts. 2 PETER 1:19

JULY 25

A man from Elmira, New York, came to see me in my office. He put his head in his hands and said, "Everything is lost. It's hopeless."

"Well," I said. "I'd like to explore this. Let me ask you a few questions. Your wife has left you, of course? And no doubt your children are all in jail?"

"What do you mean?" he retorted. "My wife loves me. Of course she hasn't left me. My kids are good kids. Of course they're not in jail."

"Well," I reminded him, "you told me everything was lost." We went on through a few more things like that. Then I said, "Look at the things you've got left! Plus God. Brother, you're in! What do you mean, you want to blow your brains out? All you need to do is blow your faith up." He found new courage and went home to straighten up his life.

If you are disheartened about anything today, forget it. Blow your faith up. Look to the Lord Jesus Christ. Let Him get into you and change your thinking.

Then Jesus declared, "I am the bread of life. He who comes to me will never go hungry, and he who believes in me will never be thirsty." JOHN 6:35

JULY 26

We are given the gift of life. And that is a wonderful thing. But the strange thing is that, having the gift of life, we apparently do not know how to use it. We mess it up. We limit it. We even desecrate it, though it is extraordinarily valuable to us. Many people, no matter how long they may have lived, have never yet grasped the secret of how to handle it. And that is a tragedy.

What, then, is the secret? In the sixth chapter of John's Gospel are these enormous words: "I am the bread of life." (That is, "I put substance into life.") "He who comes to me will never go hungry." What a thought! And it goes on to say, "He who believes in me will never be thirsty."

Do you ever get hungry? Not the hunger for food, but the hunger for something else, something deep? If you accept Him as the bread of life, you will never be hungry. And what goes for hunger goes for thirst.

Whatever you do, work at it with all your heart, as working for the LORD, not for men. . . . It is the LORD Christ you are serving. COLOSSIANS 3:23–24

JULY 27

Be someone! What is that supposed to mean? Nowadays everyone wants to be a big shot. What is a big shot? I've heard a big shot defined as a little shot who keeps on shooting. But there are a great many phonies among big shots, as well as a great many fine people.

In any case, to be a big shot or a celebrity is not a goal worthy of a real person. I would say a real person wants to be his or her best self. That is, a real person wants to realize all the potential inside. He or she wants to bring into focus every God-given talent. Such a person wants to attain the best results, not for himself, but for the world and for God. To be someone in that true sense is the highest realization of one's self as a child of God.

We need a reassessment of values. The end and aim of life is to be an organized, integrated, dedicated, useful, outgoing, loving, helpful individual worthy of the approval of God.

Some trust in chariots and some in horses, but we trust in the name of the LORD *our God.* PSALM 20:7

JULY 28

Once I had the great honor of speaking to the troops in Vietnam. At one place where I was to speak, I noticed a detachment of men on a hill-top about half a mile away. I asked, "Who are those men out there, General?"

"That's your security," said the general.

I sat there thinking it over and looking at those boys. And I said, "General, I don't feel right about all this security. Those boys—what is their security?"

"Their security," he replied, "is their training, their arms, and Almighty God."

"Well," I said, "I don't have the training or the arms, but I'll put my trust in God." And I thought, "Do I really mean that? Am I ready to go into the dangers of human existence with calmness and peace in my heart, knowing that in life or in death He will take care of me?" I turned to the general and quoted 1 Peter 5:7, "Cast all your anxiety on him because he cares for you." This is the only real security.

It is for freedom that Christ has set us free. Stand firm, then, and do not let yourselves be burdened again by a yoke of slavery. GALATIANS 5:1

JULY 29

Daniel Negris was a musical genius. As a young man, he began smoking marijuana, then he tried heroin and soon became addicted. He lost job after job. He realized that he needed help, but he didn't know where to turn.

Each time Daniel went on a tour, his mother put a Bible in his suitcase. He never read it; but one night, in deep despair, he took out the Bible and idly flipped through the pages until he saw these words: "If you are tired from carrying heavy burdens, come to Me and I will give you rest."

Trembling, he fell to his knees and prayed, "Lord, forgive me and take away my burden." Immediately he felt cleansed of sin and guilt and was overwhelmed by God's love. And he said, "I never touched drugs again. My recovery has been total."

Who did that for him? The One who is able to put power into anyone. Turn to Jesus. Take the power He gives. Your life will become so wonderful that you will thank God all the time for the miracle of it.

You are the God who performs miracles; you display your power among the peoples.

Psalm 77:14

July 30

An old friend of mine was a salesman. When I first knew him, he was one of the most depressed, defeated, negative individuals I've ever known. He was a lovable fellow but was getting nowhere fast. God had endowed him with a tremendous personality, but it was soft and flabby and had no force behind it. As I got to know him better, I saw that he was afraid. He was afraid of people, of economic conditions, of himself. He tried to cover up this fear with ingratiating sociability. But he didn't get any orders, and even I know that is what you have to do to be a successful salesman. At length, he talked with me about this problem and I prayed with him. All I ever did was to lead him to Christ. But that was enough, because he went on from there to be successful as a person and successful as a salesman.

And they were calling to one another:
"Holy, holy, holy is the LORD *Almighty; the whole earth is full of his glory."* ISAIAH 6:3

JULY 31

Modern science sets up a roadblock to questioning. Even some poetry teaches us that this whole visible universe is but a reflection of vaster realms beyond. The beauty and the loveliness and the charm and the love and the joy of this world are but tokens of that greater world of immortality. Sensitive people become aware of it. For example, Wordsworth wrote at Tintern Abbey: "I have felt a presence that disturbs me with the joy of elevated thoughts."

What is this sublime ecstasy that, even amid commonplace things, sometimes surges through the human heart and suffuses the whole world with glory? This could very well be a reflection of immortality—that greater, lovelier world intertwined with and superimposed upon this world.

Our Heavenly Father, help us live so that not only do we have strength and joy ourselves, but we may help others and build Your kingdom on earth. Through Jesus Christ, our Lord. Amen.

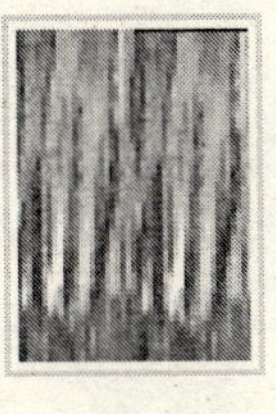

The Lord is my strength and my song; he has become my salvation. Psalm 118:14

Cast your cares on the LORD and he will sustain you; he will never let the righteous fall. PSALM 55:22

AUGUST 1

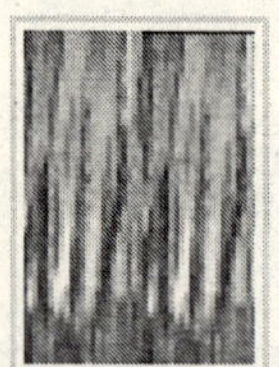

"Our Lord, we belong to you," says Psalm 55. "We tell you what worries us, and you won't let us fall." That is the first thing to remember in dealing with the toughest problems. The second is to equate the toughness that is within you with the toughness of the problem. Almighty God knew what He was doing when He created you and me. He built toughness into us. It has been built into the soul and the mind. You are tough. And you have a Savior who is the toughest man who ever lived. He is the kindly, gentle Jesus, but do you think Christianity would have endured for two thousand years if He were just a gentle man? Not on your life. Jesus Christ is tough in His faith, in His insights, in His strength, and in His wisdom. If you accept Him, you get Jesus Christ built into you and nothing can overwhelm you. So when you have a tough problem on the outside, say to yourself, "I equate with this outer toughness an inner toughness, the toughness of my faith and strength."

"For hardship does not spring from the soil, nor does trouble sprout from the ground. Yet man is born to trouble as surely as sparks fly upward." JOB 5:6–7

AUGUST 2

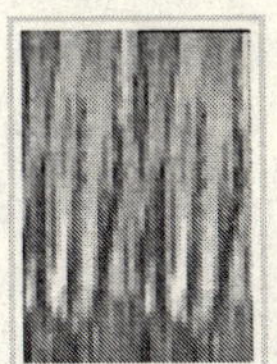

It is written in the book of Job that "man is born to trouble as surely as sparks fly upward." We cannot escape from problems, but we are called to struggle with problems and overcome them. So we may as well learn to handle problems. How do you go about doing that? Well, there is a great text in the Gospel of John that says, "The Spirit will show you what is true" (John 14:17). The Christian religion is built upon perception, upon insight, upon understanding, upon wisdom. And there is a wisdom about problems. One of the basic elements of this wisdom is the profound philosophy that sees a problem as a part of the creative process of testing and growth.

If we didn't have problems, we'd have to invent them, because our directional facility would be lost without problems. Problems help to steer a course through the years.

You are my hiding place; you will protect me from trouble and surround me with songs of deliverance. Psalm 32:7

August 3

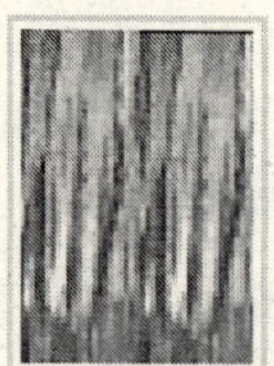

Never give in! You don't need to, for the Lord God will help you. Follow the "stick-it-out-and-never-give-up" principle. And keep in mind another idea: the "keep-God-in-it" principle. No one can be strong, vital, and heroic without the presence of God. This is a big, overwhelming world and we are small. It is like the prayer the Normandy fishermen offer when they go out on the deep waters to fish. Before they cast off their little boats, they pray, "O Lord, take care of us. The sea is so vast. We are so small." And He does and He will.

I tell you from the bottom of my heart: The secret of meeting life victoriously is how close you are to God, how deeply and sincerely you receive Jesus Christ into your life. And I guarantee you that if you give your life to God, if you commit your life to Christ until this becomes your consuming passion, you will have an immunity—not from difficulty, but from defeat. And that is all we can ask.

Let the peace of Christ rule in your hearts, since as members of one body you were called to peace. And be thankful. COLOSSIANS 3:15

AUGUST 4

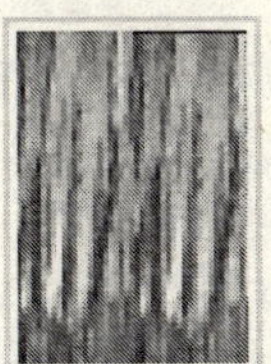

You can relax the soul by filling your mind with great words from the Scriptures about God. Say them to yourself and let them sink deeply into your mind. Let me suggest several texts: "You will keep in perfect peace him whose mind is steadfast, because he trusts in you" (Isaiah 26:3); "Come to me, all you who are weary and burdened, and I will give you rest" (Matthew 11:28); "Peace I leave with you; my peace I give you. I do not give to you as the world gives. Do not let your hearts be troubled and do not be afraid" (John 14:27).

In order to be an effective person, able to live and participate and lead, you need emotional control, serenity of mind, and what the Quakers call "peace at the center." You need the steadiness and sustaining power that can be yours only if you learn the relaxed approach to problems. So develop inner peace. And the way of doing this is open to us all.

Train a child in the way he should go, and when he is old he will not turn from it.

Proverbs 22:6

August 5

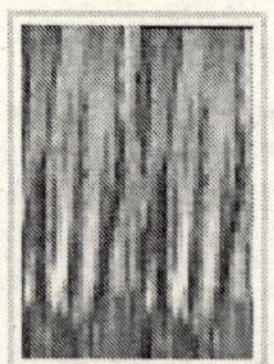

A famous man of letters said that when God wants to make a point with His children, He plants His argument in our instincts; the writer suggests that in deep feelings that cannot be put into words the greatest truths of life are communicated.

I personally had my doubts in my younger days. He who never has to fight a doubt is not a thinker. I sometimes receive letters from parents who are troubled by their children's doubts. A mother will write, for example, that she is worried about her son because he questions everything—he doubts. And I will advise her, "Thank God for your son's questioning. It means that he is alive, that he thinks. You cannot hand faith down, in packaged form, like an heirloom to your children. They must find it and develop it for themselves."

When you have to struggle to develop faith, the faith you discover is really your own. It will be a stronger faith if it has had to overcome the pain and struggle of doubt. I can only tell you now that I haven't the slightest doubt about immortality.

Great peace have they who love your law,
and nothing can make them stumble.
Psalm 119:165

August 6

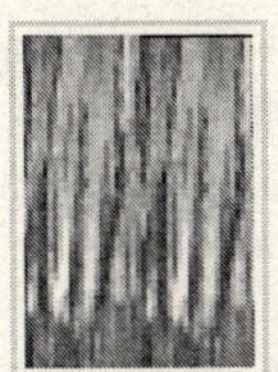

One time I was to speak at a luncheon for a group of professional people. The presiding officer was a doctor. He looked out at the group and said to me, "If I could reduce the tension and strain under which these people live, I would reduce my caseload. I can't remove those things. But," he said, "there is one Doctor who can." He then quoted from the 119th Psalm, verse 165: "Great peace have they who love your law."

Now what is God's law? The laws of nature are a part of it. When Almighty God created us, He knew we could never live as He intended without influences of serenity and beauty and healing peace surrounding us. So in order that our souls might grow great and strong, He set us in a world of great loveliness governed by natural laws. Love God's law, then you will have within you great peace.

The LORD is my strength and my song; he has become my salvation. PSALM 118:14

AUGUST 7

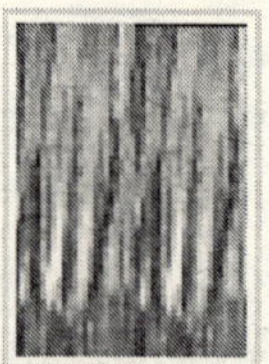

When you go to church or when you are in deep prayer, there is someone with you far greater than any person, someone who knows you through and through. He tells you that you are greater than you think—that these conflicts, these obsessions in the mind pale to the blessings He gives. He tells you to let the troubles go. He tells you that you can have a sound mind. So let your fears go.

The Lord Jesus came and taught and died on the cross—for what reason? To save us. Save us from what? To save us from sin; to save us from our weak, defeated selves; to save us from our notions, our obsessions, our prejudices, our hates, our fears; to cleanse us in our minds. That is the great secret, for God has not given you a spirit of fear. You got it yourself, and you can let it go yourself, with His help. Right now, today, you can begin. Depending on the depth of your faith, you can complete the process whereby you shed all your fear and anxiety.

Before the mountains were born or you brought forth the earth and the world, from everlasting to everlasting you are God. Psalm 90:2

August 8

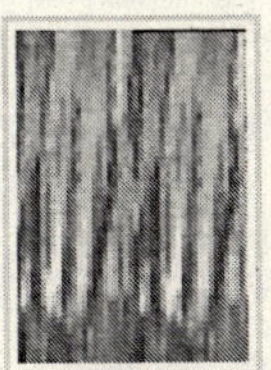

In Switzerland, my wife Ruth and I went up to a high valley six thousand feet above sea level, surrounded by the Bernini Peaks. We lingered for only five minutes. But those five minutes will forever remain in memory. All around us stretched a pristine world, golden sunshine, snow gleaming like myriad diamonds, and a blue sky above. I was so overwhelmed that I didn't even tell Ruth how I felt. But that night I said to her, "I have today spent five minutes in immortality."

If mountains can be that beautiful, so can a human being. This is the greatest form of immortality known to us in this life—not the splendor in nature, but spiritual radiance manifesting in man. A strange thing about us: we have evil in us as well as good in us. We have high desires and we have low desires. But Almighty God can change people and bring forth the immortality that is within them.

"Submit to God and be at peace with him; in this way prosperity will come to you." JOB 22:21

AUGUST 9

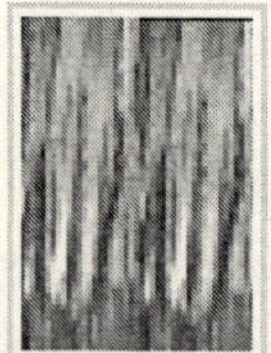

Consider today a Scripture passage so wise that it contains the answers, or the method for obtaining the answers, to your problems. It is Job 22:21: "Submit to God and be at peace with him; in this way prosperity will come to you."

I realize that embracing problems isn't a popular notion. We often encounter an insipid notion that the best thing we can do for people is to free them from all their problems so that they never again have any pain, any difficulty, any hardship, any struggle. Well, no proper-thinking person would adhere to such an idea. Almighty God has made problems an inherent part of the universe—but why? What is He trying to do? What is it all about? He wants to grow strong people: people who tussle with difficulty and grow tough in their minds and in their spirits, the kind of people on whom a great world can be built.

Though I walk in the midst of trouble, you preserve my life; you stretch out your hand against the anger of my foes, with your right hand you save me. PSALM 138:7

AUGUST 10

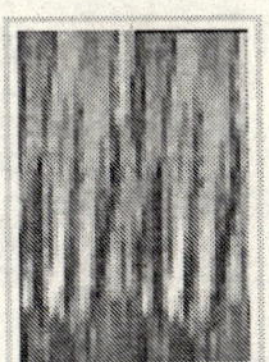

These are exciting times! A lot of people grump and whine and keep reminding you that this world is full of trouble. Well, years ago in Syracuse, New York, I knew a preacher by the name of David Keppel, an Irishman from Belfast. He was almost ninety. I was in my thirties then. One day I was telling him what a terrible state I thought the world was in.

"In Ireland we have a saying," he explained, "'when there is trouble on earth, it means there is movement in heaven. The more trouble on earth, the more movement in heaven.'" Which is a way of saying that the kingdom of God is going to come down out of heaven to replace your troubles in this world.

Who ever lived through more exciting times than these? We see more equality of status among races and expanded opportunities than our ancestors dreamed of fifty years ago. Wonderful things are happening today.

"But those who suffer he delivers in their suffering; he speaks to them in their affliction." JOB 36:15

AUGUST 11

What is the remedy when you're upset? I find it in the book of Job: "But those who suffer he delivers in their suffering; he speaks to them in their affliction."

Now what does that mean? It means that when you accept God's direction and build it into your life, no one can make you inwardly troubled. It doesn't make any difference how many people around you are trying to make trouble; they can only trouble you as you allow them to do so. When you have a deep inner quietness, the trouble others try to make for you, or the trouble you think they try to make for you, is absorbed and has no power over you.

And when you have deep inner quietness, receiving it from God, then trouble that you've been causing yourself fades away. It is lost in the depth of His quietness. So when you're upset, draw upon God for quietness and receive it. Then you will have control, orderliness, and a sound philosophy for life.

"Surely God is my salvation; I will trust and not be afraid. The LORD, the LORD, is my strength and my song; he has become my salvation." ISAIAH 12:2

AUGUST 12

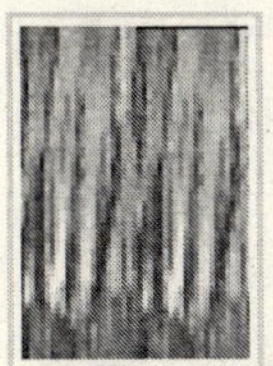

Commit yourself to God. You are a child of God. God made you. God gave you life. You are His. When your life on earth is ended, God will take you to Himself. You are God's all the way—unless by an act of will you turn away from Him, which would be the most dangerous thing you could ever do in your life, because then the power goes. So put yourself in God's hands—trust Him, believe in Him, don't doubt Him, stay with Him—and He will give you the power to do anything with yourself. But your belief has to be belief in depth, no mere surface belief. It has to go down deep. To get the kind of power I am talking about, you must really believe.

The power to change your life comes in seven magic words: "I can do all things through God." With all the strength and perseverance you can command, start practicing faith. Put your trust in God and just go calmly on your way.

An anxious heart weighs a man down, but a kind word cheers him up. PROVERBS 12:25

AUGUST 13

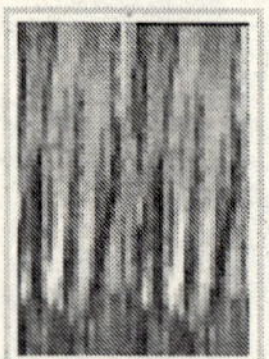

I was impressed by something I read about John Masefield, the poet. He used to perform what he called "the practice of the getting of tranquility." Each night he wouls sit in a chair and repeat to himself, "This body is a sacred thing. It is the temple of the soul. God created it for my use. God is putting His quietness upon my body." Then he would put his hand on his heart and say, "The hand of God is in this hand and I put this hand on my heart. Let not my heart be troubled. I believe in God." By this time his body would be quiet, free from the quivering tensions of the day.

Next he would say, "I hereby empty my mind of all jealousy. I hereby empty my mind of all resentment. I hereby empty every impure and evil thought out of my mind. I drain my mind." And then: "I now fill my mind with goodness and with love and with forgiveness and with hope."

With practice, Masefield gained inner peace and achieved victory over tension.

But I trust in you, O Lord; I say, "You are my God." Psalm 31:14

August 14

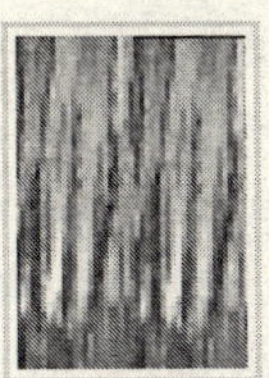

I met a lady who said to me, "I heard your wife make a speech at the church I belong to—and she said something I will always remember." The woman explained that she had been struggling in prayer for something she wanted and God wasn't answering her prayers. Mrs. Peale, in that speech, remarked that there are three ways God answers prayer: yes, wait awhile, and no. "And when she said that," the woman told me, "I knew I had my answer. It was no. But I hadn't wanted to take a 'no' answer."

"Maybe that 'no' answer is going to lead you to some great experience," I said. "Later, on some bright day, you will realize, 'If He had not said no, this wonderful thing I now have would not have come to me.'"

The attitude that really leads to life in all its fullness is that of a child walking with Him, loving Him, trusting Him, seeking to serve Him. Prayer in this attitude can change your life wonderfully.

The Lord *is good, a refuge in times of trouble. He cares for those who trust in him. . . .* Nahum 1:7

August 15

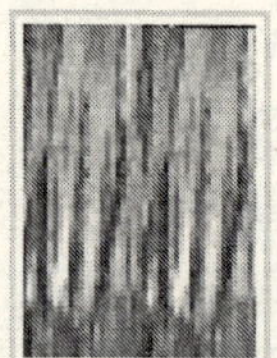

I wish to give you a statement that is worth serious pondering. It is from the prophet Nahum, who said, "The Lord is good, a refuge in times of trouble. He cares for those who trust in him." This statement says three things. First, God is good. Second, He protects. You can depend upon Him, no matter what comes. Third, He knows intimately and personally everyone who trusts Him.

Everyone, at one time or another, has been faced with an unsatisfactory situation. The first thing you must recognize is that some unsatisfactory situations cannot be changed; some you just must live with. But the power of God is so great that there is not much need to dwell unduly upon this; it is mentioned merely because one should acknowledge the fact.

The Roman philosopher-king Marcus Aurelius once said, "Adapt thyself to the things among which thy lot has been cast." Men say these things because they recognize the so-called inevitable difficulties in life. Well, that is heroic indeed. But life would be bleak if all you could do about it was to endure it.

The Lord is my strength and my shield;
my heart trusts in him, and I am helped.
My heart leaps for joy and I will give
thanks to him in song. PSALM 28:7

AUGUST 16

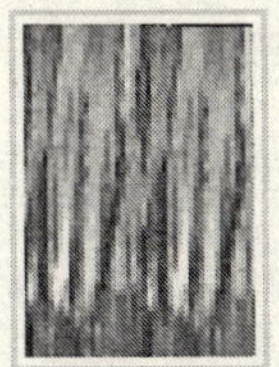

Psalm 28:7 declares, "You are my strong shield, and I trust You completely." That is a tremendous affirmation. I don't know how you begin each day, but here is a suggestion. Instead of rising in the morning and telling yourself, or your wife or your husband, all the difficulties and emergencies you have to face, forget all that and just stand and stretch yourself tall and say, "The Lord is my strong shield." Start the day like that often enough and you will develop composure, confidence, greatness of spirit, understanding, perceptiveness, clear thinking, and the right answers. That is the secret. "The Lord is my strong shield."

Our Father, we thank You that there is within us much more power and strength than we have yet allowed to come into action. Grant that by identifying ourselves with You, we may let the life in us flow out in satisfying power and effectiveness. Through Jesus Christ, our Lord. Amen.

"Enter through the narrow gate.
For . . . small is the gate and narrow the
road that leads to life, and only a few
find it." MATTHEW 7:13–14

AUGUST 17

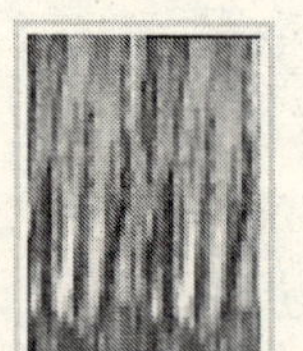

Do you get in your own way? You might be your most difficult obstacle. To live effectively, you must solve this problem.

Some time ago, I spoke at a convention in Atlantic City. At the end of this meeting, I saw a man whom I have known since we were youngsters. He frequently used to be in my prayers, because he'd become a heavy drinker. After the meeting he said to me, "I finally got wise to myself. I sure got all fouled up. I messed up years of my life. But that's all gone by now. I finally got wise."

"How did it happen?" I asked.

"I went back to the church where I grew up," he told me, "and I found the Lord and He changed my life."

This man is now one of the most devoted lay workers for the church in his community. But every time he sees me, he says again, "What a pity to have wasted all those years! It took a breakdown to get me to where I didn't go on messing myself up anymore." That is rather uncultured language, but it describes plainly what happens when you get in your own way.

". . . my unfailing love for you will not be shaken nor my covenant of peace be removed," says the LORD, *who has compassion on you.* ISAIAH 54:10

AUGUST 18

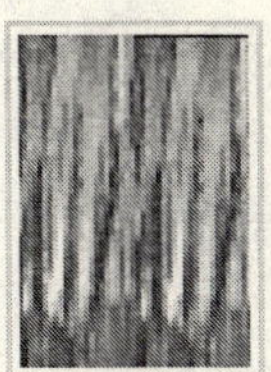

I read an article by a doctor about an experience he had had. He was at home when the telephone rang. A man's voice said, "Will you please come to my house? My wife is having hysterics." So the doctor drove to this couple's beautiful country home and listened as the wife poured out all her troubles and implored him for something to "hold on to." At that moment, the husband came in with three glasses of whiskey and said to his wife, "This will help your hysterics." He said to the doctor, "This will help you too."

Well, the doctor put the glass on the floor and said, "This whiskey is nothing to hold on to. Why don't you turn to God?" He sat and talked to them about God and Jesus Christ. When he left, the hysteria was gone and peace was beginning to come.

When you put yourself into the hands of Jesus Christ, He calms your agitation and upset. You become quiet and are able to handle your problems confidently and intelligently.

Create in me a pure heart, O God, and renew a steadfast spirit within me. PSALM 51:10

AUGUST 19

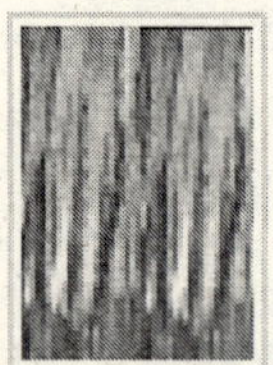

A businessman arrived late to a meeting at our church. He announced, "I am tense because I was late. I am going to relax the tension in me. In fact, I am going to practice my technique for overcoming tension."

"How are you going to do that?" I asked.

"I am going to think about Jesus." He added, "And I am going to relax my body. I have a rather peculiar practice. I imagine that my body is a big burlap bag of potatoes. Mentally, I take a pair of scissors and cut the end of the bag. All the potatoes roll out, and I am the bag that remains. Now I ask you, is anything more relaxed than an empty burlap bag? I can just feel my whole body falling into complete relaxation."

There was humor on the man's face, but also dead seriousness. "I want to live a long life," he said. "I feel I have a contribution to make to my country and my God, and I want to be healthy for the long pull. And in order to do it, I must practice relaxation of body, mind, and soul."

"'Nevertheless, I will bring health and healing to it; I will heal my people and will let them enjoy abundant peace and security.'" Jeremiah 33:6

August 20

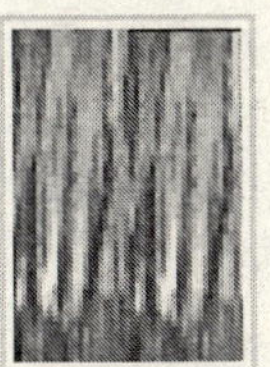

Power always comes from a calm center. Have you ever seen a tornado tearing the sky? I have. It is a sight, believe me! It has astounding force. It can lift up a house and deposit it a mile away. It can take a great board and drive it like a nail through a wall. The poet Edwin Markham said, "At the heart of the cyclone tearing the sky . . . is a place of central calm." That is to say, a cyclone derives its power from a calm center.

The human being also derives power from a calm center. We have to learn how to get rid of tension, how to live relaxed. To do that, acquaint yourself with Jesus and be at peace. I will go so far as to guarantee that if you will commit your life to Jesus Christ, if you will accept God as the guide of your life, and really live this out, you will have no further problems with tension or stress that you can't handle.

The relaxed person is the powerful person.
Practice word therapy—serenity, civility, patience, equanimity.

So what shall I do? I will pray with my spirit, but I will also pray with my mind; I will sing with my spirit, but I will also sing with my mind. 1 CORINTHIANS 14:15

AUGUST 21

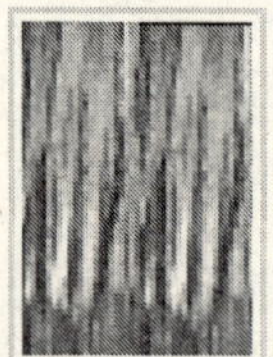

I made a list of some of the most enthusiastic human beings I have known. And by analyzing these people, I came up with three essential attributes they all seem to have in one degree or another.

First: These enthusiastic people were very much alive. They were interested in things, concerned, eager. They were sensitive to events and to people and to conditions. They were thrilled by the world, they were excited.

Second: They participated. They gave their whole selves to life. They threw themselves into things.

Third: They all had a deep spiritual motivation that freed them from inhibitions frustrating the free flow of their personality.

Focus mentally and spiritually upon all that is right about life. Because life is mighty good. A lifetime on this wonderful earth doesn't last long, either. It is here today and gone tomorrow. So love it while you can, and you'll be full of enthusiasm.

"He who is not with me is against me, and he who does not gather with me scatters." MATTHEW 12:30

AUGUST 22

The call comes to each of us individually. Are we going to give our lives to Him, or are we going to give our lives to something else? That is the issue.

We had better be with Him. We will never be truly happy unless we are. We will never find abiding peace unless we are.

Betray Him and you betray yourself; betray His call to discipleship and you betray your own future. And if a society continues to reject Him, it brings woe upon itself.

But human beings have goodness; human beings have God in them. When they see the truth, they respond and they respond gloriously. When we identify with Him, we cease to betray ourselves and our society ceases to betray itself. In new faith, we lay the groundwork for a new and glorious fulfillment of the greatest ideals and principles ever known. So let's come alive. Let's go forth as redeemed people to redeem the life of our time.

This is love for God: to obey his commands. And his commands are not burdensome, for everyone born of God overcomes the world. . . . 1 JOHN 5:3–4

AUGUST 23

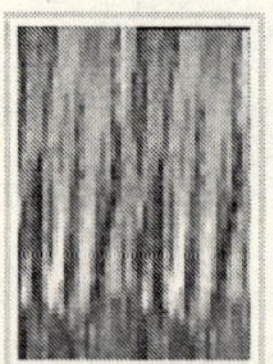

Christianity has often been made out to be a soft kind of thing, something pleasant and nice. But Christianity is the toughest religion ever formulated in the history of the world. What is its symbol? Its symbol is a cross. Not one of those chaste gold crosses that hangs around a lady's neck, but a tough crossbeam of wood—splintery and hard. That is the symbol of Christianity.

This may sound oratorical and poetic, but it isn't. It is practical through and through. It is what we must do now as a nation: this country will have to get back to a strong belief in the authority of government under God and have an enormous spiritual buildup if it is going to survive the confusions of our time. It is also what we need as individuals. Christianity is a tremendous religion, for it makes tremendous people who, when the going is not-so-good, know what to do. They just draw nearer to God and keep on keeping on—and victory comes.

Cast your cares on the LORD and he will sustain you; he will never let the righteous fall. PSALM 55:22

AUGUST 24

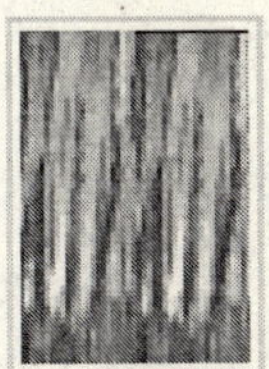

The other day I was sitting in a luncheon meeting with some business people, and I got to talking about a problem with the man sitting next to me. "Norman," he said, "don't ever let a problem worry you."

"What do you do, Bob, about a problem?" I asked.

"I do everything I can think of; I give it all I have. Then I put it in God's hands and leave it there. Sometimes, I come up to a fine line where it looks like I'm going to be defeated, but if I put the problem in God's hands, He takes care of it."

In other words, he was telling me what I am now telling you. Before our meeting was over, the problem was solved in a beautiful way. And as we parted, Bob handed me this note: "Norman, do you see what happens when you let God take care of things? He moves people a lot better than we earthly guys." Who says that Christianity isn't practical? It is the most practical philosophy of human life ever formulated.

For to us a child is born, to us a son is given. . . . And he will be called Wonderful Counselor, Mighty God, Everlasting Father, Prince of Peace. Isaiah 9:6

August 25

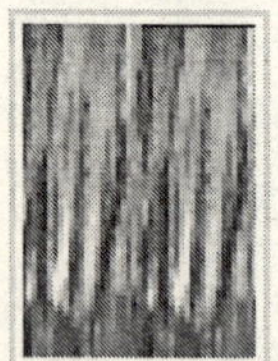

There is a great passage in Isaiah that tells us: "He will be called Wonderful Counselor, Mighty God, Everlasting Father, Prince of Peace." So that is part of the good news. There will come a time when Rachel will not be crying for her children. There will come a time when our own children will not be broken; there will be no maimed bodies in the earth. There will come the time foreseen in Tennyson's vision of which he wrote: "Til the war drum throbbed no longer and the battle flags were furled/In the Parliament of Man, the Federation of the world . . ." It will come, I do believe.

Then there is this other great promise, the other part of the good news. "I have come that they may have life, and have it to the full" (John 10:10). That who might have life? All of us. Everybody wants life in its fullest, and there is no one who can offer it to you save Jesus.

"The thief comes only to steal and kill and destroy; I have come that they may have life, and have it to the full." JOHN 10:10

AUGUST 26

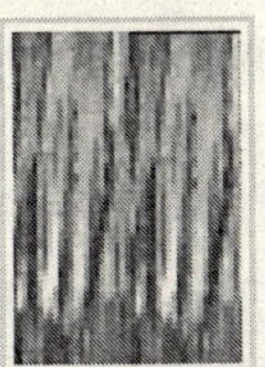

While in France one glorious Sunday at the Palace of Versailles, I watched as the marvelous fountains were turned on. The water burst forth with a gush and a roar and an upthrust as though reaching for the sun, dancing and singing. In the same way, when you get God in your life, you get so excited that you can hardly endure it. It makes life good.

"I have come that they may have life, and have it to the full," says that marvelous passage in the tenth chapter of John. You see, Christianity is designed to produce not glum, sour, growling, griping people, but happy people, lilting people, victorious people, enthusiastic people. All this takes into account the pain and problems in the world. Despite problems, and even out of them, God brings to people a consciousness and plan of victory.

He will have no fear of bad news; his heart is steadfast, trusting in the LORD.

PSALM 112:7

AUGUST 27

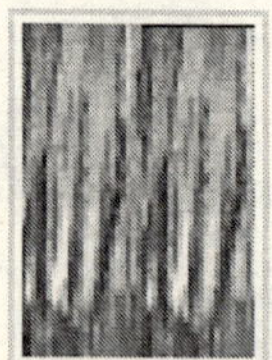

I came across a passage from Washington Irving's *Sketch Book*. "Little minds," he said, "are tamed and subjugated by misfortune, but great minds rise above it." What a picturesque phrase! "Little minds are tamed and subjugated by misfortune." But great minds—humanity touched by the glory of God—rise above misfortune. Never accept defeat.

We have cultivated in recent years a "soft" philosophy—namely, that it is the right and privilege of everyone to be pampered and shielded from the harsh, cruel vicissitudes of human existence. It is true that in the name of Christ, we are to bear one another's burdens and so fulfill His gospel. And it is our duty to care for those less fortunate than we and those who suffer without opportunity. Social awareness, social love, and social service are part of living as Christ taught. But they are not supposed to minimize the fact that a human being should stand in regal, persistent strength and face life heroically in the name of Christ.

He put a new song in my mouth, a hymn of praise to our God. Many will see and fear and put their trust in the LORD. PSALM 40:3

AUGUST 28

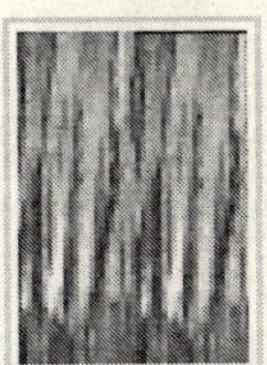

I stopped for lunch with a friend whom I've known for many years. This man is really one of the most inspirational men I have ever known. I greeted him by saying, "I just met a man who told me it was impossible to be happy anymore."

"No happiness?" he asked. Then he reached in his pocket and pulled out a card. This is what it said:

TAKE TIME TO LAUGH: It is the music of the soul.

TAKE TIME TO PLAY: It is the source of perpetual youth.

TAKE TIME TO PRAY: It is the greatest power on earth.

TAKE TIME TO LOVE AND BE LOVED: It is a God-given privilege.

TAKE TIME TO BE FRIENDLY: It is the road to happiness.

TAKE TIME TO GIVE: It is too short a day to be selfish.

I was impressed by this but said to my friend: "There is one thing left out. I'd like to add it, if you don't mind."

TAKE TIME FOR GOD: It is the way to life.

And it is, too.

"And everyone who has left houses or brothers or sisters or father or mother or children or fields for my sake will receive a hundred times as much and will inherit eternal life." MATTHEW 19:29

AUGUST 29

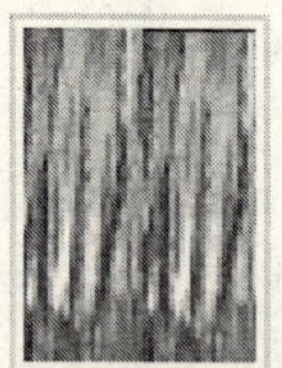

Our forefathers grew great and sturdy and strong because they drew strength from the sky and the hills and the streams—the forces and the wonders of nature. Enthusiastic people are those who live in relationship with nature and with God. So activate your mind and let it flow out and become a part of the world. Thrill to the world, thrill to people. Heed the Bible, which tells us we should walk in newness of life. That is a powerful idea. We're not supposed to be old, dead, dull, desultory. He who embraces the gospel walks in newness of life. Life is new every morning and fresh every evening. Anyone who tells you that the Bible is a dull book hasn't read it, for the Bible positively glows with excitement and enthusiasm. It is the Book of Life. Be renewed not merely on the surface of your mind, but in the deeper spirit that activates your thoughts. Love life and life will love you back.

He saved us, not because of righteous things we had done, but because of his mercy. He saved us through the washing of rebirth and renewal by the Holy Spirit. TITUS 3:5

AUGUST 30

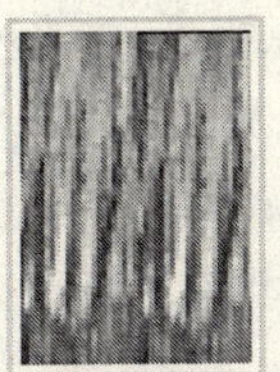

I believe that everything that is good and worthwhile in this world can be found in Jesus Christ. If you want mental life, you will find it in Him, for He has the clearest mind that ever entered into human history. If you feel your health is deteriorating—that you're growing old, that you are low in energy, vitality, and strength—I earnestly urge you to give yourself to Him, for through Him you can experience a renewal, a rejuvenation, a rebirth in the body. Even if it be God's will that you suffer from some malfunctioning or malady or disease, you can find through Jesus Christ strength, vitality, and power in your soul that will lift you above all of the defeats and vicissitudes of this life. So I earnestly lay before you the claims of Jesus Christ upon you. I know that if you commit yourself to Him and surrender yourself to Him, you will be fully alive and every day of your life can be a good day.

Then, because so many people were coming and going that they did not even have a chance to eat, he said to them, "Come with me by yourselves to a quiet place and get some rest." MARK 6:31

AUGUST 31

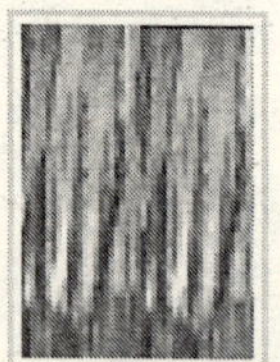

We can reduce the pressure in our lives by the practice of creative silence. Most of us today have no idea how to practice creative silence. But it's a great art, which we all should learn. Rabindranath Tagore, the great Indian poet, said, "Every day wash your soul in silence." What a good thought that is!

If you want to master pressure, I would urge you to yield yourself everyday to the silence of God. If we encouraged our young people in this practice, they would develop into more efficient men and women. So I offer the suggestion that in every schoolroom in the land, once, every day, there be a brief silent period. Just plain, non-sectarian silence. I would hope, of course, that some child in this silent period just might start thinking about God. Every family should have a quiet time every day. Everyone in business—or in any place of work—could well have a quiet time each day in his office. Just shut the door, push the papers aside, and be silent. A person communing with the silence will hear right things in it and find new peace.

September

Look to the Lord and his strength; seek his face always. 1 Chronicles 16:11

There is no fear in love. But perfect love drives out fear, because fear has to do with punishment. The one who fears is not made perfect in love. 1 JOHN 4:18

SEPTEMBER 1

The Christian faith is a tremendous thing. It can be the greatest force in your life, and it's your hope for life here and life beyond. It can do anything for you that you will admit that it can. Faith can take the limitations from you and set you free from fear.

If you have a fear that you don't seem to be able to handle, bring it to Jesus and apply His techniques for overcoming it. Say to yourself, "I now determine I will be rid of this problem." That is the first step. You determine to get rid of it. Then surrender the problem to Jesus Christ absolutely, and believe that you will be relieved of your fear. Finally, start living the Christlike life to the best of your ability.

You can make your life what you want it to be through belief in God and in yourself. Start and end every day, and in-between times, too, by thanking God for everything.

Your word is a lamp to my feet and a light for my path. PSALM 119:105

SEPTEMBER 2

I rather like the idea of taking a new thought pattern to change your condition in the same way you'd take medicine to heal you. And how can you take faith, when that is the medicine you need? You can take it either through your eyes or through your ears. For example, suppose you read the Bible. The printed words are reflected as an image on the retina of the eye. This image is transmitted to the mind where it conveys an idea, and the idea affects the diseased area of the mind with its healing potency. This is why you should read the Bible.

The other way you can take faith is through your ears. Suppose you come to church. You hear the reading of the Bible; you hear the great music; you hear the sermon; you hear the prayers. All these make impacts on the eardrum. And these travel to the mind, by a process that I do not pretend to understand, and reach the diseased area where the fears are. If you do this sufficiently and earnestly, you can be healed of your fears, your apprehensions, and your anxieties by the strong message of faith.

I love the Lord, *for he heard my voice; he heard my cry for mercy.* Psalm 116:1

September 3

A man wrote telling of how he had come through a crisis. "My left hand," he said, "was caught in a rotary mower that was turning at full speed. I clutched my left hand as blood poured through the cotton work glove. I won't even try to recount what happened from that moment on. I got depressed. Life turned flat."

Then he read an inspirational article by W. Clement Stone on how to draw on your faith when the going gets tough. "That was the turning point for me," he declared. "I said, 'Take me over, Lord. Bring what You want out of this.' And when I said that, I began to feel a sense of peace and, finally, power."

What is your difficulty? How painful is it? There is no difficulty that is as big as you are, if you ask for and accept the help of Jesus Christ. Jesus Christ is bigger than any sin, any failure, any difficulty. If you put your life in His hands, you grow along with Him.

. . . stand firm. Let nothing move you. Always give yourselves fully to the work of the LORD, because you know that your labor in the LORD is not in vain. 1 CORINTHIANS 15:58

SEPTEMBER 4

We want to live in peace with our fellow man; I am sure one of the great signs of the times is the ecumenical spirit that brings Catholic, Protestant, and Jew together in closer fellowship. But I'm also sure that the followers of the Jewish religion want to preserve the great tenets of Abraham, Isaac, and Jacob, and that the Catholics want to preserve the great traditions of their faith. And so do we Protestants want to preserve the great heritage we have from Luther, Calvin, Wesley, Zwingli, and those heroes of the Reformation who went to the stake for their faith.

We are too quick to compromise our convictions. We give in too easily to being timorous, afraid, apathetic, indolent. We don't fight. If you believe something—I tell you as a minister of Jesus Christ—stand up and fight for it no matter what happens to you. And if we live like that, we will never grow old; life will seem good and we will have enthusiasm all our days.

He who did not spare his own Son, but gave him up for us all—how will he not also, along with him, graciously give us all things? ROMANS 8:32

SEPTEMBER 5

A friend of mine once felt that he was completely defeated. Then one day, walking gloomily along a street in Pittsburgh, he turned a corner where, though he did not yet realize it, destiny awaited him.

On a church's high iron fence was a big bulletin board with a Scripture quotation posted on it. The text there seemed to reach out and grip my friend as he passed. It read: "If God is for us, who can be against us?" (Romans 8:31).

He went to his hotel and picked up the Bible. He read and read and read, finding that his whole being was being refreshed. And in that hotel room, he finally prayed, "Dear Lord, I dedicate my life to You."

In the days that followed, the same old problems were there, but they didn't defeat him anymore, for now he had an inner assurance, an uplift of thought. He had discovered in a flash of a moment how to change his defeats into victories.

Thanks be to God for his indescribable gift!

2 CORINTHIANS 9:15

SEPTEMBER 6

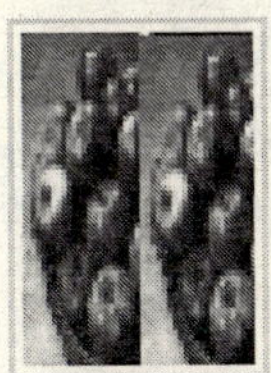

Thanks givers are blessing receivers. I believe it is a law of human life that there's a correlation between inner attitudes and outer manifestations. That is to say, what we are within ourselves, we tend to have or create outside us. For example, if your mind is full of hate and resentment and ill will and grudges, you can be sure that you will manifest these things in the life outside your inner soul. We act out what we think. If you're filled with fear, anxiety, worry, and apprehension, you manifest these attitudes so that your life becomes one of fear and anxiety.

By the same token, if in our minds we entertain thanksgiving, we manifest blessings. The more thankfulness a person cultivates, the more he will open to himself the power flow, the vast wealth of heaven. Blessings will pour out upon him.

And whatever you do, whether in word or deed, do it all in the name of the LORD Jesus, giving thanks to God the Father through him. COLOSSIANS 3:17

SEPTEMBER 7

You can't be a commander of life unless you learn the great art of keeping your head in any crisis. And how is that done? "Let the peace of Christ rule in your hearts" (Colossians 3:15). The secret of attaining self-control is the application of practical spiritual principles. The Bible is filled with techniques that are so simple that anyone can understand them. And these, when believed in and applied, will in due course give victory over any lack of self-control or lack of calmness.

Here are the steps: When confronted with a big problem, think. Apply all of your mental powers to it. Second, pray for God's guidance, because you will never come out right as long as you think wrong. Third, do all you can do about it. Fourth, put it in the hands of God. Let Him take over and trust Him for guidance and for the outcome. These four principles constitute a basic scientific spiritual formula that will work for the great or the simple.

That if you confess with your mouth, "Jesus is LORD," and believe in your heart that God raised him from the dead, you will be saved. ROMANS 10:9

SEPTEMBER 8

With God's help, I preached the same sermon in the pulpit every Sunday for thirty years. It has had a little variation, but it is the same theme: If an individual will surrender his life to Jesus Christ, accept Him as Lord and Savior, and condition his life according to His will, he will have the precious secret of life. I believe that today even more so than in the days gone by. I believe there is no human problem, no human weakness, no human frustration that cannot be solved and overcome—a victory attained—if a person will build his life around Jesus Christ and live by His principles. To me it is just that simple.

Our Heavenly Father, touch each of us, we pray, with deep and serious thought. Help us to commit ourselves to keeping the faith, until we finish the course. Through Jesus Christ, our Lord. Amen.

Like newborn babies, crave pure spiritual milk, so that by it you may grow up in your salvation, now that you have tasted that the LORD is good. 1 PETER 2:2

SEPTEMBER 9

Let God's Spirit strengthen your inner spirit. Draw upon your own unused strength. How is this done? First—and I know I am claiming a lot when I make this statement, but I wouldn't make it unless I believed it—we must realize that nothing is impossible. Jesus says in Matthew 17:20–21, "Nothing will be impossible for you." It doesn't mean you are going to get everything you want. But it does mean you can move out of the area of the impossible into the realm of the possible.

Human beings are endowed with a tremendous capacity to grow and to outgrow. All life is growth. The minute a baby is born, he begins to grow. The minute you put a seed in the ground, it begins to grow. Unless you grow, you die. And the secret of growth is to outgrow. The person who has a conscious desire to outgrow can do so by drawing upon his own unused strength.

When I am afraid, I will trust in you. In God, whose word I praise, in God I trust; I will not be afraid. What can mortal man do to me? PSALM 56:3–4

SEPTEMBER 10

Life tends to frighten people, for it can be pretty ferocious sometimes, pretty mean. But while fear is pervasive, a Christian, if really a Christian, shouldn't ever be frightened of anything. (I speak now of abnormal fear, not of normal caution.) If a person is truly living a Christian life, he should not be afraid of anything except God. And when we speak of having "the fear of God," we really mean living with great respect for God.

In Psalm 56, there is a passage that reads, "Even when I am afraid, I keep on trusting you." If you really believe this and really have it in your heart, you have a power against all difficulty. Life is just packed full of great, big difficulties, and sometimes you say to yourself, "Circumstances are too big for me. I can't handle them. I haven't got what it takes." Oh, yes, you have. There is no difficulty in this world that you can't handle. This I firmly believe, and this faith is justified by experience with many people.

Better the little that the righteous have than the wealth of many wicked; for the power of the wicked will be broken, but the LORD upholds the righteous. PSALM 37:16–17

SEPTEMBER 11

No good thing will be withheld from a person who lives a good life. Uprightness means honor, truthfulness, purity, decency—just general goodness. But sometimes we see instances that conflict with our understanding of goodness.

From the days of Job until now, we have seen instances where the righteous suffer and bear heartache and pain, while the evil flourish like a tall tree. I've even had people tell me, "It never pays to be good." They contend that the smart ones get away with their wickedness, but that good people don't get any reward. An old farmer once told me, "God doesn't pay all His debts on the first of January." And he continued, "I've watched these evildoers over many years. They may get away with it for one year, five years, ten years, thirty years, maybe forty years. But I've lived a long life, and evil pays in its own coin in the end. Whereas those who are good do suffer, and there is no promise that they won't, they come out on a higher value level." No good thing is withheld from those who are upright.

Look to the LORD *and his strength; seek his face always.* 1 CHRONICLES 16:11

SEPTEMBER 12

A woman wrote to me saying, "My husband awoke one morning, drank several cups of coffee, and sat at the table looking so depressed that I couldn't help thinking to myself how very old and dejected he looked. Occasionally he emitted a giant sigh, followed by, 'I'm afraid I can't make a go of it. I'm afraid I'm licked.'"

She persuaded her husband to repeat affirmations after her. "He turned to me," she continues, "and said, 'I feel a little better already.' So off he went to work, repeating to himself, 'I go forth in the name of the Lord.' After a few days of this, his shoulders were thrown back and he was breathing deeply of the fresh morning air as he walked to his car. I thought, as I turned from the window, 'How alive he is now!'"

Certainly. God is life. This husband had put God out of his life. He was taking only shadows and fear into his life. But when he began to walk with God, new faith cleared the quirks and shadows from his mind and canceled out his fear.

The LORD has dealt with me according to my righteousness; according to the cleanness of my hands he has rewarded me. PSALM 18:20

SEPTEMBER 13

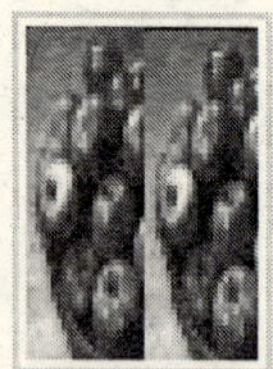

George Romney, before he became governor of Michigan, was president of American Motors Corporation. At one point, the corporation was almost bankrupt. Everyone was lost in gloom, but Mr. Romney remained hopeful and enthusiastic. He kept telling his associates the situation would turn out all right. One of them asked him, "But George, what's going to save the company?"

"God is going to save it," George said. "God always helps people who are trying to do the right thing."

So, to recap: Don't get upset, remain calm. Think. And in the name of Jesus Christ, always do the right thing. God always helps people who are trying to do the right thing. The way to put these fundamentals into practice is to acquaint yourself with Him, so that you have His strength, so that you can be at peace. For then you can think and then good will come.

Hope deferred makes the heart sick, but a longing fulfilled is a tree of life. PROVERBS 13:12

SEPTEMBER 14

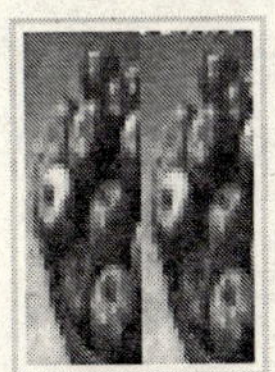

A preacher friend of mine came to see me and started pacing the floor, saying, "I want to describe the church I hope to have some day." He pictured it all meticulously, specifically, to the smallest detail. He got me so excited that I leaped to my feet, exclaiming, "The church is already built! It is built in your mind. All you need to do now is finish the job." Ten years later, I dedicated his church and it was exactly what he had described to me ten years before.

What do you want to build out of your life? How high do you want to go? If you can only think to the rooftop, that is as far as you will go. But you can think your way without limit to the stars. What you are now is what you have been thinking for a long time. What you will be ten years from now depends on what you think from now on. If you want a great life in the future, think great thoughts.

But those who hope in the L*ORD* *will renew their strength. They will soar on wings like eagles; they will run and not grow weary, they will walk and not be faint.* ISAIAH 40:31

SEPTEMBER 15

A major-league baseball pitcher once pitched a game in Kansas City on an afternoon when the temperature was 105 degrees in the shade. Halfway through the game, he suddenly felt weak, listless, too washed out to continue.

But this ballplayer was a creative, practical Christian, so he walked around the pitcher's mound for a moment, repeating to himself a Scripture from the fortieth chapter of Isaiah: "But those who hope in the LORD will renew their strength. They will soar on wings like eagles; they will run and not grow weary, they will walk and not be faint."

He finished the game with energy to spare and reported that he never had a better time in his life with more feeling of mastery than in that game. This Christian discovered a great truth: the power of God is not only concerned with ethical precepts or with sociological and theological matters, but in a deep sense it has to do with the re-creation of the believer.

For the Lord *loves the just and will not forsake his faithful ones.* Psalm 37:28

September 16

What is a weakness? A weakness is a deficiency in the personality. It is a defect. It is a disorganized area in a human being's nature. What is your policy toward your weaknesses? Or have you a policy? Do you just idly settle for a weakness? Perhaps you say, "Well, this is the way I am. I'm weak. There is nothing I can do but put up with myself like this and make the best of it." Is that your attitude?

One of the great reasons for studying the gospel and attending church is to help us overcome weaknesses and become strong. In the book of Daniel are these resounding, electrifying words: "Those who remain faithful will do everything possible." What a sentence! It is a masterpiece. The people that know their God shall be strong—and not only be strong; they will amount to something. They will do tremendous deeds. The ones who remain faithful will do everything possible.

Brothers, I do not consider myself yet to have taken hold of it. But one thing I do: Forgetting what is behind and straining toward what is ahead . . . PHILIPPIANS 3:13

SEPTEMBER 17

One of the factors that contributes to mental health is the art of forgetting. Lest you think I rate forgetting too highly, I cite one of the great passages of the New Testament: "Forgetting what is behind and straining toward what is ahead . . ." (Philippians 3:13). In other words, turn your back on past mistakes; put them out of your thoughts. The wisest book ever written tells you to forget your failures and go ahead.

"Well," you may say, "I believe that; but how do you do it?" It is difficult, you say, to put the memory of frustrations and disappointments out of your mind.

Whoever said it was easy? I am only saying it is necessary. If you carry on your mind all the failures and disappointments of the past, lugging them into the future, you'll have too great a weight upon you, and you'll be broken by it.

How then can you forget? My answer is: By will. By positive determination. By disciplining yourself.

A cheerful heart is good medicine, but a crushed spirit dries up the bones.

PROVERBS 17:22

SEPTEMBER 18

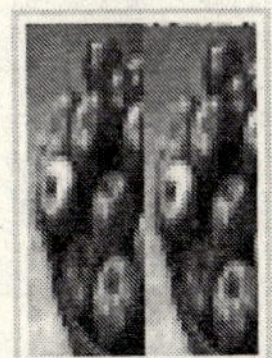

I visited my old hometown and thought about my boyhood days. I remembered the time I'd been eating unripe apples, and I suffered for it. I called a doctor. He came and poked around at me and asked me what I had been doing. He gave me some peppermint and said, "You just take that and quit eating unripe apples. You will be all right." Then he put his hand on my head and said, "Son, I can cure your stomach. That is easy. But if you get bad thoughts in your mind, it will take a greater doctor than I am to cure you. So don't let bad or sick thoughts get in that head of yours."

How you think can even change the impact of sickness, physical deterioration, and aging. Christianity is life, friends. Jesus said, "I have come that they may have life, and have it to the full" (John 10:10). And if you are going to have life, you have to cope with illness and deterioration and aging. And how you think has an important bearing on the aging process.

Be on your guard; stand firm in the faith; be men of courage; be strong.

1 Corinthians 16:13

September 19

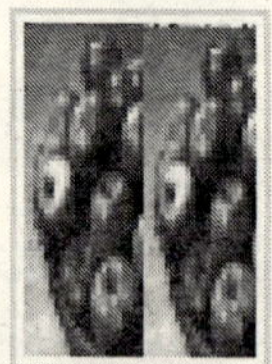

We live in an insecure world. Your body is no more secure than your ability to resist disease and infection. Accidents can happen to anyone at any time. This world is insecure. Yet you should never come to the point where you say, "Life is over for me; I am through. I can't do anything anymore. I haven't any confidence; I have no sense of security." Remember that the Lord is faithful. He will strengthen you and guard you against all evil. Don't live with too much caution.

It may seem strange that a man would stand in a pulpit and advocate throwing yourself into life, even at the risk of getting hurt. But I have observed that people who try to keep from getting hurt never amount to anything. Only those who throw themselves into risky circumstances—regardless of whether they may get hurt—become really great people. When you live daringly, you do many stupid things; you often make a fool of yourself and people criticize you; and you may fail at one thing and another; but in the long run, you will accomplish great things.

If any of you lacks wisdom, he should ask God, who gives generously to all without finding fault, and it will be given to him. JAMES 1:5

SEPTEMBER 20

All preaching should have practical applications, for Christianity is a way of life that really works—when it's lived properly. This includes making right decisions. In the long run, you determine what your life will be by your decisions. You can decide yourself into failure or into success, into mental turmoil or into mental peace, into unhappiness or into happiness.

A man remarked to me, "Let's face it: life goes the way the ball bounces." I don't go for any such idea as that at all. There is a deeper reality. We can control the bouncing of life's circumstances and outcomes as we learn the art of making right decisions.

And how do we learn it? I repeat: "If any of you lacks wisdom, he should ask God, . . . and it will be given to him." Believe, really believe, that there is an answer for you and that God will give you the wisdom to find that answer. People who have become great people have been those who have discovered that God will guide them through the problems of their lives.

You have made known to me the path of life; you will fill me with joy in your presence, with eternal pleasures at your right hand. PSALM 16:11

SEPTEMBER 21

What depletes energy? Is it something in the physical being, some malfunctioning, some sickness? Are you tired because you are overworked? I doubt it. Energy is seldom depleted due to work alone. The factors resulting in losing energy usually originate in our minds. We think tired, depletion, exhaustion, or we nurture hate thoughts, resentment, guilt, or prejudice. These habits siphon off our energy.

If you keep your thoughts alive, clean, and healthy, and if you keep yourself in good physical condition, you can have abundant energy all your life. Almighty God, who created you in the first place, who gave you life, did not finish the creative process at that point. He not only creates; He re-creates. Through Him you can have new life, new vitality, and new energy every day of your life. In fact, you can possess energy that never runs down.

God looks down from heaven on the sons of men to see if there are any who understand, any who seek God. PSALM 53:2

SEPTEMBER 22

One day I was working on a sermon. The house was quiet, but I couldn't get the sermon outlined to save me. I finally said to my wife, "Let's take a walk."

The ground was covered with deep snow, so we put on our boots and went out. We had our dog Tonka with us. After walking a half mile, Tonka sat down, and Mrs. Peale and I stood beside him. We looked across the valley at the great snow-clad hills. There was not a sound to be heard save the gentle wind in the trees and the singing of the water in a nearby stream—peace, quiet.

After a while, I said, "Let's go back." And when we got back to the house, I sat down and had the sermon outlined in about fifteen minutes. Something happened to my whole being when I let go and got out into the harmony and peace of nature where there is power. The secret is to live with relaxed power. When your attitude is easy-does-it, the power can come through.

For I know that through your prayers and the help given by the Spirit of Jesus Christ, what has happened to me will turn out for my deliverance. PHILIPPIANS 1:19

SEPTEMBER 23

J. C. Penney told of how he lived through the Great Depression when he had to face the hard fact that he had lost some forty million dollars. How would you feel if you lost forty million dollars? Well, J. C. Penney became terribly ill and put himself into a sanitarium.

One night, he got the notion that he was going to die. He wrote farewell notes to his family, made his peace with God, and fell into a troubled sleep. But when he opened his eyes and saw sunlight streaming into this room, he realized he had another day of life. He got out of bed, went down the hall and found a group of people singing, "God will take care of you."

As he sat listening, he felt two great loving arms go around him, and he knew that God loved him and would indeed take care of him. From that time on he was past being afraid, for he had found the love of God. He regained his health and set about rebuilding his great enterprise.

I have fought the good fight, I have finished the race, I have kept the faith.
2 TIMOTHY 4:7

SEPTEMBER 24

God makes you strong enough by His supportive presence. That is what He is: supportive. By His power He makes you strong enough to stand against anything.

Unfairness, injustice, hate, pain, sickness, weakness, infidelity—such are the enemies of human beings. Time and time again, a person falters under the onslaught of all this. Sometimes, after you have battled long and been thrown back many times and so many difficulties lie in your path, life throws the whole book at you, and you feel like giving up.

Have you ever felt like giving up? I have. I'd hate to tell you how many times I've felt like giving up. But do you know something? You must never give up. Never. You must do like Paul: You must fight the good fight. You must finish the course. You must keep the faith. No, as a Christian you must never give up. As a human being you must never give up. And if you know this fact, this truth, that He whom they call Emmanuel is with you, you never will give up.

In this way they will lay up treasure for themselves as a firm foundation for the coming age, so that they may take hold of the life that is truly life. 1 TIMOTHY 6:19

SEPTEMBER 25

When you truly take hold of life, it is life indeed. Thousands of human beings have discovered this truth—some in dramatic ways, others in quiet, sudden insights. But there are millions more people everywhere trying to find life. Paul tells us where to find it. So help yourself to life. There is a generous supply for you. Take hold of life, which is life indeed.

When you get that life, you begin to develop a subtle insight; your mind gets sharpened. You get what is known as God's guidance, and you develop perceptiveness. You are then able to handle the frustrations and difficulties of life and not let them throw you. You know then that you can take the mistakes, the sorrows, and the troubles, and weave them into a pattern.

Our Heavenly Father, we thank You for the power we may receive from You. Help us, Lord, to take this power, which is so freely offered to us, and live on a level we have never heretofore known. Through Jesus Christ, our Lord. Amen.

Turn my eyes away from worthless things; preserve my life according to your word. PSALM 119:37

SEPTEMBER 26

Before a speech in San Francisco, a man approached me. "I came here tonight," he said, "because I believe in your philosophy that you never need to be defeated."

And he told me of his own experience. "Life just ganged up on me, and I felt I was completely through. Finally, I decided I couldn't live that way. So my wife and I started a little program. Every morning we read the Bible and we prayed. Out of this practice, I got some ideas. And these ideas helped me rebuild.

"I decided I would never accept defeat. Then I decided to start thinking creatively and spiritually. I stopped feeling sorry for myself. I got reacquainted with the God of the new start. Then I got God's directions on how to rebuild."

There was a full moon over San Francisco that night. It was fresh and clear, and everything was bright and beautiful—but more beautiful than anything else was the look on the face of this man who had decided never to accept defeat.

Trust in the LORD *with all your heart and lean not on your own understanding; in all your ways acknowledge him, and he will make your paths straight.* PROVERBS 3:5–6

SEPTEMBER 27

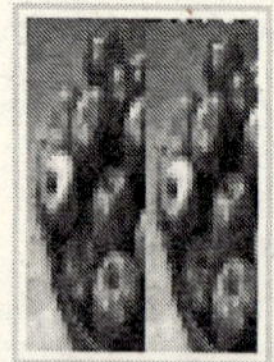

I've heard it said so many times that "you've got to face the facts." Take a man of about fifty-five years of age who loses his job and doesn't know where to get another one. A well-meaning friend says, "Jack, let's face it. When you're fifty-five, it's pretty tough to get another job. You might as well face the facts." Or consider a couple who got married and raised children but then began to grow apart, and some well-meaning person says, "Well, you might as well break up. You'll never get together again. You might as well face the facts."

But in each of these situations, a wise friend should say, "Yes, this is tough. But be thankful we have a big God, and He will help you to straighten out that situation." The issue behind the problem is: How much are you willing to trust God? I tell you, friends, I honestly believe that if you trust Him completely, with all your heart, you'll never go wrong. Because He is rightness itself. There is no error in Him. And if you stay with Him, there will be no error in you.

The highest heavens belong to the Lord*, but the earth he has given to man.* Psalm 115:16

September 28

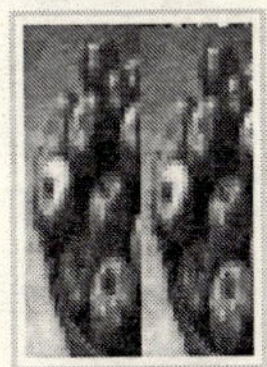

A newspaper carried an item entitled, "There's a Fortune in Your Attic" that claimed there are several billion dollars in the form of unclaimed securities lying around in old trunks and elsewhere.

Now don't rush out immediately to ransack old drawers; but if I may borrow the phrase, there is a fortune in the form of potential strength, power, joy, and peace in the attic called the human mind.

God who created you told you that He gave you dominion—not over any person, but over the circumstances of life. So don't go on defeated and crawling through life on your hands and knees. We need a new emphasis on the greatness of man. As Wordsworth says, "Trailing clouds of glory do we come from God, who is our home." Essentially, man is a tremendous being—a marvelous creature. That means you. It means me. Greatness!

Those who know your name will trust in you, for you, LORD, have never forsaken those who seek you. PSALM 9:10

SEPTEMBER 29

A missionary's wife in central China during World War II knew the Japanese were approaching her city. She was with her baby girl, two months old, and her son, just over a year old. Her husband had been taken to a hospital, himself ill. He was one hundred and fifteen miles away and would not be back for perhaps a month. The poor woman was filled with fear—she was alone and unprotected, in bitter January weather.

When morning came, she realized that she was without food for her children. She pulled off the calendar page. That day's verse stated simply: "So then, don't be afraid. I will provide for you and your children" (Genesis 50:21). There was a rap at the door. "We knew you would be hungry," said a longtime neighbor, "and you didn't know how to milk the goats. So I have milked your goats. Here is milk for your children."

Will you try to explain this away, handle it on an intellectual basis as just pure coincidence? When you come right down to it, what is coincidence? It is an act of God in the midst of time.

But these are written that you may believe that Jesus is the Christ, the Son of God, and that by believing you may have life in his name. JOHN 20:31

SEPTEMBER 30

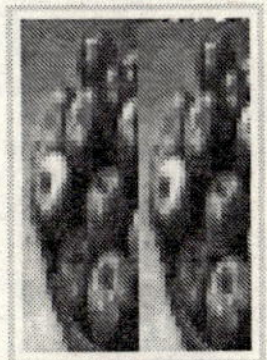

A woman wrote that she had become an alcoholic. One Sunday she saw herself in the mirror—not merely her outward form, but the defeated inner spirit. "I fell on my knees," she wrote, "and cried, 'O God, what a mess I have made of myself! Please, dear God, help me.'

"Then I got up and sat in a chair. The radio was on and a voice said, 'God will help you. Turn your life over to Jesus Christ. Your life will be different if you do.' It really got inside of me and I knelt down again and prayed, 'Dear Lord, I know the answer. I give You myself, I give You my problem. You take it.'"

This woman was cured instantly. She lost her desire to drink. Peace came to her, and strength, cleanliness, hope, new life. What do you call such an occurrence? Well, you call it a miracle. It was a spiritual rehabilitation by a power that works when a person really takes it. Real faith works miracles.

October

Great is our Lord
and mighty in power;
his understanding has
no limit. Psalm 147:5

You hear, O LORD, *the desire of the afflicted; you encourage them, and you listen to their cry. . . .* PSALM 10:17

OCTOBER 1

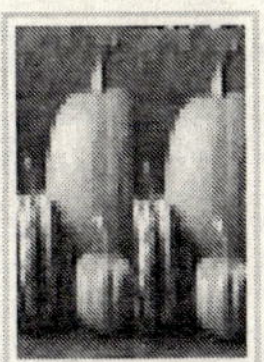

As long as you live, no situation is hopeless. As long as you have life and God, as long as you have Christ and your own intelligence, why should any situation be hopeless? It is because you don't believe in yourself anymore, and you don't really believe in God or in Jesus Christ. Actually, you don't believe in life itself. Start believing and get strength, such as is promised you, from God, who is good.

The statesman Mirabeau, whose clear thinking influenced the course of the French Revolution, once said, "Nothing is impossible to the man who can will." I believe that. What is will? It is the determination, the commitment, that you will do something. "

Nothing is impossible to the man who can will." To have strong will, it must be backed up by faith. So strengthen that will of yours by strengthening your faith. God is good. He is a tower of strength. And He listens to you. So instead of regarding an unsatisfactory situation as hopeless, face it with a will. Then you can change it.

But may all who seek you rejoice and be glad in you; may those who love your salvation always say, "The LORD be exalted!" PSALM 40:16

OCTOBER 2

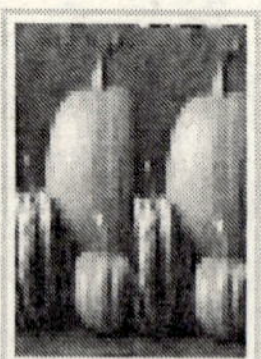

Governor Charles Edison of New Jersey told me of the time when his father's laboratory at Menlo Park caught fire and burned down. The great inventor was sixty-seven years old, I believe. He stood there, his son told me, watching years of work go up in flames. "My heart ached for him," Charles Edison said. "He was no longer a young man. But then he spotted me and shouted, 'Charles, go find your mother. Bring her here. She'll never see anything like this as long as she lives!'"

And the next morning Thomas Edison remarked, "There is great value in disaster. All our mistakes are burned up. Thank God we can start anew." Great people do not allow the vicissitudes of life to defeat them. They have something within them that rises victoriously above the losses and disappointments. Whatever comes, life is good. And the thing that makes a person most aware of its goodness is to know God. Leo Tolstoy, one of the greatest men of letters who ever lived, said, "To know God is to live."

Blessed is the man you discipline,
O Lord, *the man you teach from*
your law. . . . Psalm 94:12

October 3

How can a person defeat the problem of tension and live with quiet power? Is there an answer? The answer is, "Blessed is the man you discipline, O Lord, the man you teach from your law." That is from Psalm 94, verse 12. There is a law by which a person can be organized in his emotional life. It is as certain as the law that lifts the tides. It is not man's law, but God's law. Think God's way, live His way, and you will be freed from tension. You can live with quiet power.

The law of God created you and created me. Every once in a while, you ought to look at yourself and say, "Think of the complexity of this body with which I am blessed." And it functions perfectly when kept in harmony with His law. But if your attitudes become contentious, selfish, or hostile—or if you take this wonderful instrument and drive it too hard—then tension, stress, and anxiety take over. But when you bring yourself back into harmony with God's law, the tension abates and good health returns. The law of God is the law of organization, of harmony, of control.

How much more, then, will the blood of Christ . . . cleanse our consciences from acts that lead to death, so that we may serve the living God! HEBREWS 9:14

OCTOBER 4

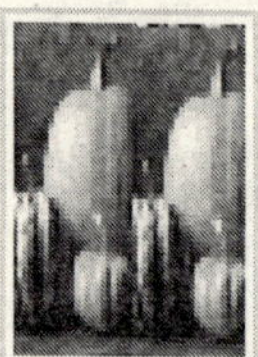

If any man is honest with himself, he knows the sin that is in him; he knows the weakness that is in him. And he ought also to know he should confess it to God and ask Him to forgive him and release him from it. And the Lord, who loves him, will respect him for his honesty. So will any good minister respect him. I've had the worst things confided to me by people who conclude by saying, "You'll never speak to me again. You thought I was a fine person."

"I think you're finer now than I ever thought you were before, because you have the sincerity and courage to come clean about your wrongdoing and you want God to change you," I say to them.

So don't be defeated; don't be weak; don't be wicked. Remember there is the power of God to help you follow through on your prayers. If a person will really pray and will surrender up the evil things that he thinks and does and says, it is incredible what can happen to him.

He said: "In my distress I called to the LORD, and he answered me. From the depths of the grave I called for help, and you listened to my cry." JONAH 2:2

OCTOBER 5

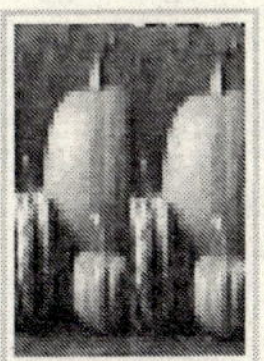

Vincent Tracy did more good for alcoholics than almost any man I know. He and I were together for a Christmas night radio program and he said to me, "Back in 1948, life and my weaknesses were more than I could take. I started across the Brooklyn Bridge and headed for the Bowery, where I could get a handout. On the bridge I stopped and looked down at the cold water. The urge to jump was strong. But something kept saying to me, 'Keep on across the bridge.' And over on the Bowery, I suddenly started praying: 'Please dear Lord, won't You come to me and help me?' Instantly a great light burst into my mind. I walked away from the Bowery saying the Lord's Prayer, with my hand in the hand of Jesus. And I've been walking along the road with Him," he concluded, "ever since. Without Him, I wouldn't be anything."

"With Him, Vincent," I said, "you're a very great deal." Vincent Tracy was humble enough to be wise. He came to Jesus and became a wiser wise man.

Being confident of this, that he who began a good work in you will carry it on to completion until the day of Christ Jesus. PHILIPPIANS 1:6

OCTOBER 6

I read about a young man who suddenly found himself at the top of his class in college, whereas previously he had been rattling around near the bottom. Somebody asked him how he had done this. He replied, "I went to a handwriting expert who told me I was a natural-born extrovert. When he told me that, on the basis of his science, I was an extrovert, I believed what he said. I began to act like an extrovert. That is why I'm no longer near the bottom of the class."

You may say this is superficial. It isn't superficial at all. Paul, in his letter to the Philippians, affirms, "Christ gives me the strength to face anything." You have heard that for years. If you really believe it, then you know that spiritually you are a released extrovert. Go out and be that. It is an old and thrilling theme that I just love. No one has ever changed my opinion that a human being has in him illimitable powers. He usually lives and dies without ever bringing more than a tiny fraction of his potential into action.

You guide me with your counsel,
and afterward you will take me
into glory. PSALM 73:24

OCTOBER 7

In the seventy-third Psalm we read these words: "Your advice has been my guide, and later you will welcome me in glory." There are many things you and I do not understand. But if you live with Him so that He guides you with His counsel, you will find your destination in eternal life.

God gives Christians a deep, sensitive perceptiveness and understanding of truth. This is what a Christian has that makes him different from other people. He has truth. Error is reduced in him. The great issue of life is: How much error have you; how much truth have you? If you live by error, you will go wrong and come to wrong ends. Error means that which is wrong. Truth means that which is right. To people who love Him, who study Him, who live with Him, Jesus gives a sensitive, keen perceptiveness of truth. That means you don't need to go stumbling through life ineptly, failing at what you try, miserable and helpless. You have available to you the answers that answer.

Let us draw near to God . . . in full assurance of faith, having our hearts sprinkled to cleanse us from a guilty conscience and having our bodies washed with pure water. HEBREWS 10:22

OCTOBER 8

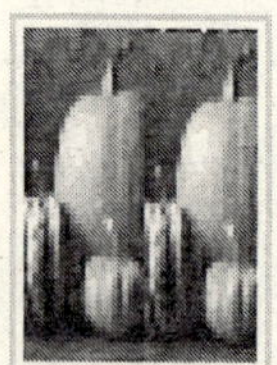

I received a letter from a man who told me that he was just five years old—that he had been resurrected that many years ago. "I've been around for fifty-one years," he wrote, "but I was dead for all but the last five of them." And he went on to explain, "Some years ago I was making a good deal of money in real estate, but I started drinking. I lost everything. I became a bum. One day I stopped at the clubroom of Alcoholics Anonymous. I found one of your sermons lying on a table. I stuck it in my pocket and shuffled out. Passing a park bench, I sat down and read that sermon. You said that Jesus Christ was greater than any human weakness. I thought about that and found myself saying, 'Jesus Christ, change me!' I went back to my room and slept twelve hours. When I woke up, I was free of my weakness. It was that simple. I am a resurrected person. Once again, I've become a successful businessman."

We continually remember before our God and Father your work produced by faith, your labor prompted by love, and your endurance inspired by hope in our LORD Jesus Christ. 1 THESSALONIANS 1:3

OCTOBER 9

To be a true optimist, you have to be rugged and tough in mind. An optimist is a person who believes in a good outcome even when he can't yet see it. He is a person who believes in a greater day when there is yet no evidence of it. He is one who believes in his own future when he can't see much possibility in it.

A lot of people live under a cloud. But up above the clouds, the sun is always shining. Down here, on the surface of the earth, groping around in the shadows under a low ceiling, a person may not feel optimistic. But you ought to begin to practice optimism. Send up into the mass of dark clouds bright, powerful optimistic thoughts, a bright optimistic faith. By so doing, you can actually dissipate the clouds and have an entirely different life. Constantly send up into the overcast sky that is blanketing your mind bright thoughts of faith, love, hope, thoughts of God, thoughts about the greatness of life.

My soul yearns, even faints, for the courts of the LORD; my heart and my flesh cry out for the living God. PSALM 84:2

OCTOBER 10

I once spoke with a gentleman who seemed to be on top of the world. His attitude astonished me somewhat, because I knew how much trouble he had been through. You've heard it said, "It never rains, but it pours." Well, it really poured on him. But he endured it all, and more than that, he came through victoriously. "You are a remarkable, indefatigable human being," I told him. "You really are something special. How come?"

He grinned and said, "Years ago, I discovered a philosophy that will stand up under anything. Nothing can break it—and I mean nothing. And it can be stated in five words: Keep believing—never lose faith."

The writer of Psalm 84:2 knew the same truth: "My soul yearns, even faints, for the courts of the LORD; my heart and my flesh cry out for the living God." What a picture! Here is a man who was really up against it and would have folded had he not been able to see that, despite how bad everything was, the goodness of the Lord prevails!

But now he has reconciled you by Christ's physical body through death to present you holy in his sight, without blemish and free from accusation. COLOSSIANS 1:22

OCTOBER 11

I sometimes read the obituary notices in the papers; the obituaries do not have the romance they once had. When I was a boy growing up in Ohio towns, they used to fill three or four columns. They told the most interesting things about people. From reading those notices you could pick up some wisdom.

Well, some years back, the New York papers carried the obituary of Mrs. Knox of the Knox Gelatin Company. She evidently ran the business herself. She must have been a dynamic and intelligent lady, but rather cryptic, too, and perhaps a bit difficult to work with, for she had a sign in her office warning people about making mistakes. And this is the way it read: "He who stumbles twice on the same stone deserves to break his own neck." Well, that is pretty hard-boiled. Let us everlastingly be thankful to the good Lord that He has more patience than Mrs. Knox.

"His master replied, 'Well done, good and faithful servant! You have been faithful with a few things; I will put you in charge of many things. . . .'" MATTHEW 25:23

OCTOBER 12

A man offered to drive me to the airport if I would talk with him about a personal problem. On the way there, he confided all his troubles, worries, disappointments, and unhappiness.

I said to him, "The only way to free yourself from it is to stand up against it now and practice happiness."

"How do you practice happiness?" he asked.

I cited the example of John Wesley, who, in his maturity, was one of the greatest men of faith in all the world. At an earlier time in his life, Wesley had no faith whatsoever. So he hit upon the device of acting as though he did have faith. And in due time, he did have faith. You can bring about the ideal condition by persistently acting as though that ideal condition already existed.

Our Heavenly Father, help us never to be discouraged nor overcome. Grant that we may enter into the life of our time with creative power to make it a better world. Through Jesus Christ, our Lord. Amen.

"But so that you may know that the Son of Man has authority on earth to forgive sins. . . ." Then he said to the paralytic, "Get up, take your mat and go home." MATTHEW 9:6

OCTOBER 13

One morning after I preached in a church in New Jersey, there suddenly appeared in front of me a woman who bluntly demanded, "Tell me why I itch all the time."

I talked with her at some length. It gradually came out that this woman's father had provided in his will that his estate was to be divided equally between his two daughters. Later this woman got the idea that her sister had "double-crossed" her, and so she built up an enormous resentment and a terrible sense of guilt.

Fortunately, she was a strong person, with the wisdom to insist, "I am my own sickness. I must get myself healed." And that is exactly what she did. She took love and forgiveness and goodwill into her; the hatred went, and so did the itching.

Know the truth about yourself and know the truth about God, and you will be set free and become an entirely different person.

"For where two or three come together in my name, there am I with them."

MATTHEW 18:20

OCTOBER 14

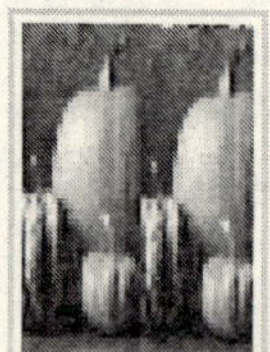

Prayer can change your life. I strongly recommend that you learn the art or science of prayer and put it to work in your life. Now this may seem to you to be just one more religious idea, without much life or sparkle to it. But that is where you would be wrong. It is the way to life itself.

When I say this of prayer I do not speak of the mere mumbling of words. I do not mean formal affirmations either, although formal prayers sometimes help and some formal prayers are touched with the glory of God. What I mean is a deep, fundamental, powerful relationship of the individual to God, whereby his whole mind and heart become changed and he receives power from God within himself. I have seen such prayer change the lives of many.

God's peace deeply imbedded in your mind can often have a more tranquilizing and healing effect upon nerves and tension than medicine. God's peace is itself medicinal.

Therefore we will not fear, though the earth give way and the mountains fall into the heart of the sea though its waters roar and foam and the mountains quake with their surging. PSALM 46:2–3

OCTOBER 15

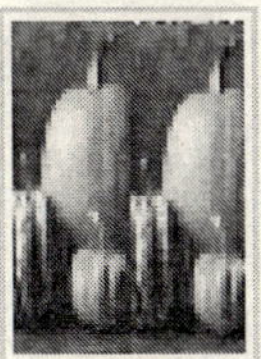

Years ago, I spoke with a chaplain who had returned from a year in Vietnam. As chaplain, it was his duty to go out and bring back the wounded men. One time, he was crawling through the mud toward one man, when his strength suddenly left him. He felt he could not go any farther.

"But just at that instant," he said, "a long shaft of sunlight came down to a spot just in front of me and rested upon a flower. It was the only vegetation left. There came to me in that instant," he continued, "the Scripture in 2 Corinthians that says, 'God . . . made his light shine in our hearts to give us the light of the knowledge of the glory of God in the face of Christ.' New heart came to me; new strength filled my body; and a new determination made me know I could bring back that wounded man."

Every one of us knows that deep trouble of the human spirit known as disheartenment. But just then, if you will look for it, God will repeat His miracle. He will shine in your heart.

Immediately Saul fell full length on the ground, filled with fear because of Samuel's words. His strength was gone, for he had eaten nothing all that day and night. 1 SAMUEL 28:20

OCTOBER 16

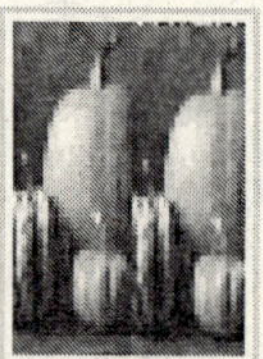

A famous physician has said that fear is the commonest and subtlest of all human diseases. And an equally famous psychologist has declared that fear is the most deteriorating enemy of human personality. Now these men, being scientists, are referring not to normal fear, but to abnormal fear. Normal fear is both proper and desirable. It is a mechanism designed by the Creator for our protection.

Abnormal fear is another matter. If you step over the line that separates it from the normal, you find yourself in a region of grotesque shadows and darkness, obsessions, and mental distortions.

But Almighty God never intended that anyone should live like that, and He has provided an approach by which you can have so much faith that you can live unafraid. There is a power by which you rise above the dangers and uncertainties of human existence and have power over them.

He who conceals his sins does not prosper,
but whoever confesses and renounces
them finds mercy. PROVERBS 28:13

OCTOBER 17

There is nothing that can keep you or keep me out of the glorious new world of Christianity in depth—save our own reluctance to embrace it.

"Well," I can hear someone say, "my trouble isn't as serious as that. But I'm not a good person. So how do you expect me to step into that new world? I must confess to you, sir, that there is a great deal of sin in my life. I'm weak. I'm a pushover for temptation. I haven't got the strength to give of myself as you say I must in order to enter into this experience. I can assure you that in the depths of my heart I desire it. But what about all these blemishes in my conduct, all these sins, all this hate, all this lust, all this dishonesty? How can I separate myself from these?"

How? By changing, that's all. Anyone can change if he has the desire to change and the will to change and will let Jesus Christ bring about that change.

Great is our Lord *and mighty in power;*
his understanding has no limit. Psalm 147:5

October 18

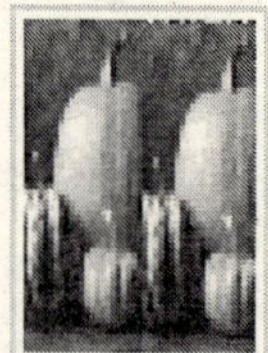

One day, a radio and television producer I know was sitting in the airport reading the New Testament. A soldier sitting next to him said, "You know, I don't think Jesus ever lived at all. It's all a myth and a fairy tale. He never lived."

"It's funny you would say that," the producer said, "because He was with me here just a minute ago."

"He was with you a minute ago?" asked the soldier. "Is that why you look so peaceful and so happy?"

"Yes, and you, too, can be peaceful and happy if you will let Him help you get rid of your conflicts and fears. He loves you as much as He loves me."

The soldier took my friend's hand and said, "Okay. I think maybe you've got something here. I'll try."

Now all that any of us can do is to try. And as we try, God will meet our feeble efforts much more than halfway. He will give us the power to stand up against fears, disappointments, frustration, opposition, misunderstanding—everything—and we will walk with our heads above it all into victory.

Give thanks to the God of heaven. His love endures forever. PSALM 136:26

OCTOBER 19

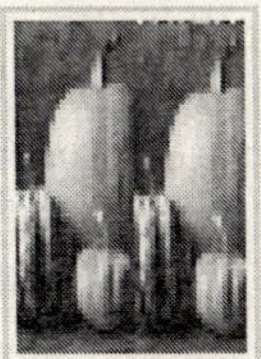

Isn't it wonderful to meet a person who is really alive? Not long ago I found myself talking with a man who positively sparkled with vitality. "Tell me," I said, "where did you get so much faith and enthusiasm?"

"I heard you speak at a meeting," he explained. "There was something in your talk that day that changed my life. It was a single sentence."

That sentence was Psalm 118:24: "This is the day the LORD has made; let us rejoice and be glad in it."

"And in what way has this changed your life?" I asked.

"That verse helped me realize that if I take just this one day and do my best, then when night comes I can give thanks to God and go to sleep, knowing that He watches over me."

Not every day is going to be a pleasant day. Not every day is going to be an easy one. Life brings to each of us some share of pain, struggle, sorrow, heartache. But even in a day that is full of suffering and difficulty, there lies hidden a nugget of something good.

That if you confess with your mouth, "Jesus is LORD," and believe in your heart that God raised him from the dead, you will be saved. ROMANS 10:9

OCTOBER 20

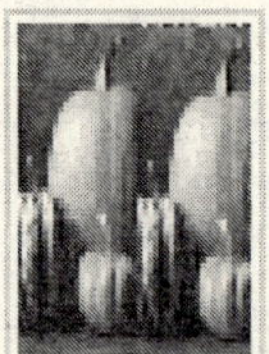

Some years ago, I received a call to come to a hospital to see a patient—a medical doctor. On my way to the hospital, I remembered that a doctor by this name had been mixed up in some crooked business. I went into the hospital room and asked, "I don't know you, do I?"

"No," he replied. "But I know you. I want you to get me out of this place. I have a stomach condition, and it has developed because I hate so many people. I want you to operate on me and get this hate out of me."

"Doctor, I have a suspicion about you," I said. "What have you got on your conscience besides hate?"

After a pause he admitted, "Doctor Peale, I am absolutely full of rottenness and sin."

He told me all the dirty things he had done and there were plenty. He wanted to change. And before we got finished in that hospital room, he did just that, for he said to the Lord Jesus Christ, "I will go with You all the rest of the way." And he did, too. He got the error out of him and got the truth in him.

Such confidence as this is ours through Christ before God. Not that we are competent in ourselves . . . but our competence comes from God. 2 CORINTHIANS 3:4–5

OCTOBER 21

Charles M. Schwab, one of the great American industrialists, said: "A man can succeed at almost anything for which he has unlimited enthusiasm." My friend Raymond Thornburg gave me a wonderful quotation from Anatole France, who said, "I prefer the folly of enthusiasm to the indifference of wisdom." George Matthew Adams said, "Enthusiasm is a kind of faith that has been set afire."

Sir Edward V. Appleton, the British physicist whose scientific discoveries made worldwide broadcasting possible and won him a Nobel Prize, was asked the secret of his achievements. Now what would you think a scientist of that caliber might say? Well, Sir Edward V. Appleton answered, "It was enthusiasm. I rate enthusiasm even above professional skill." It is a fact that people who do not have the skill of the professional, but have enthusiasm that the professional lacks, achieve things. They have the motivational force.

So we fix our eyes not on what is seen, but on what is unseen. For what is seen is temporary, but what is unseen is eternal. 2 CORINTHIANS 4:18

OCTOBER 22

I remember a sign I saw in Syracuse, New York. The winters in upstate New York are rugged, and the spring thaws break up the roads very badly. One spring, near Watertown, I actually saw a sign some farmer had put up that said, "Choose your rut well. You'll be in it for the next twenty-five miles." When people get into ruts in living, it's for longer than twenty-five miles. But you don't have to stay in a rut. You can get out of it.

Each of us, I believe, should at intervals re-study his activities and redefine his goals. At times, a person ought to appraise carefully what he is doing and ask himself the question, "Why am I doing this?" We do our work each day, and maybe we do it the best we can. But why are you doing that particular work? What are your objectives, your goals? Could you tell me what your goal is? Or is it fuzzy, hazy? We need to sharpen our thinking and bring our goals into focus.

Consider it pure joy, my brothers, whenever you face trials of many kinds, because you know that the testing of your faith develops perseverance. James 1:2–3

October 23

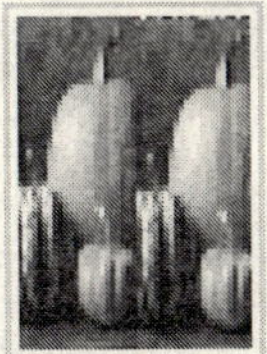

A good friend of mine thinks of the world as "God's tumbling barrel." A tumbling barrel is an industrial device for smoothing pieces of metal. It's a revolving drum into which workers put shaped metal pieces that have burrs or rough edges and an abrasive.

The barrel is then rotated. One piece tumbles against another, and the abrasive rubs steadily against them. After some time, the drum is opened, and the pieces are spilled out. The burrs have disappeared, the rough edges are gone. The metal parts are now in shape to function properly in a finished product.

In my friend's mind, this ingenious process suggests the way human beings are tumbled in God's world. As we move through life we tumble against each other and are rubbed by hardships and difficulties. All this friction smooths our rough edges, rounds our personalities, and forces us to use our minds and make ourselves better people.

See to it, brothers, that none of you has a sinful, unbelieving heart that turns away from the living God. But encourage one another daily. . . . HEBREWS 3:12–13

OCTOBER 24

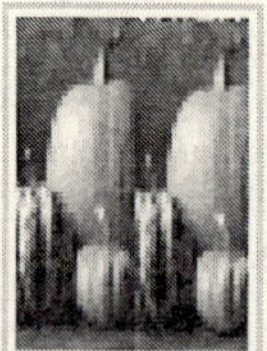

An old man from a small New York State community appeared on a national television show. The program's host was one of the greatest quipsters in the business, but he nearly lost the show to this old man, who was so full of light and fun that he had everybody rocking with laughter.

The host finally said to him, "Sir, you are the happiest man I ever had on my show. How did you get to be so happy?"

"Why, son," said the old man, "every morning when I wake up, I have two choices for the day. One choice is to be unhappy. The other choice is to be happy. So, faced with those two choices, I choose to be happy."

Now what that happy old man was referring to is one of the greatest powers that you and I possess: the power to choose. By the power of choice, you can either make your life creative or you can destroy it. Somebody said that history swings on small hinges. Similarly, human life develops according to small decisions. We determine our future by our immense power of choice.

If we confess our sins, he is faithful and just and will forgive us our sins and purify us from all unrighteousness. 1 JOHN 1:9

OCTOBER 25

A man once wrote, "I was getting near the bottom and couldn't find any way to stop the descent. One day, I went down to the lakeshore and I began to pray. 'God,' I said, 'I need Your help desperately. Please give it to me now. Not later—now.' At that exact moment, I was filled with a sense of incredible peace.

"I was forty-five years old. I had never really believed in forgiveness. I carried my sins like a sack on my back. I thought it possible that they might be forgiven, but I couldn't believe they could be forgotten. Now it's as though they had vanished. I feel pounds lighter."

This is the reason we believe, with all our hearts, in a Gospel of power that can touch a defeated man and give him power and life again. Believe in God's power, yield yourself to it, and start at once to live differently, in accordance with His will, so that you may be lifted from defeat to victory, from weakness to strength, and from sadness to joy.

"By faith in the name of Jesus, this man whom you see and know was made strong. It is Jesus' name and the faith that comes through him that has given this complete healing to him. . . ." ACTS 3:16

OCTOBER 26

What we need today is a greater emphasis upon big, strong people. When I was a boy they used to teach us in school that there is a great something a human being can use, which is known as willpower. Later on, a generation of more laid-back educators decided this was corny. But they sure produced a corny situation when they abandoned it! The mental health situation in this country worsened when they abandoned stressing willpower.

There is a power in an individual whereby he can decide, "I will. I will it to be. This is my decision. This is it—with the help of God." Naturally, willpower is much like whistling in the dark unless you combine it with God's help. But there are rugged people who with God's help take failure or difficulty or disappointment in their stride, extract from the experience whatever know-how it can give them, then relegate it to oblivion. And these people are inspiring.

. . . Forgetting what is behind and straining toward what is ahead, I press on toward the goal to win the prize for which God has called me heavenward in Christ Jesus. PHILIPPIANS 3:13–14

OCTOBER 27

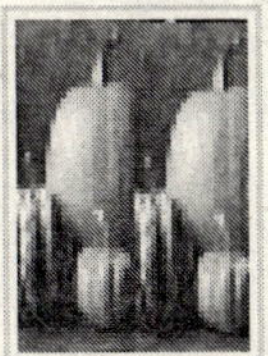

A young man came to see me. He had been a teacher in a secondary school. He was highly educated, highly trained, scholastically the best. Naturally when the headmaster retired, he thought he would get the job. But the board brought in a man from the outside. Offended and angry, the young man quit.

I said to him, "Look, I understand that you are a man of great potential and great capacity, but you are ruining yourself with resentment. The thing for you to do is to forget the whole incident. Go back and apply for a position on the faculty."

Well, he never mentioned it again. He went back on that faculty. Later, when a school needed a headmaster, the board chairman recommended him because he had developed so impressively after mastering the art of forgetting—and he became a headmaster.

What misfortune are you nursing in your mind? Forget it. It's a great art; I've seen many people do it. It's difficult. But it's the way to mastery.

"Therefore everyone who hears these words of mine and puts them into practice is like a wise man who built his house on the rock." MATTHEW 7:24

OCTOBER 28

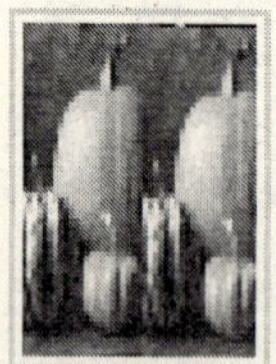

Little did the thousands who heard Jesus' words on the hillside that day realize that what they were listening to would be honored by multitudes twenty centuries later. Nor that scholars through the ages would say that these simple statements represented the greatest wisdom mankind would ever hear. As Jesus finished His sermon, He said that a person who had heard and lived by these teachings could be compared to a man who built his house upon a rock. Though all the elements conspired to knock that house down, they could not prevail—it stood, for it was built upon a rock.

Friends, you really listen to something when you listen to that passage of Scripture! Why don't you, this very day, read again the Sermon on the Mount in the Gospel of Matthew? If you read this passage and if you live by it, you will have what it takes; nothing in this world—and I mean nothing—will be able to beat you down.

. . .we consider blessed those who have persevered. You have heard of Job's perseverance and have seen what the Lord finally brought about. The Lord is full of compassion and mercy. JAMES 5:11

OCTOBER 29

Two gentlemen I knew suddenly found themselves without jobs. What did the two men do? One said to the Lord, "I don't understand why this developed, but I know that You have an answer for me."

Then he made a list of the hundred top executives of great American business organizations. To these men he wrote a letter. He told these presidents exactly what his record was and was absolutely honest. He had seven offers, one of which led him to the very thing in life that he could do best.

The other fellow went all to pieces. And he hasn't made anything of his life even yet, I am sorry to say.

If you adopt the outlook that something great can be done with your trouble, you can do something great. Your outlook determines your future.

Satisfy us in the morning with your unfailing love, that we may sing for joy and be glad all our days. PSALM 90:14

OCTOBER 30

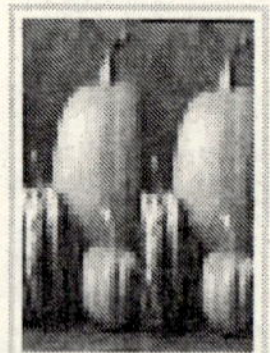

I wish to remind you of one of the greatest and most helpful facts in this world—namely, that you can start life new every morning. This ought to be comforting for everyone who feels discouraged about yesterday or who thinks the future looks hopeless. This assertion is not based on wishful thinking, but upon the solid, factual authority of the Bible itself. In Psalm 90:14 are these sparkling, resplendent, upbeat words: "Satisfy us in the morning with your unfailing love, that we may sing for joy and be glad all our days."

In his poem, "The Song of Diego Valdez," Rudyard Kipling has a line that is a gem. He refers to "the God of fair beginnings." It makes no difference to God what mistakes you've made, what failures you have had. He does not hold them against you. He is the God of fair beginnings. God is big. He forgets, He forgives, He writes it off—because He is fair. No matter how badly things have gone, He always makes it possible for you to make a new beginning.

For physical training is of some value,
but godliness has value for all things,
holding promise for both the present life
and the life to come. 1 TIMOTHY 4:8

OCTOBER 31

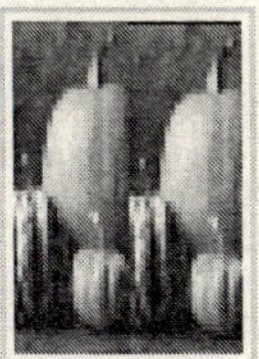

There are many people this very day who will die years before they should because they are not masters of themselves mentally and emotionally. For this reason, the subject of how to develop inner calmness may be considered during a service of divine worship. The purposes of worshiping God include pondering His word and conditioning ourselves to live according to His will. But worship is also part of spiritual healing.

Where is the healthiest place anybody can be on Sunday morning? The highway? Not on your life! A golf course? Well, I'm not going to minimize the health-giving value of golfing, but I have difficulty in understanding why it must be Sunday morning at church time. No, the healthiest place to be Sunday morning is in church, where one receives a healing treatment of the mind and of the soul and of the body. Every person should go forth from worship with the peace of God ruling in his heart.

November

THE LORD IS GOOD TO ALL;

HE HAS COMPASSION ON ALL

HE HAS MADE. PSALM 145:9

Therefore we do not lose heart. . . . For our light and momentary troubles are achieving for us an eternal glory that far outweighs them all. 2 CORINTHIANS 4:16–17

NOVEMBER 1

One of the greatest human beings I have ever known was an old man who lived in Syracuse, New York. One time I went to him for advice about a problem.

He said, "Well now, son, tell me all about it." I had no trouble doing that, because my mind was full of it. When I had finished he said, "You know, God has a sense of humor. You know what He does? When He has a wonderful possibility for you, He buries it at the heart of a big difficulty and He hands you this difficulty. So if you know the mind of God, you thank Him for the difficulty, because you know that, with His exquisite sense of humor, He has buried a bright possibility at the heart of that difficulty."

"But how do you find this bright thing that has been buried in the difficulty?" I asked.

"You surround the difficulty with prayer and faith and good hard thinking," answered Mr. Andrews, "and melt it down. After a while, in the midst of it, you see this bright, shining thing, this potential good."

Do not be afraid, for I am with you; I will bring your children from the east and gather you from the west. ISAIAH 43:5

NOVEMBER 2

Believe the great fact that God is with you. And with God's help, what can stand in your way? I have no doubt that you believe in God one way or another, but do you really believe that God is with you, on your side, by your side, in you, helping you? When you have this overwhelming faith in God, when you really believe in Him, and then call upon Him, He will answer and show you mighty things that you never knew.

As you practice this thought, you will become aware that He is also showing you a greater truth. "Do not be afraid, for I am with you" (Isaiah 43:5) is probably one of the greatest statements ever made in the history of human life on this earth. "Do not be afraid, for I am with you." We are taught this but we do not keep it in mind. Think big. And think the biggest thought of all—that you are not alone, that God will always help you.

"I will give you the keys of the kingdom of heaven; whatever you bind on earth will be bound in heaven, and whatever you loose on earth will be loosed in heaven." MATTHEW 16:19

NOVEMBER 3

One night I spoke in Webster Groves, Missouri. A man asked if he could drive me back to my hotel. He said, "I want to tell you a story of spiritual victory.

"I was a failure. I was completely down. Then a friend said to me, 'Frank, I want you to read the Bible. Stick to Matthew, Mark, Luke, and John; and when you come to a passage that strikes you, commit it to memory.'

"One day I came upon Matthew 16:19, where Jesus tells Peter, 'I will give you the keys of the kingdom of heaven.' I knew Peter had messed up his life, just as I had. I took it to mean He would give the keys to me too. Each day in my prayers, I unlocked the kingdom of heaven, and blessings started flowing into my life."

That man had had his life changed. He had found Jesus Christ and accepted Him as his Savior. Moreover, he had learned to pray in such a way that he developed perception and understanding. The keys to the kingdom are available to all God's believers.

All the ends of the earth will remember and turn to the LORD *. . . for dominion belongs to the* LORD *and he rules over the nations.* PSALM 22:27–28

NOVEMBER 4

It is said that the United States of America was formed by the convergence of two streams of history. One took its rise in the thinking of the philosophers of classical antiquity: Socrates, Plato, Aristotle, Cicero. These men believed that the human mind must always be free.

The other stream took its rise when Moses addressed a nation of slaves and told them that they were children of God, that other men should not put shackles on their wrists or lay whips to their backs.

The confluence of these two great streams of thought formed a government predicated upon the greatness of the human mind and the sovereignty of the human soul. I have enormous faith in the continuity of these ideals in the American people. You cannot break a nation built upon such foundations, unless that nation becomes arrogant, forgets its great heritage, and, worse than all else, turns away from God.

Because you are my help, I sing in the shadow of your wings. PSALM 63:7

NOVEMBER 5

Everyone needs to know how to stand up to a tough situation. The answer to this problem may be given in a concise statement. The one sentence is very simple, but if it is believed in and used, it can help you stand up successfully to any tough situation, no matter what kind it may be. This may seem to be claiming a great deal, but the claim is a valid one. And we find this great truth in Psalm 63:7: "Because you are my help, I sing in the shadow of your wings."

We can put this truth another way: Don't struggle so hard. Don't get yourself worked up. Don't fill your life with tension. Do the best you can with any situation and then commit it—that means put it completely in the hands of the Lord, trusting absolutely in Him, and He will bring it to pass in a right and proper manner. This is an old truth, but the wisest and most astute of men and women have believed it, have applied it, and have found that it will absolutely, positively work.

How can we thank God enough for you in return for all the joy we have in the presence of our God because of you? 1 THESSALONIANS 3:9

NOVEMBER 6

William L. Stidger was a distinctive preacher, but at one time he had a nervous breakdown and sat for months in abysmal gloom. He emerged from this by the practice of thanksgiving.

One day a friend said, "Think of people who have benefited you and ask yourself whether you have ever thanked them." Stidger gave it some thought, then wrote a letter to an old teacher. Presently he received a letter written in the shaky handwriting of an aged lady. "Dear Willy," she wrote, "I taught school for fifty years. Yours is the first letter of thanks I ever received from a student and I shall cherish it until I die."

This brought a ray of sunshine into Stidger's mind and he wrote another letter and another and another, until he had written five hundred letters! In the years that followed, whenever depression began to seize him, he would take out his copies of the letters of thanks he had written to people; and the happiness he had felt while doing it would well up in his heart once again.

Whoever gives heed to instruction prospers, and blessed is he who trusts in the LORD. PROVERBS 16:20

NOVEMBER 7

Happiness is not, as some might assume, a light or frivolous topic. Many tend to play down happiness as a superficial objective. But such an attitude is contrary to the facts of human nature. To be truly happy is to be drawing upon the essence of life. Furthermore, happiness fosters healthiness.

A physician once said that happiness corrects imbalances in a person's being. Imbalances, he said, tend to produce sickness, weakness, and deterioration. Balance tends to produce health, strength, and growth. Therefore, genuine happiness brings healthiness.

Happiness will not be found in soft sweetness. It will not be found in moonlight and roses. Happiness in depth—and that is the only kind of happiness that will stand despite trials and continue to be happiness—is to be found through struggle, hardship, pain, suffering, difficulty. It is a joy that is bathed with tears and consecrated by effort. If you are experiencing pain today, look carefully in it for a golden nugget called happiness that has been buried there.

We will not all sleep, but we will all be changed. . . . For the trumpet will sound, the dead will be raised imperishable, and we will be changed. 1 CORINTHIANS 15:51–52

NOVEMBER 8

There has never been anyone like Jesus in all the history of mankind. He is incomparable because He had the truth and has it now. He has love for people and a strange, mysterious power to change men—to take the bad out of them and put the good in, to take weakness out of them and put strength in, to take hate out of them and put love in, to take dishonesty from them and make them honest. Jesus can change anyone. Because all of us, deep down in our hearts, want to be better than we are; we continue to follow Him, hoping, praying, and dreaming. One day we meet Him, and we are changed.

It is for this reason that today untold millions around the world shout acclaim to Him. "Heaven and earth will pass away, but my words will never pass away" (Matthew 24:35). You shall pass away; I shall pass away. But if we are in Him, none of us will ever pass away. We will be immortalized in His truth, which is deathless.

Remember your Creator in the days of your youth, before the days of trouble come and the years approach when you will say, "I find no pleasure in them." ECCLESIASTES 12:1

NOVEMBER 9

I was once interviewed by reporters from a hometown of mine—Findlay, Ohio. They asked me the usual questions. Finally, one of them asked, "Dr. Peale, have you any advice for young people about how to work for a good future for themselves, and, beyond that, how they can help make the world a better place for people everywhere?"

With that question in mind, I would suggest that the essential first step would be to let God release a fuller measure of our potential.

Everyone has potential. God put it in you. That is a tremendous word: potential. Eleven men once got their potential freed and began to use it, and they turned the whole world upside down with their message of Christ. They were so dynamic that wherever they went, they turned things upside down, bringing new life, new understanding, and new joy. Did anyone ever say that about you? How to release our potential—this is the challenge.

He makes me lie down in green pastures, he leads me beside quiet waters, he restores my soul. He guides me in paths of righteousness for his name's sake. PSALM 23:2–3

NOVEMBER 10

One can learn various techniques for strengthening one's faith. I think preachers make these concepts so general and abstract sometimes that a person can't quite get hold of them. So I will mention a few specific, simple techniques for faith building. For example, there was a timid, inferiority-complex-ridden young woman who lived in Brooklyn and worked in Manhattan. She came to our clinic for counseling. "How can I get over these fears?" she wanted to know.

The counselor suggested she memorize specific passages in the Bible and say them over to herself from time to time during the day. This she did. On her daily subway trip, she discovered she could repeat Psalm 23 three times and the Lord's Prayer twice. That is how she got her mind imbued with the great presence of God and with the truth, "I won't be afraid. You are with me." And by this means, she developed faith. If you repeat Psalm 23 every day of your life, paying attention to its meaning, the fears would begin to ease out of your mind.

Now the LORD is the Spirit, and where the Spirit of the LORD is, there is freedom.
2 CORINTHIANS 3:17

NOVEMBER 11

A story is told of an incident during the Nazi occupation of Denmark in World War II. The Nazis told King Christian that they were going to put the Nazi flag on every building in Denmark, saying he could fly the Danish flag beneath the Nazi banner.

King Christian replied, "If you put a Nazi flag over the Danish flag, in ten seconds a Danish soldier will pull it down and send up the Danish flag."

"That soldier," they threatened, "will be shot."

"All right," said the king, "I will be that soldier."

They never shot him. Then when they were going to proscribe the Jews and there make them all wear Star of David armbands, the king put a Star of David band on his own arm and protected his Jewish subjects. There are still people who will risk everything for freedom.

For the word of God is living and active. Sharper than any double-edged sword, it penetrates even to dividing soul and spirit . . . it judges the thoughts and attitudes of the heart. HEBREWS 4:12

NOVEMBER 12

Many years ago, in a farmhouse in the Midwest, a seventeen-year-old boy was in a coma, desperately ill. The doctor said, "I see no reason why this boy should die. What he needs is a faith transfusion, a desire to live. In some way he is near death because the faith isn't there to pull him through." He said, "If a transfusion like that doesn't happen, he will die before morning."

When the doctor said that, a farmer drew near and started reading to the boy from the Bible. Hour after hour, he drove those healing thoughts into the boy's unconscious mind until near dawn when, suddenly, the boy gave a sigh. His eyes opened, he looked at the man and at all the people in the room; he gave them a smile and fell into a deep, untroubled, normal sleep.

The doctor checked his vital signs and said, "The boy will live!" And he did live. Saved by what? By faith and prayer and thought. The problem had its solution right within itself, as all problems do.

. . . God, who has saved us and called us to a holy life—not because of anything we have done but because of his own purpose and grace. . . . 2 TIMOTHY 1:8–9

NOVEMBER 13

I remember an experience of my old friend E. Stanley Jones, the famous missionary. During his first few years in India, he labored under a heavy sense of personal inadequacy. He began to think he would have to give up his missionary career.

At a meeting in Lucknow he had a remarkable experience. He was praying and he seemed to hear a voice asking, "Are you ready for this work to which I called you?" Silently, he confessed that he just didn't seem to have the strength. Then the voice said, "If you will turn it over to Me, I will take care of it."

But there is a catch. You can't expect God to help you repeatedly unless you help Him. The furtherance of His kingdom on earth comes about through human beings trying to help and serve. That is how He ordained it should be. God wants to have the love and help of people.

Our Heavenly Father, we thank You for the great truth that we are not alone, that You are always with us and always will be, to the end of our lives and beyond. Through Jesus Christ, our Lord. Amen.

Then he touched their eyes and said, "According to your faith will it be done to you"; and their sight was restored. . . .

MATTHEW 9:29–30

NOVEMBER 14

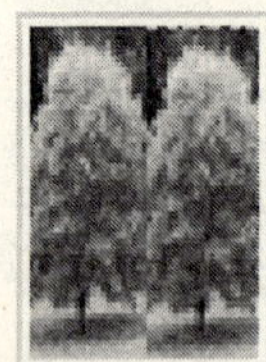

Pray big. Think big. Believe big. The Gospel of Matthew, chapter 9, verse 29, declares, "According to your faith will it be done to you." In other words, your life is going to be great in proportion to how greatly you believe. Believe little, you get a little life. Believe weakly, you get a weak life. Believe fear, you get a life of fear. Believe sickness, you get a sick life. Believe big, and you get a big life.

Jesus said, "Everything is possible for him who believes" (Mark 9:23). Which means what? That the person who believes is going to get everything he wants? No, it doesn't say that. But it does mean that if you believe big, you move things out of the realm of the impossible into the realm of the possible. Christianity is the religion of the incredible, the religion of the astonishing, the religion of the breathless. You bring to yourself what you believe.

They were all trying to frighten us, thinking, "Their hands will get too weak for the work, and it will not be completed." [But I prayed,] "Now strengthen my hands." NEHEMIAH 6:9

NOVEMBER 15

Are your human relationships what you want them to be? Would you like them to be better? Then why aren't they better? Maybe it is because you fail to realize your full capacity. If all the members of some group of, say, several hundred persons would suddenly realize their full capacity, do you know what they could do? They could change this world. If we would just all catch it!

But how do you catch it? How does one get a power that is plenty for the work of God's kingdom? One thing is certain: you can't manufacture it yourself. Human beings are weak. We are only as strong as we are strong in God. God promises you infinitely more strength. But you've got to reach for it. You have to take it. You have to want it. You have to accept it. Then you have the full complement of power.

Surrender yourself completely to Jesus Christ and build your life around Him. Live the way He wants you to live, even though it's hard at times. Do this, and you will have the power.

"I, even I, am he who blots out your transgressions, for my own sake, and remembers your sins no more."

Isaiah 43:25

November 16

Rest in the Lord, wait patiently, have faith in Providence and God's love. In this way, you actually get your life under new management. What happens when a business repeatedly fails to show a profit? Usually it gets new management, doesn't it? A human life that hasn't been going well likewise calls for new management. Does everything go wrong for you? Why? Poor management. Are you nervous and tense and tired? Why? Poor management. Are you resentful and grumpy and bitter, full of hate and miserable as a result? Why? Poor management. You are making life hard for yourself because you don't think right, you don't act right, you don't plan right. Get your life under new management. Do it by opening your mind and heart to Jesus Christ. Take Him into your thinking and living.

I have been crucified with Christ and I no longer live, but Christ lives in me. The life I live in the body, I live by faith in the Son of God. . . . GALATIANS 2:20

NOVEMBER 17

If you are failing at anything, chances are it is because you have an image of yourself failing. Do you know what you are doing? You are hypnotizing yourself with a limiting idea. When you come to church, when you read the Bible, and when you listen to Jesus Christ; when you lift up your eyes and look on Him, He eliminates the limitations you have imposed upon yourself. I know this is a fact. It all depends on what you think of yourself. The image you and I have of ourselves determines the actual state of our lives. The Christian religion teaches us not only how to live good moral lives and how to have faith so we will be received into eternity, but also how to live as children of God here and now. What Jesus Christ wants to do is to knock the shackles off our minds and remove the limitations of our lives.

The LORD is good to all; he has compassion on all he has made. PSALM 145:9

NOVEMBER 18

Many Americans have long since forgotten the romance of the simple basic blessings of this life. A Japanese businessman remarked to me once that his people "still know how to contemplate and love the simple, basic things of human existence." He told me of a Japanese custom called a snow-viewing party. This is usually held on a night when the moon is full, by someone who has a large picture window with a beautiful garden outside. The guests gather. There are no cocktails, there is no hubbub, no empty conversation, no hand-shaking. You sit and look through the picture window at the snow, at the stark, bare trees with little flecks of snow on them, at the great rocks capped with snow. You spend an hour or two, in silence, viewing the snow and thinking and meditating. Then you rise, bow, and go home. That is all, but you have had an hour of quiet fellowship with sensitive, appreciative people. Life is good; and you walk along thinking long thoughts about how lovely the world is. So let us give thanks for the deep basic things of human existence and for family, friends, and loved ones.

Every good and perfect gift is from above, coming down from the Father of the heavenly lights, who does not change like shifting shadows. JAMES 1:17

NOVEMBER 19

After two years of professional baseball with the St. Louis Cardinals, Frank Bettger hurt his arm and had to give up baseball. He spent two years in a dismal job, then he switched to selling life insurance. His first ten months in this new work were the most discouraging months of his life. He would make many calls without selling a single policy.

Finally, Bettger decided to "burn up the paths" in life insurance, just as he had done in baseball. The next day, he sold a policy to his first prospect. That was the beginning of a spectacular career. Insurance people tell me that Bettger is regarded as having been one of the greatest salesmen in the history of life insurance. And on the subject of developing enthusiasm, Bettger says, "There is only one rule. To become enthusiastic, act enthusiastic."

Practice enthusiasm in even the most commonplace things and presently the immense power of enthusiasm will begin working wonders for you.

And this is his command: to believe in the name of his Son, Jesus Christ, and to love one another as he commanded us. 1 JOHN 3:23

NOVEMBER 20

A young man told me his grandmother was always doing good, so I decided to look her up. After finding the house, eventually I saw an elderly lady coming down the road, carrying a big basket on her arm. And she was singing—beautifully and melodically—at the top of her voice.

"Are you Mrs. Wright?" I asked.

A big smile crossed her face as she said, "Of course, that's who I am. What do you want to see me about?"

"I had a letter from your grandson and he says that you are an angel on two feet," I explained. "Please tell me how you got to be so happy."

"I just love everyone," she answered. "When you have the Lord Jesus in your heart, you love everyone and it's like birds singing. It's like music all day long."

Jesus said: "I will give you the keys of the kingdom of heaven" (Matthew 16:19). The greatest of all keys to the kingdom of heaven is to have Jesus in your heart. And this is the greatest of all formulas for happiness.

Praise be to the God and Father of our LORD *Jesus Christ! In his great mercy he has given us new birth into a living hope through the resurrection of Jesus Christ from the dead.* 1 PETER 1:3

NOVEMBER 21

Do you know what the greatest word in the New Testament is? It's *life*. Hunt through the New Testament to find how many times the word *life* appears, and you will be amazed. Associated with the word is another word—*new*. The whole emphasis of the New Testament is on newness. The Bible is the most modern thing in the world. It is more modern than today's newspaper, for it deals with life that is new.

In 1 Peter 2:9 are the words, "[God] called you out of darkness into his wonderful light." What is light associated with? Morning, the new day. And again, in Ephesians 4:23–24, we are told: "Let the Spirit change your way of thinking and make you into a new person." And, again, the Bible says, "Therefore, if anyone is in Christ, he is a new creation; the old has gone, the new has come!" (2 Corinthians 5:17). That is the word: new, new, new! Fresh, new world. New life.

Do not be overcome by evil,
but overcome evil with good.
Romans 12:21

November 22

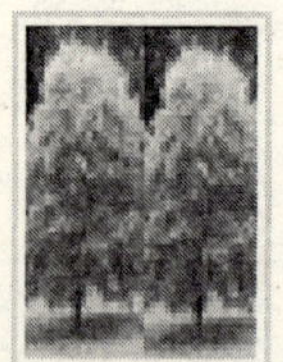

People talk about the evils of our society—the breakdown of morality, the rising incidence of crime, the growing paganism of our generation, and the dishonesty rampant in human affairs.

Sometimes people say, "It's so bad that you can never do anything about it. These things are so deeply rooted in the wickedness of human nature that you can never eradicate them. It's an impossibility."

It is my humble judgment that the remedy for these social impossibilities is for individuals to be so stimulated and motivated, to become so identified with God, that they become part of His process of overcoming impossiblilities.

"Here I stand; I can do no other," said Martin Luther. It was he himself, individually, who stood for principles so forcefully that he initiated great changes in the social order. Individuals overcome impossibilities.

. . . you may have had to suffer grief in all kinds of trials. These have come so that your faith . . . may be proved genuine and may result in praise, glory and honor when Jesus Christ is revealed. 1 PETER 1:6–7

NOVEMBER 23

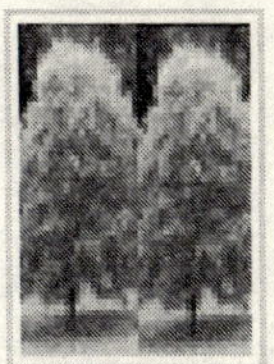

You may say, "You don't know the difficulties I have. There are so many problems. I have inner conflicts and all kinds of trouble. Yet you tell me not to be depressed." But let me ask you: Would you want all those problems and troubles to be taken away from you? Who made this world? Some whimsical being? Some devilish individual? Or was it someone with wisdom? You know it was someone with wisdom because everywhere you find order and law; and wherever you find order and law, you are beholding signs of intelligence. This world was created by an intelligent God. He put you in it, and He put some trouble in it along with you. Why? Because He wants to make a great person out of you. If He didn't care whether you ever amounted to anything, He wouldn't have put any difficulty in your life.

"Consider the ravens: They do not sow or reap, they have no storeroom or barn; yet God feeds them. And how much more valuable you are than birds!" LUKE 12:24

NOVEMBER 24

Discouragement is one of the most pernicious diseases of the human spirit. It weighs heavily upon the mind, making its judgments grotesque and unsharp. It saps energy. It destroys creative possibilities. It renders us ineffective.

And let's face it, oftentimes there is much cause to be discouraged. If I wanted to, I could give you quite a talk on all the things you might find to be discouraged about. But I don't think it's my job to tell you how bad things are. You know that already. My theme is that you can do something about it. You can learn to handle and get above discouragement. Out of discouragement, rightly handled, great things come.

Our Heavenly Father, we know that all things are a demonstration of the spiritual. Grant that we may have the wisdom to see this in our lives and fill us with wonder and joy. Through Jesus Christ, our Lord. Amen.

You were taught, with regard to your former way of life, to put off your old self, . . . and to put on the new self, created to be like God in true righteousness and holiness. EPHESIANS 4:22–24

NOVEMBER 25

Jesus promised that if people would believe in Him, really believe in Him, and follow Him, a wondrous thing would happen to them. He told people that they could discover a whole new world of real living. If He were standing among us today, He would say to any of us who feel confused, unhappy, restricted, defeated, or depressed that we need not be this way at all—that if we reorganize our thoughts and affirm our faith, we can discover a marvelous new world of real living. He is the only man in history who has delivered such a promise.

There may be some who say, "I wouldn't want to change my life for the world. It is perfect. I like it just as it is." Don't ever settle for what you already have, no matter how good it may seem to be. No matter how wonderful your life is, it can be more wonderful. You can go from level to level into an ever-new world of real living. This is why Jesus lives and is a real, contemporary personality when all other great figures pass away.

". . . Everything is possible for him who believes." Immediately the boy's father exclaimed, "I do believe; help me overcome my unbelief!"

Mark 9:23–24

November 26

I think it may be said that a pastor sees people as they really are. Having had this experience for many years, I have an exalted respect for human beings, because I've seen them struggle against the greatest imaginable odds and gain victories through the power of God.

I've observed one thing that has never ceased to impress me. The person who has a certain great truth in his mind can never be defeated by anything and will ultimately win victories, though he may have to go through the deep waters now and then. That great truth is the belief—the obsessive belief—that God is always with us. When you believe this, you are not alone, never, under any circumstances. When you live with this belief, you are never rejected, you are never forsaken, you never walk by yourself. God is with you—this is the greatest source of strength a human being can have.

Give thanks to the L*ORD*, *for he is good.*
His love endures forever. P*SALM* 136:1

NOVEMBER 27

Have you had a hard time this past year? Psalm 136:1 tells us we should give thanks for it. Hard times struggled with in the name of Jesus become victories by and by, and we are stronger people for having wrestled with those problems. Have you had sorrow? Through your tears, give thanks for it, for it is through difficult circumstances that souls grow. Whatever life has brought, the message is to give thanks. As you do so, greater things will come.

We need to recall and give thanks for the gift of life itself. We're so accustomed to being alive that we take it for granted. The thrill and the wonderment of it elude our minds. Do you ever get up in the morning and look out the window or go to the door and breathe in the fresh air and go back in and say to your wife or husband, "Isn't it great to be alive?" Probably if you did, your spouse would have a heart attack! But life in itself is so tremendous, such a privilege, that it should be cause for deep thanksgiving.

Restore us, O God; make your face shine upon us, that we may be saved. PSALM 80:3

NOVEMBER 28

Some years ago, one of the speakers at a summer conference of the Fellowship of Christian Athletes was Paul Anderson, an Olympic weight lifting champion, said to be the strongest man in the world. He began by amazing his audience with feats of strength. After he got through these demonstrations, he preached a forceful sermon on the theme that anyone who has filled himself with the love of Jesus Christ can overcome any temptation life may bring him. He said that Christlike love is the greatest power men and women can tap. And he told the assembled athletes to use it!

Of all the people I have known, the happiest are those who have had lots of trouble, sickness, pain, or difficulty, but have overcome all these because they had a resource. And the resource they had was an acquaintance with God. They knew that, no matter how dark the shadows, God and Jesus Christ were always there. If you know that, then no matter how much trouble and difficulty you have, you are happy in your heart, because you know that the source of victory is yours.

This is how God showed his love among us: He sent his one and only Son into the world that we might live through him. 1 JOHN 4:9

NOVEMBER 29

God is so big that He has confidence in His creatures. He gives them the power of private judgment; He makes them free moral agents so that they can do what they want to do—even contrary to His will. That is a big God. If God were a little god, He would tell us exactly what to do. But He leaves us free.

You and I repeatedly make a mess of things—that's for sure. To some people, the human picture looks quite hopeless. Life is dark at times. But I hold with the faith expressed by John Greenleaf Whittier in the lines:

I know not where His islands lift
Their fronded palms in air;
I only know I cannot drift
Beyond His love and care.

Beyond this universe, Christianity tells us, is eternal goodness. The conflict between evil and good, between hate and love, goes on and on; but love is fundamental and underlies the immortality of the soul.

Give, and it will be given to you. . . .
For with the measure you use, it will
be measured to you." LUKE 6:38

NOVEMBER 30

Sam Reeve was so poor that the first time he ever wore a suit was the day he graduated from high school, and the suit was given to him by a neighbor. One day, he read this passage in the Bible: "Give, and it will be given to you. A good measure, pressed down, shaken together and running over, will be poured into your lap. For with the measure you use, it will be measured to you" (Luke 6:38). Sam decided to predicate his life on this and eventually became an outstandingly successful small businessman. He was invited to a White House conference of small businessmen who had done distinguished jobs. The president asked him, "Sam, how did you do it?"

Sam thought a moment and then answered, "I just tried to give away more than my competitors. I try to find my pleasure in giving," he said, "and let the getting part take care of itself." I tell you, if you really believe in the Bible, you've got to believe in this. If you want a life full of blessings, a life out of poverty, a life victorious over difficulties, if you want things to flow your way, you practice that.

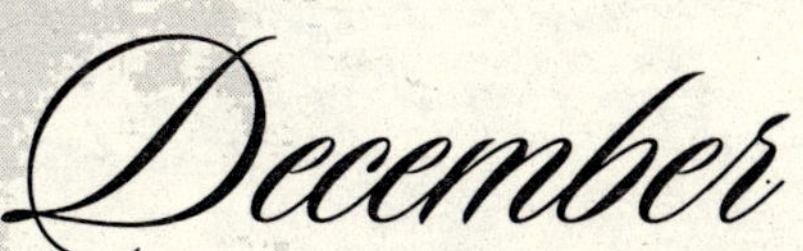

December

"For God so loved the world that he gave his one and only Son, that whoever believes in him shall not perish but have eternal life." John 3:16

I pray that out of his glorious riches he may strengthen you with power through his Spirit in your inner being, so that Christ may dwell in your hearts through faith. EPHESIANS 3:16–17

DECEMBER 1

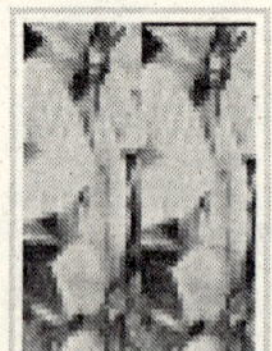

Christianity is a fountain of power—the greatest power in the universe. After His Resurrection, Jesus said to the disciples, "But you will receive power when the Holy Spirit comes on you" (Acts 1:8). That was the beginning of the Christian faith, a power promise.

How much power do you have? Do you have a great surging river of power or do you have just a little rivulet that carries you through some things but fails you in others? The law of supply is a great concept. And this law of supply is offered to anyone who will practice the magic of believing.

This doesn't mean that you are going to get rich. Christianity isn't designed to make you rich. Christianity isn't interested in whether you are rich or not. The Bible says, "Be generous, and someday you will be rewarded." You shall have every one of your needs satisfied if you practice the magic of believing.

And the God of all grace . . . after you have suffered a little while, will himself restore you and make you strong, firm and steadfast. 1 PETER 5:10

DECEMBER 2

God knows that human beings need help. No matter how strong they may be or what attainments they may have to their credit, they are still faced with many problems that upset them. Even though their faces may look calm and peaceful, people may be upset to one degree or another.

Only a short time ago, a man came to my office whose name I think would be known to nearly everyone who has any knowledge of the American business world. He manages a vast industrial empire. He is one of those men born to leadership, a strong, powerful character. And he sat in my office and asked me, "Can I unload my mind to you?"

"Go ahead," I said. And he was with me for a long time, for he had lots to unload. There he sat in front of me, a powerful, famous man, but at the same time just a human being whose mind was terribly upset. He had come to talk with me because he wanted me to tell him how Jesus could help him. I was touched. And he was touched. And he was helped.

". . . if anyone says to this mountain, 'Go, throw yourself into the sea,' and does not doubt in his heart but believes that what he says will happen, it will be done for him." MARK 11:23

DECEMBER 3

"If you have faith . . . you can say to this mountain . . ." Now what does Jesus mean by "mountain"? Well, obviously not a mountain made of stone or earth. You couldn't remove such a mountain by faith. Or maybe you could, but there would be no meaning to it. There would be no sense in it. No, what are referred to here are the difficulties of life piled one upon another. If you have faith and do not doubt it, you can say to those difficulties, "Go, throw yourself into the sea"—which is another way of saying, cast out of sight, gone for good—and they will be. That is what the Bible says. And I personally am simple enough to believe it. I believe it because I have seen this truth demonstrated many times. The believer is conferred power over difficulties.

. . . If a man's gift is prophesying, let him use it in proportion to his faith. If it is serving, let him serve; if it is teaching, let him teach. ROMANS 12:6–7

DECEMBER 4

Through extraordinary intelligence, hard work, and by the application of the basic laws of successful achievement, W. Clement Stone has made huge sums of money. But I never knew a man who gave so much money so generously as does Mr. Stone. It appears that his chief reason for making money is to help people. For example, he has helped more prisoners to find new life—and more boys to find a future—than anyone I know of. He started life with nothing. He said that the Lord just gave him the gift of making money.

But I've noticed that a lot of people who make money hang on to it. Some of the tightest people I've ever known are people who have made money—they've got the idea that it is for them alone. If you have the ability to acquire wealth, you should learn the equally important art of how to give it for mankind. You are a steward of God, who made everything and owns all values of this world.

"The King will reply, 'I tell you the truth, whatever you did for one of the least of these brothers of mine, you did for me.'" MATTHEW 25:40

DECEMBER 5

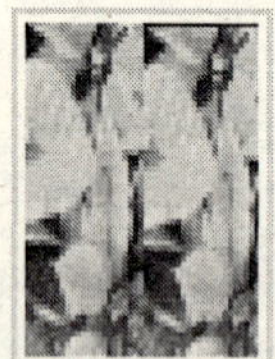

Frank Boyden was headmaster of Deerfield Academy at Deerfield, Massachusetts, for over sixty years. When he first took charge, the Academy was heavily in debt. But if you go there today, you will see the most marvelous campus. I asked Frank Boyden one day, "How did you get this place built up?"

"Whenever I got to rock bottom," he said, "I'd talk to the Lord about it. The Lord would say, 'Frank, give some more.' I would tighten my belt and give more of my own money, more of myself. And the blessings have just rolled in—because I wanted to make good men out of little boys and I gave of myself to do it."

I will tell you this: If you are missing blessings in your life, if the flow of prosperity has been inhibited, the thing to do is start giving! Even when you haven't anything to give, give anyway. This is what is offered you through the law of supply. The law of supply works only as long as you give.

"Do not store up for yourselves treasures upon earth . . . But store up for yourselves treasures in heaven. . . : For where your treasure is, there your heart will be also." MATTHEW 6:19–21

DECEMBER 6

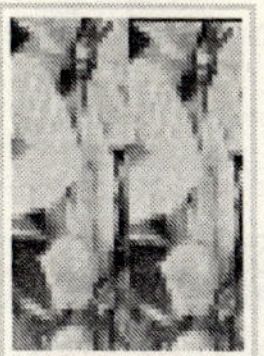

Jesus delivered a message that would bring peace, goodwill, happiness, and creativity to all the world. And it was as if He said, "This cannot be except by your own choice, for you have been created free moral agents. You can turn it down if you wish. You can support it if you wish. It cannot be realized without you."

Think of all the blessings that ensued from the vast onward march of Christendom over the past two thousand years! But still it is not enough. The forces of materialism and evil grow so fast that we have to keep building our Christianity ever higher and broader and deeper. And the people who will give themselves to this task are going to be the people who see blessings beyond all calculation. You have to give. If a person doesn't give, he doesn't get. If he does get and doesn't give, he doesn't keep. It is a spiritual law.

"And when you pray, do not keep on babbling like pagans, . . . for your Father knows what you need before you ask him." MATTHEW 6:7–8

DECEMBER 7

Prayer is a mental process. Oftentimes a person will complain, "I've prayed and prayed and I didn't get what I wanted." You didn't? Well, who said you were supposed to get what you wanted? Prayer isn't a device to get you what you want. Prayer is a means of bringing you to the point where you will accept what God wants. If you're using it just for getting what you want, you're engaging in an improper and degraded use of it.

The Lord does want good things for us all, and if with all your heart you pray for something that is wholesome and constructive, you are likely to receive it. But sometimes the thing you pray for is something you shouldn't have. We are like children—we want what we want when we want it. But to be a Christian means to be a mature person. You learn to say, "This is what I'd like to have, Lord, if You think it's all right for me, but if You don't, then give me what You want me to have or show me what You want me to do."

Yet I am poor and needy; come quickly to me, O God. You are my help and my deliverer; O LORD, do not delay. PSALM 70:5

DECEMBER 8

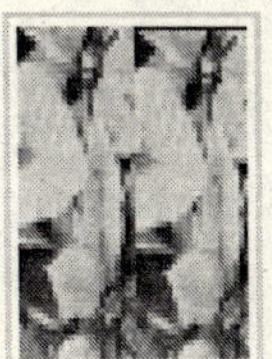

I received a letter from a young man in Texas. He began: "Until about two years ago, my life was governed by sick, consuming fear. I prayed to God for help, but when the answer came, it was not what I'd had in mind. It was an idea: 'Go to the library and get a book on psychology and find out why you are afraid.'

"I went to the library, and what caught my eye that day was something you had written, *A Guide to Confident Living.* Confident living—that's what I needed all right! And the idea of a personal God and His presence in our lives strongly appealed to me. I became a church member. Reading the Bible took on a new meaning. God touched me.

"My life has changed. It is not a bed of roses by any means. But I am calmer now. I know that God never turns His back on anyone who sincerely seeks Him."

This is the key to the formula. Let God touch you and you become a victorious person, whose mind has been freed from fear by being filled with faith.

"Love the LORD your God with all your heart and with all your soul and with all your mind and with all your strength." MARK 12:30

DECEMBER 9

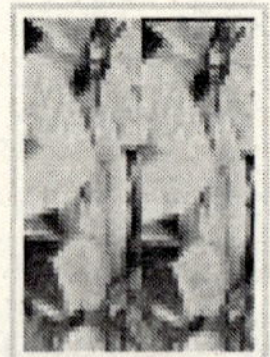

When I first met Paul Chow, he had brought his family from Shanghai to freedom in Hong Kong. He wanted to come to America. Even though I practice positive thinking, I warned him, "It will be difficult for you to get to America."

"I know," he assured me, "but difficulties are the things the Lord handles."

And the day came when, standing in the pulpit at Marble Collegiate Church, I saw a wonderful face and thought, "It looks like Paul Chow." Sure enough, it was. Well, I found that Paul and his family were living on a street that was more dismal than anything I'd seen in Hong Kong. I exclaimed to my wife, "Imagine a man going to the trouble he went to only to land in a place like this. I won't let them stay there." We found a home for them in Pawling, New York. And the Chows became one of the most beloved families in the community. Against great odds, this man became a tremendous person, because he had Jesus in his heart.

All this also comes from the L*ORD*
Almighty, wonderful in counsel and
magnificent in wisdom. ISAIAH 28:29

DECEMBER 10

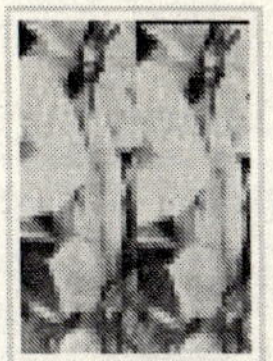

W. Clement Stone is a philosopher who says you should read the Bible with the idea that God wants to do wonderful things for you. You get exactly what you are looking for, he says. If you seek inspiration, you become inspired. If you seek knowledge, you become informed. If you seek wisdom, you become wise. If you seek health, sickness disappears. Seek good and it comes to you. Seek success and it will come to you. Know specifically what you want and then keep your mind on that which you want—and off the things you don't want. If you keep thinking about what you don't want, you'll get what you don't want. But if you think about what you want, it is likely to come to you.

Our Heavenly Father, we thank You for the great truths that are given to us out of Your holy word. Help us therefore to commit ourselves to You in completeness. And then will come victory after victory.

I thank Christ Jesus our LORD, who has given me strength, that he considered me faithful, appointing me to his service.
1 TIMOTHY 1:12

DECEMBER 11

When an old friend's last will and testament was read, it contained the following declaration:

"I desire to testify and give thanks for: the goodness of God, who has blessed me far beyond my merit; godly parents; the patience and devotion of my wife; the Christian character, love, and loyalty of my darling daughter, my son-in-law and their family, and my grandchildren; the rich fellowship of my friends; the kindness and cooperation of those with whom I have been associated in business; the opportunities for service in the community and in the church; the strength for daily toil; the joy of living; the inexpressible reward of striving, even in an imperfect way, to follow Christ; and the glorious certainty of life eternal and abundant. These comprise my real possessions."

My friend had so many blessings because he was constantly activating the flow of blessings by giving praise and thanks to the Source of it all.

For the Lord *will vindicate his people*
and have compassion on his servants.
Psalm 135:14

December 12

The Empire State Building is a marvelous structure. Seeing it reminded me of a boy who lived in downtown New York City in devastating poverty. At the age of thirty, he was elected to the New York State Assembly and was assigned to the committee on banking; he had never had a bank account up to that time. He was so discouraged trying to read the bills that came before him that he almost decided to quit.

I am talking about Alfred E. Smith, four-time governor of New York. And he later realized his dream of building the tallest building in the world, the Empire State Building. Once I sat with him in that building and said, "Governor, you have had a great career. Tell me about it."

He smiled and replied, "My mother always believed in me. She said there was something in me that God would bring out if I allowed Him to do so."

So if you are not satisfied with your life, say, "Lord, help me to bring out the greatness that is within me." What God can make out of a person is astounding.

Jesus looked at him and loved him. "One thing you lack," he said. "Go, sell everything you have and give to the poor, and you will have treasure in heaven. Then come, follow me." MARK 10:21

DECEMBER 13

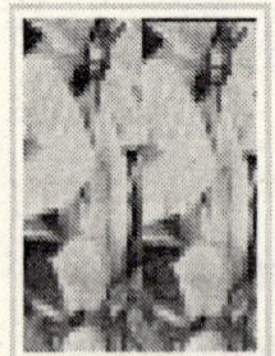

During the Depression of the 1930s, the air was filled with gloom. One night I went out and walked in Walnut Park, with fear clutching at my heart. How were we going to live? How were we going to keep the church going? How were we going to pay bills?

When I came home, my wife said, "Now, look. You are my husband, but you are also my pastor. And you are doing better at the first than you are at the second. I want to tell you something, Norman. All we need to do is to give."

"But we haven't anything to give."

"We will give of what we have. I'll promise you this," she continued—and I remember looking into her lovely face as she said it—"if you will rededicate yourself to Jesus Christ and give your money and time to God and to the church and to human beings, God will always take care of us. You can forget being afraid." That was a long time ago, and He has always taken care of us. We have had blessings. Why? Because I deserve them? No! But that kind of faith will always bring blessings.

The LORD will watch over your coming and going both now and forevermore.

PSALM 121:8

DECEMBER 14

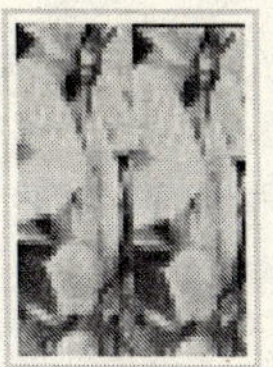

I liked to hear my grandmother, Laura Peale, pray. She could pray as could few persons I have known on this earth. My brother and I as boys used to spend summers with her and our grandfather. Each night she put us to bed with the Bible and that old Methodist magazine, *The Christian Advocate.* I can see her yet, with those concave glasses people used to wear, reading stories out of a magazine and the Bible.

Then she would take us upstairs and put us into a comfortable feather bed, and she would blow out the kerosene lamp. She knew we might be afraid in the dark, so she would put one hand on Bob's head and one on mine and say, "Dear Lord, let these boys know that You watch over them all night long. Keep Your eye on their pillows while they sleep tonight." Then we would hear her soft footsteps going downstairs, and we would drift off to sleep. As long as I live, I shall remember the sweet, beautiful, loving prayers of my grandmother.

"'A tithe of everything from the land, whether grain from the soil or fruit from the trees, belongs to the LORD; it is holy to the LORD.'" LEVITICUS 27:30

DECEMBER 15

Ernest L. Wilkinson wrote a booklet on tithing, and one day we got to discussing the subject. He said, "The way to unlock the flow of power is to give." And he told me about a man in Grand Rapids who made furniture.

This man got into difficulties and practically went broke. He was able to save the factory, but his credit was thin. The banks wouldn't loan him money, so a few friends loaned him enough to get started again. Then he got the idea of tithing—giving ten percent of his income and his time to the Lord. When he was ready to start his factory again, he knelt in his office and said, "Lord, this plant, such as it is, is Yours. I accept You now as my partner and I will give the first ten percent all the rest of my life to You." His business grew and he brought blessings to other people.

The basic spiritual law of the universe, demonstrated by Jesus Christ who gave His life, is that blessings come from giving yourself away. If you can believe this, all things are possible.

When the angels had left them and gone into heaven, the shepherds said to one another, "Let's go to Bethlehem and see this thing that has happened, which the Lord has told us about." LUKE 2:15

DECEMBER 16

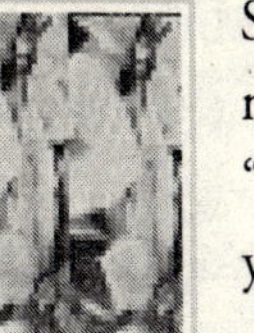

Some years ago, a man named Bob waited for me after the Sunday service and said, "Tomorrow I have to go to the hospital. Would you pray for me right now?"

I put my hand on his shoulder and said, "Okay, Bob, I don't want you to think that the hand on your shoulder is the hand of Norman Peale. You just believe that the hand of Jesus is on your shoulder. Will you?"

He looked at me and said, "Yes, I will." I prayed. Then he said to me, "I give myself to Him."

Later, Bob came along on a trip to the Holy Land. Looking at Bethlehem from a site known as the Shepherd's Cave, Bob was so moved he could hardly speak. He pointed toward the city and said, "Norman, what would have happened to me had He not been born, had I not taken Him as my Savior?" I looked into his face and I thought to myself: The wise men still come to Bethlehem. And they still find their answer. They find a power that changes their lives.

Then they cried out to the LORD in their trouble, and he delivered them from their distress. PSALM 107:6

DECEMBER 17

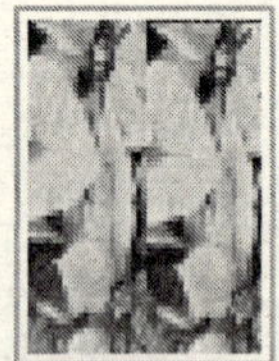

We encounter some real troubles in life. Anyone living on Earth will know of someone who is having a grievous time with real troubles. I think there are certain basic things we can do when we're in trouble to keep our troubles from overwhelming us. The first is to remember God and have faith in His providence. Look to Him for guidance. And from this there follows a second basic idea: Since we are children of God and can look to Him for help, we ought not to quake in the presence of trouble, nor run away from it, nor pretend it isn't there—but face it, stand up to it, take hold of it, and deal with it. Actually, the more you try to run away from trouble, or evade it, the more overwhelming it becomes; while if only you would boldly take hold of it, you would find it that much easier to handle.

Take a long straight look at your fear and stand firmly up to it. Then practice strong action. If everyone followed the purposes of the Creator, the general thrust of life would be in our favor.

Let us hold unswervingly to the hope we profess, for he who promised is faithful. HEBREWS 10:23

DECEMBER 18

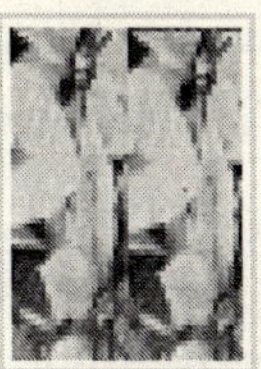

When I was a boy, several people told me they didn't think I would be able to make much of anything out of my life. So I was comforted to read an article by Alston J. Smith in which he mentioned a number of distinguished men and women who early in their lives had been the butts of brutally discouraging remarks—including Thomas Edison and Louisa May Alcott.

One of the functions of the church is to help people who have lost faith in themselves, who are overcome with difficulties and problems, by reminding them who they are. There isn't anyone who hasn't within himself tremendous possibilities. You should never let the fact that you have problems and difficulties overcome you. If you have a whole armful of difficulties, you may be sure the Lord likes you. And He knows that you have what it takes to dig down into this difficulty and that problem and come up with bright and shining good.

Humble yourselves, therefore, under God's mighty hand, that he may lift you up in due time. 1 PETER 5:6

DECEMBER 19

Some people seem to be afraid to partake of any optimism put to them—as though there were something blasphemous about taking a hopeful view. Pessimism thrives, the intellectuals say, because the world is in so much trouble. Certainly it's in trouble. When hasn't it been in trouble? This is the nature of human existence. The bright fellows who think they are going to create a perfect world have a superficial understanding of the nature of life. It always has been a world full of trouble and it always will be. But out of this world of trouble rise people who live above the trouble.

What is your trouble? It isn't anything you can't rise above. Not by your own strength, but with Him lifting you. There is an old gospel song in which each line of the refrain ends, "He lifted me." Get lifted in the spirit, and life will have great new meaning.

"I tell you the truth, anyone who has faith in me will do what I have been doing. He will do even greater things than these, because I am going to the Father." JOHN 14:12

DECEMBER 20

I read some time ago that a well-known psychiatrist in France had added a new dimension to the psychological perception of humans. He maintains that we have not only the conscious and the unconscious within us, but a superconscious as well. And he refers to Jesus' words in John 14:12: "I tell you the truth, anyone who has faith in me will do what I have been doing. He will do even greater things than these, because I am going to the Father." Does that mean that I can do greater things than Jesus did? Or that you can? Well, that is what Jesus said! The French psychiatrist reasons that it is through the superconscious element in man that this possibility exists. A person can do things incredible for himself when he gains the kind of understanding that is a wellspring of life for those who have it.

"Do not be afraid, little flock, for your Father has been pleased to give you the kingdom." LUKE 12:32

DECEMBER 21

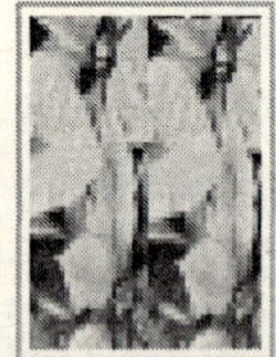

When an individual really is enthusiastic, you can see it in the flash of their eyes, in their alert and vibrant personality. You can see it in the spring of their step. You can see it in the verve of their whole being.

Enthusiasm makes the difference in our attitude toward other people, toward a job, toward the world. It makes a great big difference in the zest and delight of human existence. Do you have enthusiasm? Or have you grown dull? Lackadaisical? Indifferent? Has the zest gone out of you? Well, remember what is said in Luke 12:32: ". . . your Father has been pleased to give you the kingdom." And that implies that a person can gain an enthusiastic participation in life.

Enthusiasm lifts living out of the depths and makes it mean something. Play it cool and you may freeze. Play it hot and even if you get burned, at least you will shed warmth over a discouraged and bewildered world.

He replied, "You of little faith, why are you so afraid?" Then he got up and rebuked the winds and the waves, and it was completely calm.

MATTHEW 8:26

DECEMBER 22

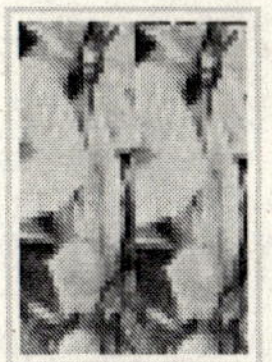

In his early life, Abraham Lincoln traveled the court circuit and stayed overnight, as was his custom, with an old Illinois farmer. One night the farmer witnessed the spectacular phenomenon known as "shooting stars." He thought the end was at hand and he got scared. Then he remembered Lincoln was asleep upstairs. He dashed up the stairs crying, "Abe, Abe, get up! The heavens are falling! The world is coming to an end!"

Lincoln got out of bed and looked out the window. He stepped back into the room, put his hand on the shoulder of his frightened friend, and said to him, "Don't you be afraid, Bill. Even if there are some shooting stars, the great constellations are still there."

When difficulties rain down upon you, it is easy to become bewildered and frightened. But if you look behind the difficulties into the eternal verities and see that the great God is still there, then you realize you need not be afraid. Because of His presence, you have what it takes to face up to anything.

It was good for me to be afflicted so that I might learn your decrees. PSALM 119:71

DECEMBER 23

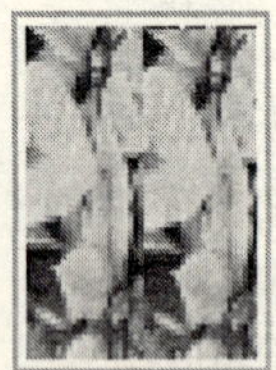

Over and over again, I have seen what can happen when a person who has been defeated becomes conscious of the words of Jesus. They cast out all weakness. Life is rebuilt around a substantial center. That is the reason you should go to church and read the Bible—to expose yourself to the powerful words of Scripture.

We need to realize that the difficulties inherent in this life are not without value, and that every defeating situation has within it a potential victory. Almighty God buries at the heart of every difficulty a nugget of gold. Overwhelmed by difficulty, a person may throw up his hands, not knowing that at the very heart of this crisis is some great value in life which he seeks. So when a difficulty faces you, don't be appalled by it, but say, "I wonder what God has put into this difficulty for me. By His grace, I am going to find it."

Therefore the Lord *himself will give you a sign: The virgin will be with child and will give birth to a son, and will call him Immanuel.* Isaiah 7:14

December 24

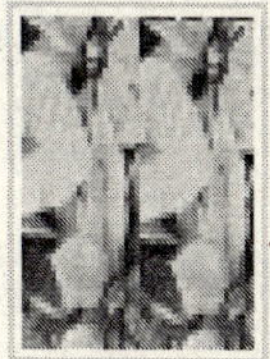

One bitterly cold, snowy Christmas Eve, Fred Henderson was making his way home. A series of blows to his business had him reeling. Then he saw the lights of home. Fred didn't feel up to the festivities but thought, "I must pull myself together. I must not let anyone know what has happened."

He put on a good act. At length, the family prepared to hear the Christmas story and Fred opened the Bible to the first chapter of Matthew. Reading, he came to verse 23: "'The virgin will be with child and will give birth to a son, and they will call him Immanuel'—which means, 'God with us.'" When he had finished, Fred went out to clear the snow from the walks. As he dug into the drifts he found himself saying, "God is with me." Peace came over him. And with it came a firm conviction that a solution would be found to his problem.

God is with you and with me. This means you can be strong enough to handle any problem that will ever come to you, strong enough to meet any difficulty, take any disappointment, bear up under any reversal.

But the angel said to them, "Do not be afraid. I bring you good news of great joy that will be for all the people." LUKE 2:10

DECEMBER 25

The great word at Christmas is joy. The old carol says, "Joy to the world! The Lord is come." "Don't be afraid," said the angel. "I have good news for you, which will make everyone happy." All the bright colors, all the lilting music of Christmas, bear out the joy with which the season is filled.

It was Jesus who brought the emphasis of joy into our human experience. When I went into the ministry years ago, a friend of mine rather sneeringly asked, "Norman, why do you want to be a preacher? I'm surprised! Are you going to be one of those sanctimonious joy-killers?" Well, not long ago the same man, after all these years, said to me, "I tried to kid myself for years that I was happy, but really I wasn't. Finally, I reorganized my life around Jesus Christ. Then I became and have remained a happy man." He added, "Why was I so dumb for so long? Why did it take me so long to get wise to myself and realize that true happiness is in Jesus?"

I pray also . . . that you may know the hope to which he has called you . . . and his incomparably great power for us who believe. EPHESIANS 1:18–19

DECEMBER 26

I would like to advance the theory that a Christian should never really be discouraged. There are some who will say I am not being realistic. Well, it depends on how you define discouragement and how you define a Christian. There is superficial Christianity and there is Christianity in depth. When an individual becomes identified with Jesus Christ, surrenders his life to Him, accepts Him as Savior, and lives with Him and walks with Him, then Jesus Christ confers upon him the power to rise above discouragement.

This doesn't imply that you are going to turn your back on the world and let it go. The true Christian is a person who participates in the world's work. He is the kind of person who says, "Sure, here's a situation. So what! Let's go to work and bring the power of God to bear upon it." He brings the same approach to his personal problems. And he discovers that he need never be a victim of discouragement.

Dear friend, I pray that you may enjoy good health and that all may go well with you, even as your soul is getting along well. 3 John 1:2

December 27

It is good to talk about the spirit because this language confers the sacredness and the inherent greatness of the individual. I went through the Bible asking God's guidance on the subject of the human spirit and came upon this verse: "I pray that you may enjoy good health and that all may go well with you, even as your soul is getting along well" (3 John 1:2). God is a generous God. Abundance is His word. Why, then, do we live in poverty and in want?

I read about a man in Oklahoma who was low financially. But he had a big soul, he loved God, and he had some insights. He took some pieces of paper and put these in his wallet. When things weren't going well, he would take out these slips of paper, on which were written verses such as 2 Corinthians 9:8: "And God is able to make all grace abound to you, so that in all things at all times, having all that you need, you will abound in every good work." So don't think I'm not preaching out of the Bible when I say there is a law of supply.

Jesus replied, "What is impossible with men is possible with God." LUKE 18:27

DECEMBER 28

The Bible is filled with astonishing passages. One of them can be found in Luke 18:27, where it says, "What is impossible with men is possible with God." Now, of course, on the surface this means that God can do things man cannot do, which is a fact that goes without question. But it seems that this verse implies that if people are identified with God in a special way, the power of God to change impossibles into possibles becomes associated with those people. This, of course, is an enormous assumption. But the Bible deals in enormous assumptions.

You, too, have it in you, as do I, to do (using an ordinary phrase) the things that cannot be done. But there is a tendency in human nature to emphasize the seemingly impossibles in life, to underscore them, to build them up. This is one reason why the life accomplishment of many of us falls at a far lower level than God ever intended it to be. To the degree that we identify ourselves with Him, we gain power over the seemingly impossible.

You will be made rich in every way so that you can be generous on every occasion, and through us your generosity will result in thanksgiving to God. 2 CORINTHIANS 9:11

DECEMBER 29

The individual who finds something useful to do beyond himself, who gives of himself, knows joy of the deepest kind. Jesus Christ stimulates people to have a meaningful life.

After a speech I made in Indiana, a man drove me to the train station. During our drive, he told me about himself and said, "I'm not happy. Why is it that, having all these things, I'm not happy?"

At the railroad station I said to him, "You have great ability. You have capacity. But you have never found any use big enough for it. Why don't you give yourself to Jesus Christ and help Him build His kingdom?"

We continued to talk, and sitting there with me beside a couple of mail trucks, this man spoke to Jesus saying, "I'll give You my life. I'll do Your job." And since that time, I have followed his activities in the area where he lives. He has been a benediction. He has uplifted young people, saved marriages, and put power in the church. And he has put joy into his own life. That is how Jesus even now brings joy to this world.

They rejoice in your name all day long; they exult in your righteousness. *Psalm 89:16*

December 30

Are good people happy people? They're on the way to being happy. They've made the start. They've gone down the road a long way, but they'll not have religion in power that brings deep joy until they penetrate the essence. I fervently pray that this might happen to us all. Let us go deeper through self-surrender, through self-giving, through desire, through earnestness, until the glory bursts upon us and true happiness surges up and fills our lives. Psalm 89:16 says it well: "They rejoice in your name all day long. . . ."

Did you ever stop to ask yourself how alive you are? God, who breathed into us the breath of life, certainly intended that a person should have fullness of life. What a pathetic thing it is that some people seem to live out their days without ever being fully alive! The greatest gift outside of the salvation of our souls is the gift of life itself. And the salvation of our souls is life eternal.

"For God so loved the world that he gave his one and only Son, that whoever believes in him shall not perish but have eternal life." JOHN 3:16

DECEMBER 31

Can people do impossible things? Of course they can. We are constantly witnessing demonstrations of humankind's immense power to do what was once considered impossible. Some foolish people believed it was irreligious for anyone to go beyond the atmosphere of the earth. But it's all God's universe. When astronauts venture into space, they find natural laws like the ones we encounter on earth. God rules the universe with law.

But have you noticed that the almost impossible is carried out by men and women who are poised and fearless? Naturally, to get people who can do the impossible, you have to get people who are identified with God. Only God can do impossible things, and only a man or woman of God can share with Him in the accomplishment of the impossible.

Scripture Index

"Those of us who have come to love and serve God have learned how practical are His teachings, how never failing His help, how ever dependable His advice and directions."

– Norman Vincent Peale

For well over fifty years, in his writings, in his speeches, and in his sermons, Dr. Norman Vincent Peale preached a simple message: the keys to happiness and success are faith in God, faith in oneself, and faith in others. He called this concept "Postive Thinking." The essential elements of Positive Thinking, Dr. Peale said, are praying, believing in and visualizing the desired outcome, and maintaining a deep and abiding faith in the unlimited power of God. Through this practice, we can begin to feel the power of God flowing through us and influencing our lives.

According to Dr. Peale, by sincerely and persistently applying the principles illustrated in these daily devotionals, we can experience an amazing improvement within ourselves and a positive change in the circumstances in which we live. We can have improved relationships and become more self-confident. We can enjoy peace of mind, improved health, and a never-ceasing flow of energy.